THE SECOND FORCE

OTHER BOOKS BY GARY EMERY

Rapid Relief from Emotional Distress (co-authored with
James Campbell, M.D.)
Own Your Own Life
Getting Undepressed
Anxiety Disorders and Phobias (co-authored with
Aaron Beck, M.D.)
Cognitive Therapy of Depression (co-authored with Aaron Beck,
A. John Rush, and Brian Shaw)

A complete list of books and tapes by Dr. Gary Emery is available
from the Los Angeles Center for Cognitive Therapy, 630 South
Wilton Place, Los Angeles, California 90005 (213-387-4737).

GARY EMERY, Ph.D., AND PAT EMERY

THE
SECOND
FORCE

REDIRECTING
YOUR RESISTANCE
TO SUCCESS

DUTTON  NEW YORK

DUTTON

Published by the Penguin Group
Penguin Books USA Inc., 375 Hudson Street,
New York, New York 10014, U.S.A.
Penguin Books Ltd, 27 Wrights Lane,
London W8 5TZ, England
Penguin Books Australia Ltd, Ringwood,
Victoria, Australia
Penguin Books Canada Ltd, 2801 John Street,
Markham, Ontario, Canada L3R 1B4
Penguin Books (N.Z.) Ltd, 182–190 Wairau Road,
Auckland 10, New Zealand

Penguin Books Ltd, Registered Offices:
Harmondsworth, Middlesex, England

First published by Dutton, an imprint of Penguin Books USA Inc.

First Printing, August, 1990

1   3   5   7   9   10   8   6   4   2

Copyright © Gary Emery and Pat Emery, 1990
All rights reserved

Library of Congress Cataloging-in-Publication Data
Emery, Gary.
The second force : redirecting your resistance to success / Gary
Emery and Pat Emery. — 1st ed.
p.   cm.
ISBN 0-525-24852-8
1. Success—Psychological aspects. I. Emery, Pat. II. Title.
BF637.S8E394   1990
158'.1—dc20   89-71483
                                                    CIP

Printed in the United States of America
Set in Caledonia

Designed by Steven N. Stathakis

To Josephine, Lavona, and Olvis

"None but yourself who are your greatest foe."

—HENRY WADSWORTH LONGFELLOW

CONTENTS

CONTENTS

ACKNOWLEDGMENTS

This book is a synthesis of insights and wisdom from many different sources. We are indebted to many people. Among them are Michael J. Apter, Syd Banks, Harry Benjamin, J. G. Bennett, Sharon C. Brown, Roger Callahan, Robert S. deRopp, Abdullah Dougan, Monty Dunn, Dan Dunne, Robert Fritz, Joseph Goldstein, G. I. Gurdjieff, Mike Hernacki, Robert Kausen, Hazrat Inayat Khan, Pirvilayat Inayat Khan, Anne Knowles, Jack Kornfield, Roger Mills, Jane Nelson, Maurice Nicoll, P. D. Ouspensky, Helen Palmer, Pat Paulson, George Prawsky, Richard Riso, Richard Rohr, Richard Rose, Richard Schenkman, Al Shore, David Stark, David Steinl-Rast, Darlene Steward, Rick Suarez, Colin Watson, Jo Ann Wolf, Shelly Young, and Shinzen Young.

T H E
SECOND
FORCE

INTRODUCTION

As sure as death and taxes, as soon as you want something, you'll encounter resistance. The telling resistance, the serious resistance, always comes from *you*. You are your own best friend or your own worst enemy, depending on how you handle your resistance.

Master your own resistance and you'll be able to master your whole life. Mastery comes from understanding the three forces that are always at play. The first force is your desire; the second force is your resistance; and the higher, third force reconciles your desire and your resistance.

TRANSCENDING FORCE

The three forces allow you to evolve morally and psychologically. Just as relationships grow by resolving conflicts, you grow by reconciling your desires with the resistance you encounter. Your evolution in life depends on how well you negotiate the conflict between desire and resistance.

Feelings of joy and serenity are the positive third force—the means to power and wisdom. When you find good feelings, you're able to rise above your resistance and move forward. You take action on what you can change (first force), accept what you can't change (second force), and have the serenity or wisdom to know the difference.

Good feelings are the third force, which moves you to the middle of the pendulum swing and neutralizes the conflict between desire and resistance. As you move toward the center, you rise in perspective and gain a *greater clarification of reality*. Reality becomes clear and transparent: you see what's going on and you see what you really want.

From this higher, more inclusive vantage point, conflicts, paradoxes, and contradictions disappear. You realize there are always at least two sides to everything. Your response to life no longer is "yes" or "no," but "yes *and* no." You take life in stride because you know with every gain comes a loss; and with every loss, a gain.

SUSTAINING FORCE

You can never actually *see* the third force, but the feeling is as real as enzymes, photosyntheses, and chemical catalysts. Just as you know when something "feels right," you know when the third-force feeling is in the room and when it's not.

Third-force good feelings sustain you and allow you to persevere in the face of disappointments and self-doubts in all areas. By finding a good feeling, you can rise above a job setback and keep moving toward your career goal. The third force allows you to lose weight and keep it off—when you have the feeling, any diet will work.

THIRD FORCE AS A GIFT

An artist feels the creative impulse of the third force when colors, brush strokes, design, and feelings come together and the

2

painting paints itself. Under the spell of the third force, you become the actor who steals the movie or the leader who speaks from inspiration.

When you move into the third force, you relax into the moment and experience life in a timeless, effortless flow. You feel powerful and confident that you can bring about what you want.

FEEL SUCCESSFUL

You may strive for power, position, and possessions, discounting good feelings because they are temporary and fleeting. You have it backward. You'll never reach El Dorado and gain everlasting happiness through outward success.

Rather than look for good feelings to come from your success, look for success to come from good feelings. Good feelings move you to a point of security and confidence, where you're easily able to bring about what you most want.

How you see the world reflects your level of awareness and understanding. The more third-force good feelings you have, the sharper, clearer, and more inviting the world looks. You see reality from a higher attitude. You understand that your first- and second-force thoughts ("I must succeed at all costs"; "I might fail") are simply debris that you can step over or go around as you move forward.

The path to good feelings is good feelings. The means determine the end. If you can enjoy your days, your hours, and your minutes, you can enjoy your life. Joseph Campbell's advice, "Follow your bliss," is both a prescription for a happy life and a guide to success.

VERTICAL LEVEL

The choice is self-destruction or self-realization. All of your self-defeating behaviors come from low feelings—when you feel bad, you act badly. In contrast, when you feel good, you're at your best—you make choices that easily and effortlessly lead you to what you want.

All of your low feelings come from distorted, one-sided think-

3

ing. However, when you try to change your thinking or the resulting bad feelings, you'll nearly always be unsuccessful. Because the job of your thinking is to prove itself right, you'll believe your negative thoughts more than your positive thoughts.

The secret that frees you from your own conditioned thinking process is realizing *you can work on the vertical level.*

Knowledge is on the horizontal plane—a fact is a fact. Understanding is on the vertical plane. You can understand a fact on infinite levels—from the gross to the subtle. Like a few drops of dye in a glass of water, a little understanding changes the whole coloring of your being.

When you work only with your first-force desire or the corresponding second-force resistance, you're stuck on the horizontal level. Good feelings, the third force, allow you to ascend to a higher level of perception and functioning.

Refuse to waste your time and energy fighting with yourself and trying to overcome your resistance on the horizontal level. Realize that by finding a good feeling you can raise your point of reference—and then, from this more inclusive perspective, you're able to think and act in new ways.

Good feelings allow you to become congruent with your essence, your true self. You realize, "I stand behind and am senior to all my thoughts, feelings, and actions." No need to buy into or fight your thoughts—you can simply note they are thoughts and let them rise up and pass away.

Once you understand at a deep level that you can call up or dismiss any thought, you'll be able to take an active part in your own evolution. You'll be able to bring about the internal and external qualities you most want in life.

INTERNAL GUIDE

Your feelings and their corresponding states of mind are a psychological map and an ethical guide: *anything that raises your state of mind is to your advantage; anything that lowers it is to your disadvantage.*

Once you understand the geography, you can use your feelings as a compass to indicate which direction you are headed. Sinking feelings mean you are going down and losing common sense; uplifting feelings mean you are going up and gaining wisdom.

LEVELS OF AWARENESS

Thoughts analyze and fragment reality; good feelings synthesize and make reality whole. When you feel good, you move toward greater clarification of reality. Your real self comes to the forefront and you feel complete. Good feelings are the link to others: you see others more clearly and more fairly. When you feel good, you have integrity and treat yourself and others ethically— you bring truth to everything you do.

Good feelings lead to success because the truth works. When a playwright writes the truth, the play works. When you are truthful to others, your relationships work. When you are truthful about when you are hungry and when you're not, your diet works. When you are truthful about your flaws and are truthful about what you want, your life works.

UNIFYING FORCE

Your good feelings are a guide, an inner catalyst, a fresh breath of life. To transcend any conflict, look for a good feeling and let the feeling lift you to a higher state of will, awareness, and intelligence.

By finding a good feeling, you unify your own house. Once you feel centered and integrated, you instinctively know what to do next. Your deeper good feelings bring you into the present moment and create an inner harmony that unifies you with yourself, and with what you want in life.

When you feel good, you're physically healthier: your immune system works better and you take better care of yourself. Good feelings are even more important in the psychological realm: *happiness is synonymous with mental health*. When you have a good feeling, all of your internal and external conflicts disappear.

You may be having a fight with someone, but when you find a good feeling toward the other person, you rise above your differences. You may be avoiding a task, but if you can find a good feeling toward the finished result, you transcend your resistance. If you're stuck on anything, look for a good feeling and you'll rise above the resistance and move into harmony with what you're doing.

UNDERSTANDING

You can use this book as a third force to start an education that helps you complete yourself. Good feelings are the alchemy that turns knowledge into understanding—once you feel something, you understand it.

Bertrand Russell said, "We know too much and feel too little." As you read this book, look for a good feeling. Your good feeling will turn the ideas and principles into understanding and mastery. What you have a feeling for stays with you. If you're unable to find a good feeling, put the book away and come back when you're feeling better.

The first time you read this book, read it with the light good feeling you bring to a magazine or a newspaper. After you have digested it the first time, read it again. This time, read it more slowly. Go for the deeper meaning that lies behind the words. The more you feel the ideas, the more real and alive they will become to you.

When you're ready, come back a third time. Focus on one chapter each week. During the week, reread the chapter every day and put the principles into action in your daily experiences. You'll find that, as you develop a positive feeling toward the principles, your understanding will deepen and you'll become wiser and more powerful in all areas of your life.

1

THREE FORCES

Your first force is desire. Starting with your first breath of life, you want something. As soon as you get what you want, you immediately want something else. Your desire will always be with you—no matter what you have, on some level you'll always want more.

The third force reconciles the first and second forces. Good feelings are the third force, which neutralizes the conflict by helping you get what you want. When you feel good, you rise above the gridlock, as a helicopter rises above a traffic jam. Your first force may be that you want to get into law school, and your second force may be that you're discouraged because all five schools you applied to rejected you. To apply the third force, find a good feeling toward going to law school, raise your state of mind, and you'll realize what you need to do next (you may need to study and raise your test scores, or you may need to apply to other schools).

7

UNDERSTANDING

Learning to use good feelings as a bridge allows you to design your own life. As you come to understand the dynamics between the three forces, you can consistently bring about the experiences you want.

Your first-force aims, goals, and plans motivate you to start a new relationship, look for a better job, or begin a new diet. The second force slows you down as you run into reality—you feel suffocated in the relationship, uncomfortable going on interviews, or physically deprived on the diet.

When you want something, the first and second forces are always in play. Without a third force to reconcile and neutralize the two forces, they cancel each other out and nothing happens.

In the past, you may have called on a teacher or a friend to help you through a difficult period. You may have counted on luck or other people to be your third force. You become powerful once you learn to use your own good feelings as a third force.

By finding a good feeling, you raise your level of understanding and tap into an inner reservoir of wisdom. You always have insights within you, common sense that you can bring to bear in any situation. When you feel good, instead of playing life like a two-dimensional game, you add a third dimension and are able to rise above the playing board and move forward, above internal and external resistance.

FIRST FORCE

The first force manifests itself in your thinking. In the first force, your mind is racing with thoughts and fantasies. Instead of trying to eliminate your desires, aim to clarify what you truly want. You can't have it all, but you can nearly always have what you most desire.

Realize desire is an intrinsic part of being human. The desire to conquer nature allowed early humans to survive and evolve. You may have a desire to get ahead, write a poem, help someone you love, or beat another car to a parking place. The entrepreneur expresses it by going after business; the student goes after an A;

and the mystic goes after a sense of oneness with the whole universe.

Your desires are just as much a part of you as your heart and lungs. To evolve and grow, you need first-force challenges; you need to take a stand for what you most want and most care about in life.

FIRST-FORCE BLIND

As you start to understand yourself, you will see the connection between your active first force and your second-force reaction. You know that, after an enjoyable vacation, you will have to endure an inevitable letdown. You realize that, if you give in to your desire to stay up late, you will feel tired in the morning. You know that, if you drink a lot of caffeine, you're going to feel bad later.

With understanding, you stop trying to avoid the pain and disappointment of the second force by closing your eyes to your desires ("I don't want anything"; or "I don't know what I want"). Instead of approaching life like a tennis hacker who has little desire to be a better player, refuse to let your days and weeks pass by without aim or purpose.

William Blake said, "Sooner strangle an infant in its cradle than nurse unacted desires." Rather than repress your desires, tell yourself the truth about what you really want. Make quick decisions in favor of what you want most and then act on them.

FIRST-FORCE DOMINANT

If you're all first force, you're always in motion. You push your body to exhaustion, and eventually it wears out. When you want something *too* much, you become like a "one-eyed cat peepin' in a seafood store"—all you can see is dinner.

Your first-force overdrive comes from a dread of second-force passivity. You think, "Unless I move fast and work hard, I will be run over by life." Your desire to beat life before it beats you can easily get out of hand.

Realize that your excessive first force explodes like a supernova, but eventually collapses back into a second-force black hole. Refuse to stare into the first-force sunlight and you'll avoid first-force blindness later ("I didn't want anything").

If you're first-force dominant, you're an activist—you want to put your mark on the world. This is admirable, but realize that you lose your balance when you are driven by your insatiable desires and fantasies. Dampen your desires when they become the all-consuming focus in your life.

A healthy first force comes from your essence and is something you want to encourage for its own sake. You will have resistance to your true desires, but not the violent second-force reaction that comes from trying to prove or defend yourself through your achievements.

SECOND FORCE

The second force checks creation and balances all nature. Without a second force, nature's plate would be too full. Second-force destruction makes room for new growth and new possibilities. This is the dance of nature. Without a down, there would be no up; without death, there would be no life.

Throughout your life, your excessive desires have been checked by the second force. Look at where you continually check yourself and you will see where you have too much desire. You need to reassess your priorities. If you've had many failed relationships, you've asked too much of relationships in the past. You need to make relationships less important in your life. If you've failed in your career, you've made your career too important.

REALITY PRINCIPLE

Your second force, or internal resistance, comes when your desires conflict with reality. You experience second-force resistance in your body—the part that directly interfaces with reality. You want to get started on a project, but you feel too comfortable to get off the couch. You want to give a successful presentation, but you're so antsy and irritated that you lose your fluency and overlook important details.

The second force only becomes a problem when your thoughts freeze the resistance—you give your resistance the illusion of permanency by making the obstacle global, all-encompassing, and unchanging ("It's always going to be impossible").

Thinking solidifies and feelings liquify. Thinking a task is difficult makes it difficult. You strengthen your resistance by thinking, "This must change." The more you insist an obstacle change, the more it appears to be cast in cement. The thought, "This will never change," disguises a more subtle truth: *your resistance, like everything else, is always in a state of flux and change.*

Good feelings dissolve the illusion of solidity. By finding a good feeling toward what you want, you can further clarify present reality and realize your resistance is coming from your thoughts and you can disregard any thought. With this awareness, your resistance starts to melt and fade away.

At times, your resistance may be so pervasive that you have trouble tying your shoes. Usually, you experience the second force as an uncomfortable physical sensation. You may feel too beat to exercise, or too tense to complete the forms in front of you. You may get strong cravings to have a cigarette, or you may come down with the flu right before an important exam.

SECOND-FORCE DOMINANT

If you are predominantly second-force, you are the opposite of the driven workaholic. You are too passive, too trusting, and too easily resigned. Unlike the activist who wants to dominate life, you let life dominate you.

You may be cheerful about it or you may complain bitterly. In either case, you need to balance your "no" to life with "yes" to living. Realize that, although there is great wisdom in *not caring*, you need to balance your passive energy with *active caring*.

SECOND-FORCE BLIND

From one point of view, your life can be summed up in one sentence, "It's one damn thing after another." (The corollary to this is Robert Frost's observation "Life goes on.")

Resistance is part of life. When you're unaware of the inevitable second-force, you expect to execute your plans without a hitch. You may *say*, "I know there will be difficulties," but deep down you don't *believe* it. You start strong but give up when confronted by obstacles. You're like a child who wants a puppy and is unable to foresee any difficulty in caring for it.

With wisdom, you look for the real obstacles, rather than sweep them under the rug. Before you jump into a project, check to make sure you have the capacity and the resources to pull it off. Be honest about what is required from you and what you have to give at this point in your life.

Realize that the second force is inevitable, but not insurmountable. When you do encounter the second force, refuse to make up personal theories to explain it away ("They don't like me"; "I'm not good enough"; "If only . . ."). Realize that your explanation makes matters worse. You want to see reality more clearly, not cover it up with explanations and pet theories.

Only in your fantasies can you find a world free of second force. Once you understand that the second force is ever-present, you'll no longer be fooled into thinking, "The grass will be greener in the future." Rather than drift from one job or one relationship to another, decide to face and feel your way through your uncomfortable second-force body sensations.

OWN YOUR SECOND FORCE

Achieving an understanding of the second force, which comes through good feelings, is the third force. Start to appreciate and value the second force and you'll be able to finish what you start. If you go back to school and run into difficulty, rather than drop out and take up Russian folk dancing, find a good feeling toward finishing school and decide to stick with your decision.

Be willing to be responsible for the second force you generate. Be willing to pay the price, face the challenges, and make the sacrifices to achieve what you want. Start only what you're willing to finish. Your life may become simpler, but it will also become richer and more satisfying.

A balanced life comes from a willingness to accept the second force (the uncomfortable body sensations) as much as you accept the first force. To own anything internally, from your own existence to your relationships, you have to pay for it. Refuse to let your charm, money, or friends and relatives rob you of second-force experiences. Be willing to complete the cycle and do the tough part yourself. Only through experiencing second-force resistance can you learn to appreciate the value of anything.

TRIADS

When stuck, rather than fight your resistance or increase your desire, calm down, get in touch with the feeling of the second force, and look for a third force. In all forms of creation, a third force combines the conflicting forces and produces a new result. The higher, realigning force allows the two lower forces to complement each other. More than just a combination of the two lower forces, the third force is a separate entity that allows the three forces to come together as something completely new.

In physics, the third force is the electromagnetic field that combines the nucleus and the electrons. In law, the judge is the third force that reconciles the opposing parties. In Buddhism, it is called the "middle way"; Zen master Deshimaru said, "The middle way embraces opposites, it integrates and goes beyond all contradictions." In Christian philosophy, the Holy Spirit intervenes in the struggle between good and evil. In Hinduism, Vishnu reconciles Brahma, the affirming force, and Shiva, the denying force. In Taoism, the Tao reconciles and stands above the opposition of the male yang and the female yin. In philosophy, the synthesis blends the thesis and the antithesis.

COMBINING OPPOSITES

When you find a third force, opposites naturally fall together. In mathematics, the concept of the space-time continuum reconciles space and time. Einstein said the happiest moment of his life was realizing that a man falling from the roof of a house is both in motion and at rest at the same time. This insight formed the basis for his theory of relativity.

Finding a connecting third force is the key to all creativity.

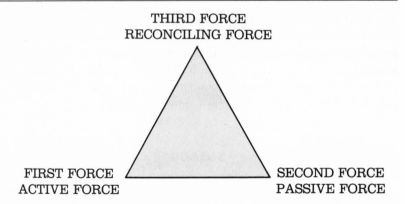

THIRD FORCE
RECONCILING FORCE

FIRST FORCE
ACTIVE FORCE

SECOND FORCE
PASSIVE FORCE

In all creations, a first force leads to a second force, out of which comes a third force, which creates a new first force.

Depending on the situation, the relationship between the three forces changes. A first force can turn overnight into a second force or a third force. The forces are constantly in motion. The job you want today becomes resistance to the time you want off tomorrow.

Just as understanding Newton's Law enables engineers to build and fly jet planes, understanding the first and second forces and the completing power of the third force enables you to stay on course toward what you want in life.

THE THIRD FORCE

Your instinct when you run into resistance is to quit or to fight with yourself. You waste your time and energy trying to talk yourself out of your resistance. Your first-force self-talk ("I can do it") stimulates second-force self-talk ("You'll never do it") and escalates the conflict. Your internal battle becomes like a bout between two equally matched sumo wrestlers. Your first-force desire pushes and strains against your second-force resistance, which tenses up and pushes back.

To move beyond the impasse, feel the second-force feelings in your body, and find a good feeling toward what you want, and shift to the reconciling third force that unifies opposites. You may want to move cross-country but are afraid to take the risk. Feel the fear in your body, and then find a good feeling toward where you want to move. From this third-force, higher perspective, you realize that your fears and insecurities are illusionary and that you have the capacity to make a move and bring about what you really want.

PLAY OF FORCES

Your life unfolds like a series of plays. In the first act, your focus is all on desire. Act two introduces the second force, your Achilles' heel, and you become blocked or thwarted in some way. Act three brings in a negative or a positive third force, which reconciles the conflict in some way. When you learn to master the third force, you can consistently create happy endings.

Fail to direct your own life, and circumstances will become the third force—you have to rely on external conditions to manipulate you into action. With understanding, you no longer have to manipulate yourself or circumstances to overcome your resistance. You no longer need negative feelings as a third force. As an alternative, look for a good feeling toward what you want and rise to a plane that lifts you above your resistance. If you want to leave a relationship, leave; no need to make the relationship so awful you must leave. With wisdom, you no longer need the fear of losing your job to get you out of bed in the morning, and you no longer need the April 15 deadline to manipulate you into doing your taxes.

Good feelings are a panacea—you can use them as a third force in any situation. When you feel good, you expand your awareness, increase your intelligence, and raise your general level of functioning in every area of your life.

THIRD-FORCE BLIND

When you lack third-force understanding, you oscillate between excessive first or second force. Move to the third-force perspective and you'll no longer bounce between desire and resistance. You realize that the first and second forces come from your thoughts. Rather than fight or buy into your thinking, learn to direct your thinking to bring about the results you want. With understanding, you avoid intoxicating first-force thoughts and toxic second-force thoughts by aiming for what you truly love and truly care about.

Just as you want to drive a car with a gas pedal that works, you want a car with good brakes. You equally respect and appreciate the first-force gas pedal, which gets you moving, and the second-force brake, which holds you back.

When you start off on a new project, the tendency is to overlook many real obstacles. All you see is green lights and open roads. Once resistance comes on, rather than fight or try to ignore it, slow down and get the lay of the land. Use the uncomfortable feelings in your body as cues: see obstacles as reality checkpoints—opportunities to pull off to the side of the road and get your bearings. Realize that obstacles point you toward your destination and help you find the best route. Pay attention to the detours and "wrong-way" signs and you'll avoid getting lost and having to double back later.

As you start out on a project, use as your touchstone the love of what you want to see happen. Realize that your deeper feelings put you in touch with your deepest wisdom and truest desires. Good feelings toward what you want allow you to connect your first-force desire with second-force reality and see the shortest route to your destination.

THIRD-FORCE DOMINANT

The first force is all in your head and has little reality base. The second force, which you feel in your body, brings in reality, but through your thoughts you make impermanent reality appear solid and worse than it is. The third force comes from your heart— you follow your heartfelt desires and honestly see what's going on in reality.

When you feel good, you move to a higher state of mind where you intuitively get in touch with all the forces. You know when the first force is needed, and you know when to slow down and avoid getting carried away with your desires. Because you know how to embrace resistance without being overwhelmed by it, you're able to bring about desired results with the least amount of effort.

Bring good feelings to whatever you are doing and then look for more good feelings to sustain you. The connecting third force comes from feelings of love, gratitude, and appreciation. Just as you want to be in good physical condition for the sake of your health, aim to feel good for the sake of your own sanity and wisdom, and for the sake of what you want to bring about in your life.

THIRD-FORCE LOBBYISTS

You have an inner first-force advocate ("Work harder"; "Change the situation") and a second-force advocate ("Quit and avoid strain"). With understanding, you develop a third-force advocate, an inner voice that lobbies for you to raise your perspective through good feelings toward where you are and toward where you want to go. Understanding makes your third-force advocate more articulate and persuasive than the two junior lobbyists.

If you're bumped from an overbooked flight, recognize how the second force starts to sabotage your desire to be happy ("This is awful, I hate airports"). Refuse to give in to this special interest. Instead, feel the frustration in your body and look for the third-force voice by making a conscious choice to feel good about the trip you're on. Adopt a friendly attitude toward the wait and merge with the reality of the situation. Create a harmonious feeling and relate to the reality of the moment ("Okay, this is the way it is").

By listening to the third-force voice, you are able to create positive experiences while you wait for the next flight. You buy a magazine, sit back, relax, look for a good feeling, and enjoy the wait.

If you find yourself ten pounds overweight, you have a choice, You can increase the lower force (fight reality and redouble your effort), or you can fully experience your discomfort, call in the third-force advocate, and decide, "Why ruin this day for myself?"

With a little understanding, you realize you'll feel better and eat less if you're gentler with yourself. When you find a good feeling toward being in shape and in good condition, you listen to the voice of reason. You exercise a little more and eat a little less.

If you're a salesperson, let go of first-force fantasies ("I've got it made. . . . A few more sales and I'll be able to buy a Mercedes") and second-force discouragement ("I'll never make another sale"). When you find a calm, gentle good feeling toward being successful at your career, you see reality clearly—you no longer promise more than you can deliver to yourself or others.

PRINCIPLES

You can create your own third force by understanding and putting into practice two principles:

· *You can choose the thoughts you want.* By choosing to hold on to the thoughts you want and to let go of the ones you don't want, you can master the three forces and design your own life.

· *You can create the state of mind you want.* The better your feelings, the higher your state of mind and the more third force you have. By focusing on good feelings, you can rise above the lower forces.

The two principles are the means for creating your own life. You can use them at any moment to create a relating third force and bring about the experiences you want. Once you master the principles, you become a conscious participant in your own life. Understand at a deep level that *your thinking, relative to your state of mind, creates your every moment* and you master your own life.

Use the two principles as training wheels to learn how to keep yourself in balance. When you are feeling too excited or too down, realize that your racing thoughts are the cause (thoughts create reality) and that you can focus on good feelings and bring about higher states of mind (feelings create states of mind). Once you are in a better frame of mind, you naturally act in your own best interests.

As if you were learning to ride a bike, as you learn to balance your own psychology, you'll need training wheels less and less. You'll naturally move up to a third-force state of mind without needing the principles to guide you and keep you steady.

2

PRINCIPLE ONE: YOU CAN CHOOSE YOUR THOUGHTS

Once you understand you can choose your thoughts, you throw rose petals instead of thorns in your path. You stop assuming that your thinking is purely an involuntary process and start taking the primary role in your own life.

With third-force perspective, you see that your first-force overpush ("Everything is great!") and your second-force resistance ("What's the use!") are just thoughts that you can disregard.

Unrealistic and counterproductive first- or second-force thoughts will still come in, but from the third-force advantage point you'll recognize them simply as mental rhetoric you can choose to disregard. The thoughts will either stay or go away; if they stay, continue to disregard them.

GUARDIAN OF YOUR MIND

Your reality, how you experience life, comes from your thoughts. Once you know for sure that your thoughts create your experiences and you are in charge of your thoughts, you are able to master any situation. At first, you will understand on a surface level that your thoughts create your experiences ("Yeah, right . . . I know that"). Then, one day, you start to feel unhappy and have real insight ("I'm only unhappy because I think I have to be unhappy"). At that moment, you'll see into reality and have a *realization*: the fact that your thinking is making you unhappy becomes real to you.

You see each thought is a harmless blank and only when you infuse a thought with the gunpowder of taking it seriously does it explode on you.

BEYOND TECHNIQUES

A man was out in his canoe eating a coconut when he had a sudden sense of the unity of all life. His whole being seemed to change at that moment. Back in his village, his neighbors asked about his newfound calm and bliss. He said, "I'm not sure how it happened. I was out in a canoe eating a coconut when this wonderful feeling suddenly came over me." When he awoke the next morning, he found the village empty. He walked to the beach and found all of the villagers out in their canoes, eating coconuts.

Techniques are on the linear, horizontal level of conditional learning, and you want to travel on the vertical path of unconditional understanding. With conditional learning, your knowledge spreads out infinitely in a horizontal direction. This gives you the illusion of advancement. Actually, you become more ignorant: the more you know, the less you know. This breeds insecurity. Discovery of new knowledge brings new questions and new problems. You constantly need more answers and more solutions.

Unconditional learning, on the other hand, leads to wisdom. Vertical learning, which raises your perspective, is basic research. You feel increasingly secure. The fundamental principles you discover transcend conditions—you find you can apply them across the board.

With techniques, you get better before you get worse. At first, techniques help you become more mindful, but eventually all techniques become mechanical. The second force comes in, and your intellect develops tolerance for the procedure, and the technique ceases to work. As with all fads and fashions, the novelty wears off, and the technique starts to put you to sleep rather than keep you awake.

INSIGHTS

What is valuable lasts—and what lasts is insight and understanding. An insight is the sudden wordless experience that comes from making a new connection. Insights come *before* thought and are qualitatively different from thought. To create the experience you want, you need third-force insights into your own functioning. Insight into your own mind/body process allows you to see that each moment a new reality rises up and then passes away. You see your inner life in a larger context—you see how, moment to moment, through your thinking, you create your experiences.

FREE WILL

A huge step in vertical learning is the realization that *you can think differently*. At any moment, you can stop the conceptual merry-go-round and get off. You may be blindly following one of your rules ("I never give anyone a second chance") and suddenly

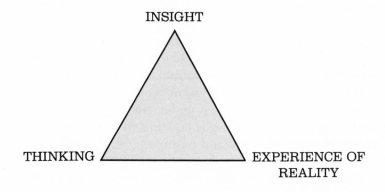

INSIGHT

THINKING

EXPERIENCE OF
REALITY

see *you* made up the rule in the first place, so you can disregard it if you choose to.

Your intellect (your thought system) throws thoughts at problems, hoping they will go away; this, however, never works, because your thoughts are the cause of the problem in the first place.

Use your racing mind as a signal that you are operating at below par, not as a sign to think more. Step back and see your thoughts for what they are—echos from your past conditioning—and then choose to let them pass by without a second thought. First, recognize that, whenever you feel excited, tense, or upset, some part of you is buying into low-level thinking; second, realize that you can set aside any line of thinking and raise your level of functioning.

In the past, you may have had insights into how two opposite experiences were directly related (bragging made you feel smaller, or you gave in and got your way). No insight is simpler than the fact that your thinking creates your experience. The connection is so simple and so obvious, you can live your whole life without seeing it. Grasping the insight is like catching on to a parlor game: you understand the trick once you relax and look for the obvious.

PSYCHOLOGICAL LITERACY

The insight that your moment-by-moment experience is constructed via thought is as plain as the printing on this page. When you first learned to read, all you saw was letters on a page. Then you had a flash of insight, and the principle of reading fell into place. You may have made the connection almost immediately, or you may have taken several years to get it—but when you had it, you had it.

In anything, you can buy or you can browse. You can look at houses for years and still be "just looking." The first step in learning to read your own psychology is to stop browsing and sincerely see how the Principle of Thought makes sense.

You set the stage for deep understanding by noting as often as you can how your thinking is creating your experiences. All of your experiences, negative and positive, give you another chance to see how your thinking is creating your reality.

Every day you have approximately forty thousand different

thoughts. As if engaged in endless batting practice, you never strike out. You always get another chance, in the next moment, to make the connection.

Once you reach a critical mass of insights, the Principle of Thought will become real on a gut level. The tumblers will fall into place and open up a door of new understanding and freedom for you. The deeper you understand the Principle of Thought, the more often you'll be able to remember it in your everyday life.

Real understanding is both a mysterious and an objective process: you know you know, without knowing *how* you know. To understand the Principle of Thought, you need first to observe objectively how your thoughts create your experiences, and second to allow yourself to feel directly in your body the truth of the insight.

Rather than build a case against the Principle of Thought, look for where you know it's true. When you're able to disrupt a line of thinking and create a new reality, look for a positive feeling to deepen your understanding. You'll find a rush of good feelings every time you have a new insight into how you function.

MIND AND INTELLECT

Your mind, in contrast to your intellect (the storehouse of thought), constitutes your ability to observe and choose thoughts. Your mind is both a witness to and a participant in how you think. Your intellect sends out thoughts nonstop—your free mind consists of your ability to let go of distorted and unhelpful thoughts and to focus instead on what is true and useful.

Right now, take a moment to think of something that's bothering you. You may be worried about a medical problem or upset with someone at work. Bring to mind all the details—what you're afraid of, what you hope will happen. Each time a thought about the situation appears, say out loud or to yourself, "Thinking," and let the thought go. Do this for ten minutes and then return to the book. This is an example of how the mind (your awareness and free will) can both call up thoughts and dispassionately watch them emerge and then disappear.

The higher your state of mind, the greater your ability to observe and direct your inner world. By finding a good feeling, you raise your awareness to the point where you can make active choices in what you think.

With this realization, you become free from the tyranny of your thoughts. When you catch yourself giving in to grandiose first-force thoughts, disregard them and focus on current reality. When you encounter second-force doubts, you can disregard them and refocus on what you want.

INTELLECT POWER

You were born with countless thinking programs and add to this a lifetime of experiences. Your intellect, or biocomputer, is so well designed it will run on its own. You can wake up in the morning and go through a whole day completely unaware that you're thinking; even when you're sleeping and dreaming, your intellect is working to solve problems and process information.

Your intellect is a wonderful tool that you can use for everything, from remembering phone numbers to solving complex mathematical problems. Your intellect is, however, limited. Einstein said, "We should take care not to make the intellect our god; it has, of course, powerful muscles, but no personality."

Although your intellect or thought system is extremely efficient, at times, like any computer, it will malfunction. You may find you want too much—your eyes will become bigger than your stomach, and then, after you overeat, you'll get a stomachache.

BIRD'S-EYE VIEW

When you get caught up in the first or second force, you press your nose so close against your computer's screen that you lose perspective. You become like a worm in horseradish: *the whole world looks like horseradish*. When you get lost in your thought system, your perception narrows and you distort reality.

Find a good feeling, and your perception widens into the bird's-eye view. With wisdom, you take the aerial view: if you are complimented, you refuse to escalate it into the Nobel Prize; and if you are criticized, you refuse to think you're a failure.

Imagine a Tinkertoy made up of a stick with three round parts

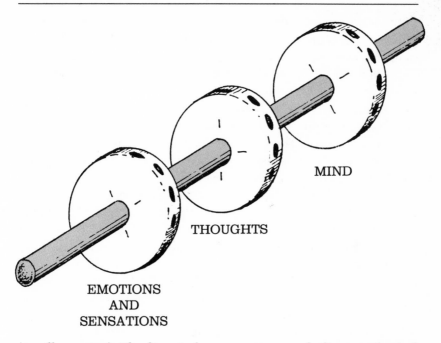

MIND

THOUGHTS

EMOTIONS
AND
SENSATIONS

(see illustration). The first circle represents your feelings or physical sensations (products of your thinking), the second circle symbolizes your thoughts, and the third circle is your mind or awareness, which is behind your thoughts. Your mind is a third force that exists outside of time and space. Your mind allows you to reconcile your inner life with your outer life.

Your mind is an inner eye that allows you to see into yourself as well as outside yourself. Your mind reflects what you're seeing at any moment in time. The calmer your state of mind, the clearer your vision. Wordsworth wrote: "While with an eye made quiet by the power of harmony, and the deep power of joy, we see into the life of things." When you're mindful, you're keenly aware of your inner and outer worlds. Your difficulties, limitations, and suffering come from being mindlessly lost in thought, while your true successes come from being mindfully in the moment.

FLUCTUATING MIND

Thinking is on the horizontal level. Your state of mind is independent of your thoughts, feelings, and actions. You can have a positive or negative thought in any state of mind. Your state of mind, which is on a vertical dimension, rises and falls moment by moment. Sometimes you're aware that you're thinking, and other times you lose your mind and take your ephemeral thoughts for objective reality.

You can directly experience your state of mind or level of awareness, but no one knows where your mind comes from, or even why it's here. The eye can't see the eye. Your observing self is too shy to be interviewed. Try to become aware of your awareness and it recedes further into the background.

You are unable to see what your mind *is*, but you can experience what it *does*. When you look at your thoughts, who is doing the looking? Your awareness stands on the riverbank and watches your stream of thought go by. In a high state of mind, you have the power not just to observe the stream, but to direct where it goes.

TRUE POWER

Start to see that you can disregard any thought and you'll create psychological space—room to maneuver, room to keep your mind on what you want, and room to accept calmly and transcend first-force drivenness and second-force resistance.

Like old ballplayers who wander up for their turn at bat, your insecure and grandiose thoughts can reappear for years. No matter how insistent they are, remember you manage your thoughts— pat them on the back and gently send them back to the dugout.

Learn to direct your thinking and you'll take the overreaching first force and the denying second force in stride. You'll stick to your decision to stop smoking and dismiss thoughts that you need a cigarette when they appear. You'll dismiss thoughts that bring you down and focus on good feelings that lift you up. You'll become saner. One recovered schizophrenic said he still heard voices, "but now I don't pay any attention to them."

WISDOM

When you're wise, you become like the Buddha, who said in the *Dhammapada*, "You are what you think. All that you are arises with your thoughts. With your thoughts you make your world." You are wiser today than when you were in high school, because you now know that many of your past fantasies and insecure thoughts (how you looked or how you sounded) were just thoughts.

Craving or greed is the self-destructive first force; aversion or hatred is the self-destructive second force; ignorance (of the difference between thought and reality) is the self-destructive third force. You dispel ignorance and gain positive third-force wisdom by seeing that *thoughts create your experience of reality, but thoughts are never reality.* When you look down in front of you, what do you see? You may think, "I see a book." But "book" is a thought or concept in your head. What you really see is color, shape, and contrasting form.

REALITY VERSUS THOUGHT

You severely handicap yourself when you confuse your thoughts with reality. Being stuck on the conceptual thought level is like being in Plato's cave: you confuse the shadows with true sunlight.

When you rely on your intellect instead of your senses, you're lost in the shadows. Zen master Huang Po said, "The foolish reject what they see, not what they think; the wise reject what they think, not what they see." Look and you'll start to see that thoughts give you a static, artificial picture of reality and feelings give you a richer, more dynamic take on reality.

If you understand the first force on the conceptual level, it will be of some value to you. However, if you can directly experience your urge to spend money and can have the insight that this is the first force in action, then you really have something. The second force will remain just words until you can directly link it to the uncomfortable body sensations that rush up when you don't want to make a phone call or do the dishes. The third force will be no more than an interesting idea until you can directly experience, with heightened understanding, the good feelings that come from reconciling an internal conflict.

SENSE OF SELF

Again your thoughts, which come from your memory, are all about your past experiences and have nothing to do with current reality. A little thought covers up a lot of reality. All of your thoughts are distorted in that they overgeneralize and give too small a picture of reality—even if they have a kernel of truth, they are still distorted. The grand distortion is that *your thoughts freeze impermanent reality.* Reality is a yeasty, ever-changing phenomenon.

Thoughts are by nature arrogant. In a rush to judgment, thoughts create a premature closure on reality. They misrepresent dynamic reality as being stable and permanent. For example, your thoughts trick you into believing you have a permanent self instead of a never-ending momentary sense of self that arises and passes away each instant.

NO PERMANENT EXPERIENCE

Your self is the experience of the momentary quality of your existence, or in other words, the experience of your experience. Self-doubt means you're experiencing doubt, just as self-confidence means you're experiencing confidence. Because you can have no permanent experience, you can have no permanent self.

The insight that your self is a process and not a thing frees you from becoming fixated on any one self experience. You know your current experience, good or bad, will soon be replaced by a new one.

If you look closely, you'll discover you have no self as an object that exists separate from your subjective experience of the moment. You'll realize that when you're seeing, you're just seeing; when you're feeling, you're just feeling; and when you're thinking, you're just thinking.

Self-concepts have no referent or counterpart in objective reality. They are illusions that don't refer to anything that actually exists. One moment you think you're a "winner," and the next moment you think you're a "loser."

NO SELF, NO PROBLEM

All self-concepts are just thoughts—excessive baggage you've picked up along the way. As if they were cataracts, the more thoughts about yourself you can drop, the clearer you see reality and the wiser you become. You discover, "No matter where I am or what the situation is, my sense of self changes moment to moment." With this insight, you no longer have an objective self you must defend or prove.

When you come to your senses, you feel the power that wells up from dropping your self-concepts and being in touch with your true sense of self. You have a sense of presence, and you take your thoughts about yourself less personally; you know that any thought about yourself can rise up and, if you leave it alone, pass away. You realize that all thoughts are impersonal and have nothing to do with you as a person—they are nothing to be ashamed of, proud of, or afraid of. You don't have to avoid, fight, or succumb to them.

OWNER OF YOUR MEMORY

Your intellect contains a huge memory bank. If you could print out all of the data, researchers estimate you would need a filing cabinet the size of Texas. Your intellect or personal computer is a miracle, but you are far greater. *You own and operate the computer.*

All of your experiences go onto a hard disk and never leave you. Your intellect has ample evidence for arguing any position. Don't be fooled by your own programs. Your thinking's job is to prove your thinking is right. Your intellect is a yes-man. No matter what you're thinking, your intellect will always try to prove you're right. Your intellect can draw on memories and rationales that make you look like Mother Teresa, or on scenarios that make you look like Charles Manson.

Your memories are tied together—one bad memory stimulates another. One man, upset over a breakup and unable to sleep, decided to get out of bed and try out a new word-processing program on his computer. He began to list the details of how his girlfriend had rejected him. After he finished, he decided to put in every rejection that he could remember. He wrote through the night. By five o'clock in the morning, he was in deep despair and hopeless about ever finding a girlfriend again.

The same brainwashing happens when you go over your bad experiences. You process your thoughts into your memory at deeper and deeper levels. Through repetition, you learn failure by heart. With insight, you see that memories are only thoughts, and you choose to experience the positive ones and let the dark ones go.

RAISE YOUR STATE OF MIND

The ultimate free lunch is that you can use your mind to raise your state of mind. Your mind naturally starts to rise and expand once you quiet your thoughts down and focus on being fully in the moment.

Just as it is true that the less you think about your fantasies and doubts the better, the less you talk about them the better. To stay in a higher state of mind, refuse to brag or complain. Writers are careful about talking about their projects beforehand; Norman Mailer said, "A tale twice told loses its creative power." Refuse to talk too much about what you are going to do, or about the obstacles you might meet along the way.

What do you have to do to feel good? *You have to be willing to give up your suffering.* Giving up suffering can be more difficult than giving up cigarettes; however, with insight and courage, you can wean yourself from familiar bad feelings. You'll find you can get used to anything, even being happy.

SCANNER

Your thought system has developed to help you survive, not to make you happy. Concerned with the survival of your body, your self-image, and your possessions, your intellect is a coping mechanism, not a source of inspiration and happiness. Left unchecked, your intellect is a relentless worrier constantly creating problems to solve. It will always create at least one major problem to worry about. As soon as you eliminate one worry, another takes its place. Because survival is your thought's foremost concern, negative memories are much more accessible than positive ones. If you have no external problems, your intellect will do a quick CAT scan of your body. Given that on the average you suffer eighty symptomatic physical episodes each year of any magnitude, from an unexplained rash on up, you usually can find a physical problem to worry about.

Although your intellect is more interested in bad news than good news, the good news is that your *mind* loves good feelings. Your natural state is joy and bliss—only your thoughts take you away from it. The secret of happiness is to stop making yourself unhappy. Quiet your thinking down and your mood and state of mind will naturally start to rise.

Your intellect can be a terrible boss, but with insight and training, you can turn it into a first-class employee. You can override your thought system's natural inclination toward negativity and replace it with a slant toward good feelings and wisdom. Use the law of use: *what you do, you tend to do again.* If you continue to disregard your negative thoughts and look for good feelings, you'll start to develop a natural tendency toward happiness.

THOUGHTS AS PEANUTS

Imagine walking through a park eating a bag of peanuts. Every now and then you get a bad one; you spit it out, keep walking, and reach in for a good one. Rather than grind on a slight or a pipe dream, spit it out like a bad peanut.

The ability to have a thought is great, but the ability to disregard a thought is even greater. Arguing with your thoughts or trying to avoid them gives them more respect and power than they deserve. Acknowledge your thoughts but refuse to negotiate with them, the way you might refuse to negotiate with terrorists.

Trying not to think about something is thinking about it. Rather than try *not* to think of your breakup or upcoming surgery, switch your focus to being in the moment—focus on driving, eating your dinner, or listening to another person.

31

If you do inadvertently swallow a bad thought, you may feel uncomfortable for a few minutes. If you're unable to shift your focus outside of yourself, voluntarily choose to experience the discomfort in your body (the more specific you can be, the better) with matter-of-fact equanimity, and the uncomfortable sensations will soon start to disappear. Give yourself radical permission to feel the body discomfort, but refuse to dwell on the negative thought; you'll discover that feeling pleasant or unpleasant body sensations is a gateway to good feelings.

Like uninvited in-laws, insecure thoughts often show up when you least expect them. Refuse to buy into them or fight them and they will tire of lurking around and leave. Your bad feelings have no life of their own. They need the heartbeat of your thinking to keep them flowing. Stop fixating on your thoughts and refocus on being in the moment, and your uncomfortable feelings will evaporate.

BIRTH AND DEATH OF EMOTIONS

Emotions consist of three elements—thoughts, feelings, and skill in handling the fusion between thoughts and feelings. Each thought has a corresponding physical feeling. The less conscious you are of the *congealing* of your thoughts and feelings (body sensations), the stronger your emotional reaction.

Second-force negative emotions (anxiety and depression) are the offspring of a negative feedback loop (NFL). First-force negative thoughts feed forward and activate negative feelings: they in turn stimulate more negative thoughts. With continuing feedback, your dark thoughts seem real and your uncomfortable feelings harden into a solid mass.

As you continue to grasp and solidify around your negative reaction, you begin to believe this is the real you. You fail to see that you're artificially manufacturing the toxic reaction and that your true self is one of bliss.

RUNAWAY GROWTH

Wisdom is knowing the difference between the container and the contents. The thinking and feeling functions are the containers, and the specific thought and sensations are the contents. Trying to gain insight into the contents prevents seeing into the container, or process. You'll never understand the underlying atomic structure of an object by looking at its form or color.

Without third-force insight into how each thought and each feeling is distinct, you're unable to tell one from the other. Your emotional reaction becomes a self-organizing and self-perpetuating system. Your thinking and feelings reinforce each other and co-mingle into an emotional flash fire. Ten units of fearful thoughts and ten units of fearful feelings can continue to multiply exponentially: the net result is not twenty units of fear, but one thousand or ten thousand units of anxiety.

ADDICTED TO THINKING

Your first-force emotions (greed and excitement) are borne out of the same incestual mating pattern between thoughts and feelings. In the affirmative feedback loop (AFL) your fantasies produce pleasant sensations which encourage more driven first-force thinking. When you lack the skill to break up this symbiotic interaction, you can, like Walter Mitty, become addicted to your own daydreams.

No one escapes periodic emotional beatings and binges. Everyone suffers. You need to have compassion—every person you meet is one of the walking wounded. You, however, don't have to spend your entire life in an emotional Super Bowl—oscillating between a punitive NFL and an escapist AFL.

DETACHMENT

You can dispel any emotional reaction simply by watching it with heightened third-force awareness and allowingness. You become free from the tyranny of your emotions once you see at a deep level that emotions are simply the fusion of tiny, subliminal bubbles of thoughts and feelings, which totally evaporate into pure energy under close examination. Your detached observation disrupts the feedback mechanism, enlarges your field of self-organization, and returns you to your natural state of calm and feelings of happiness.

Identifying with your thoughts and feelings creates and crystallizes your emotions. Careful, dispassionate investigation ("I'm not my thoughts" and "I'm not my feelings"), on the other hand, dissolves them. Small children usually get over everyday emotional upsets much quicker than adults because children feel more and think less. Instead of locking yourself into an emotional reaction by trying to think it away, take the opposite tack and *watch it to death.*

TEMPORARY STATE

You normally experience your emotions as a global, diffused mass of pain and pleasure that seems to exist more outside than inside you. By making finer discrimination between thoughts and feelings, you can raise your level of awareness to where you can see their essential impermanence: you discover that each thought and each feeling is a separate and independent burst of effortless vibration.

ILLUSION OF FUSION

As long as you remain directly in touch with the expansion and constriction of each thought and feeling, you'll never become overwhelmed by any emotion. Instead of trying to snip the knot between thoughts and feelings, loosen it by observing it. Look for the space between thoughts and feelings. By watching carefully, you can let go of something that never was really there—the illusion on fusion. You go beyond "this too shall pass," to seeing with complete certainty that your thoughts and feelings are passing away right now.

What makes emotional reactions so frightening and frustrating is not knowing what is going on. Once you understand the process, the problem resolves itself.

Given half a chance, nature (as quickly as it can) organically releases the energy bound up in your emotional reaction—this frees you to experience life as a flowing wave instead of a solid particle.

NOTING

You can nearly always short-circuit your emotional reactions before they come to full term. When you're feeling hurt at a party and have the thought, "I should tell that person off and leave," drop the thought and focus on being at the party.

If your painful emotion persists, you can transcend it by noting and feeling through your body sensation or by noting your thoughts. (Body sensations are usually easier to contact than thoughts because they have a three-dimensional quality and are directly accessible.) Note and localize the large body parts ("Throat . . . stomach . . . whole body") and use the noting as a signal to feel through the body sensation. When a thought appears, note "thinking" without buying into it and go back to experiencing your body sensations. You gain power by refusing to act on or voice your negativity. You never feel better than when you're a conscious participant in raising your own level of functioning.

MASTERY

You develop the ability to drop your thoughts and find a good feeling the same way you get to Carnegie Hall: *you practice.* Practice catching and dropping your disruptive thoughts and eventually you will do it by reflex.

When you feel down, refuse to go after the cause of your bad feelings; refuse to try to figure out why you're feeling down. This is putting the fox in with the chickens: *thinking about why you feel bad is what causes you to feel bad.*

You are unable to gain any real learning, or real understanding, from a low state of mind. Einstein said, "The world that you have made as the result of the level of thinking creates problems you cannot solve at the same level at which you created them." Remember all thoughts that come from a low state of functioning keep you in a low state of functioning.

DENIAL

Repeatedly thinking about a negative situation is sticking your head in the sand. Start to understand at a deep level that, when you're in a low state of mind, *thinking about your problems is a way of denying your problems* ("What did I do wrong?"; "What am I going to do?"). You think about the problem as a way to avoid reality—a way to avoid feeling, seeing, and accepting what is really going on.

To get past your denial, stop turning the problem over and over in your mind. You want to accept and resolve your problems, not belabor them. Forget about the problem until you feel better and your head is out of the sand. Once you're in a higher state of mind, you'll be able to see lessons you need to learn, and you'll be able to see what you need to do next.

Postpone your important thinking until you're in a high state of mind. The time to ponder and contemplate is when you feel good and are in your right mind.

In a high state of mind, you use concepts or thoughts as tools to help you clarify reality. Thoughts mindfully used as tools help you make finer distinctions and more telling analogies. The clearer and more accurate your models of reality, the greater your mastery and sense of confidence.

To avoid going the other way and becoming the tool of thought, remind yourself that thoughts are only conventions, working truths, and never reality itself. Don't become too attached to any one model—if your only tool is a hammer, the whole world starts to look like a nail. If you're able to see past thought to direct reality, your thoughts will remain helpful tools instead of terrible masters.

As you move to a higher state, you'll find you begin to think in an entirely different way. You move from your primitive, early brain to your higher-order, later brain. Once the quality of your thinking improves, you'll no longer try mindlessly to solve unsolvable problems. Instead, your thinking becomes reflective, intuitive, and inspiring.

PRESENT REALITY

Thoughts are invisible strings that tie you to the past and future (good feelings move you into the present moment). The less you think about a business loss, the less entangled you become with the past. If you keep ruminating over a past loss or a future fear, mentally note it and refocus on being in the moment. Realize that thoughts are only thoughts and you can detach from a triviality that happened twenty minutes ago or from a catastrophe that might happen twenty years from now.

To transcend the first and second forces, cut the strings and let go of what you're holding on to. Refuse to carry even the last five minutes with you. On the way home from a meeting, if you have the thought "I talked too much," dismiss it and focus on the feeling and wonder of the present moment.

Test out for yourself the possibility that, even if you drop your insecure thoughts, you'll still be safe. You can fall asleep without causing a burglar to break into your house. You'll find planes stay in the air even if you nap or read. You can stop ruminating about your mother's illness without being a heartless, uncaring son or daughter.

FREE MIND

You may be dissatisfied with a job or a relationship and want to leave, but because you are afraid to leave, you stay and remain dissatisfied. The more you push yourself to decide, the less clarity and wisdom you have to make a good decision.

The ability to make decisions comes from your free will. The higher your state of mind, the more free will you have and the greater your ability to make decisions. The irony is that, the more you insist you must decide, the more your state of mind drops, and the less ability you have to make a decision.

Your best decisions come from your highest states of mind. In a low state you have only half a mind to make a decision. You need to raise your perspective to the point where you can see what you really want and what is really going on. You'll find that in higher states of mind you have fewer decisions to make—what to do becomes self-evident—your questions answer themselves.

CREATE THE EXPERIENCE YOU WANT

Half of the story is to stop reacting to unwanted thoughts; the other half is to learn to choose actively the thoughts you want. Move to a higher state of mind and you can focus on bringing about what you want. Give your intellect clear directions and your intellect becomes your willing servant. If you tell yourself, "I want to get up at seven and drive across town," your intellect will wake you up and get you there (provided you give yourself a clear, noncontradictory message).

Give yourself the correct coordinates: *tell yourself the truth about where you are and the truth about where you want to go.* Replace your conflicting signals ("I want to be in a relationship, but I'm not attractive or lovable enough") with straightforward input ("I want to have a good, strong relationship"). Your intellect will automatically and unconsciously start to resolve the gap between where you are and where you want to go by moving toward your aim. You will start to see unexpected opportunities to bring about what you most want—almost by magic, you'll be led to the result you want.

RESOLUTION SEEKING

Everything you consciously bring about, from drinking a glass of water to having children, comes from a discrepancy between what you want and the reality of what you have. Your intellect, if given the correct first-force and second-force coordinates, will become a third force and reconcile the discrepancies between aims and current realities.

To use your intellect as a completing third force, ask yourself the first-force question "What do I want?" and the second-force question "What is happening right now that's relevant to what I want?"

You might answer, "I want to go to Europe next summer, and right now I only have two hundred dollars saved toward it"; or you might answer, "I want to make new friends, and right now I'm unsure how to do it."

REDIRECT

When you run into resistance, use this as an opportunity to redirect your focus. Raise your state of mind by moving into the moment and finding a good feeling toward what you want, and then create a new discrepancy between where you are and where you want to go. Picture simultaneously both your first-force aim and your second-force reality. The clearer you make the discrepancy, the more effectively and the quicker your intellect will work to resolve it in favor of what you want.

If you periodically focus on where you are and where you want to go, your intuition and instincts will provide you with insight on the appropriate steps you need to take. Have faith. Refuse to look over your intellect's shoulder. Your intellect works best when left alone. If you try too hard to breathe, you'll end up hyperventilating, and if you try too hard to reach a goal, you'll end up sabotaging yourself.

Your natural goal-attaining system works best when trusted to its own devices. Nature was designed to work, and humans were designed to play. Your intellect loves to bring about results—allow it to work on its own without your constant supervision and you'll find you can consistently bring about the results you want and enjoy the process as well.

3

DIFFERENT REALITIES

O nce you understand the first principle, you'll realize that your day is made up of a series of shifting subjective realities. One moment you're in a first-force reality and are convinced that your sparkling neon fantasies are true; the next moment, without your recognizing it, the lights have darkened and you are sinking into dismal second-force pessimism.

Once you understand you are watching the slide show of your mind, you refuse to react to a fantasy of being the jewel of the universe and you refuse to become desperate over thoughts that you're going to end up living in an abandoned car.

Your mind is always handing out roses and coal. Turn a deaf ear to your own propaganda and look for a good feeling. When you are caught up in first-force daydreams, you are likely to step into a manhole, and when you are engrossed in second-force dramas, you are likely to give up and lie down in the middle of the street.

With understanding, you rise from the basement to the penthouse. You see you have no need to inflate your desire for success or deflate your fear of failure. From the top floor you see the whole picture; you see what you most want, and you see the true lay of the land.

WORLD OF ART

You're an artist—you paint your version of reality thought by thought. To impress your family, you paint a picture of affluence; to get a raise, you paint a picture of dire poverty. Understand that you can choose your thoughts and you become the painter, not the canvas. You actively choose thoughts that paint an accurate and inspiring picture of life.

You can find as many different paintings of reality as there are people. All people have one commonality: each paints reality differently. You would expect the people of Timbuktu to paint their realities with strange customs and cultural differences. You know that you live in a different reality from that of a citizen of Timbuktu. Do you see that you live in a different world from that of your office mate or the person who sleeps next to you each night?

ART APPRECIATION

Much of the distracting first force and resisting second force you encounter come from other people. Understanding different realities allows you to transcend your differences successfully and connect with others.

To transcend the first and second forces consistently, you need to learn to be *nonreactive to others' pleasant and unpleasant moods.* To do this, realize that people paint their realities in their own personal styles. At times people paint masterpieces, and at other times they paint themselves into corners. People's realities come in rainbow colors that change from moment to moment. The person you live with can be green with envy over your promotion; turn white as a ghost when shocked; see red over a parking ticket; be tickled pink by the birth of a niece; develop a yellow streak about talking to the bank manager; and go into a black mood over a birthday.

The colors of people's realities vary according to their states of mind. At times you look at someone you've known for years and think, "Who *is* this person?"

People's self-portraits are constantly changing. They are blends of light, shade, shapes, design, and texture. The light you see them in depends on where *you* are standing, as well as on where they are standing.

NOT A PRETTY SIGHT

Once you grasp that people's realities are constantly shifting, you become impartial to others' unattractive sides. In lower states, people's natural beauty disappears. Just as on a camping trip you accept others even though they are grubby, you accept someone who is angry and slanting the truth. You have compassion. You know that, after a change of scenery and a hot shower, everyone sees the world in a better light.

At times people lose their free will and act like machines. It's just as futile to kick a person who is acting like a broken machine as it is to kick a broken vending machine. From your higher state, simply see the person as "out of order."

To have a happy marriage, treat your spouse like the youngest member of your family. When your partner acts badly, refuse to react to it. Remember that people eventually forget why they are feeling bad and start to feel better again.

Because each person's history is different, each person lives in his or her unique world. Each person's moment-to-moment reality is made up of his or her agenda, thoughts, feelings, and slants on the world. Take "Well, that's how *you* see it, but *I* see it differently" to a deeper level and you'll start to grasp the power and wisdom of understanding different realities.

CHANGING REALITIES

Realize that at each moment people create new realities for themselves. As if on a cross-country train trip, people pass through changing scenery. One moment they see the world as Death Valley, the next as a mountain paradise. The world remains neutral—

people paint their scenery between bites of food, while talking on the phone, and during business meetings.

Saint Jerome told a peasant, "If you can say the Lord's Prayer straight through without distraction, I'll give you this horse." The peasant said, "That sounds pretty easy. . . . Our Father who art in heaven, hallowed be thy . . . Does that include the saddle?"

SUBJECTIVE REALITIES

Given how quickly you and others can change realities, it's no wonder so much confusion exists. If you paint the world red and your friend paints it blue, what color is it? A difference in opinion is not a problem; it's just a fact. You'll no longer go to war over which is the true color once you know at a deep level that all people make up their unique versions of reality from moment to moment.

People are just like you: they form and color their pictures of the world and then project these pictures onto the world. Their states of mind determine how they see the world—to the jaundiced eye, the whole world looks yellow.

Once you see that people create their realities by their thinking, reading the morning paper becomes more enjoyable and interesting ("That's how the liberals paint the world and that's how the conservatives paint it").

FINGER PHILOSOPHY

You may point your finger at a veiled woman of Timbuktu and think, "That's wrong. It's medieval and repressive." On the other hand, the veiled woman in Timbuktu may look at a Western woman in her sundress and think, "That's wrong. It's sinful and shameful."

Once you can see the fact of different realities, you remove your veil of ignorance. You no longer get lost in another's version of reality. You understand that the way your friends and family paint reality comes from them, not from the world they are painting.

Watch for times when you point your finger at the world and think, *"That's* the way it is." Remind yourself that your finger, pointing at the world, is not the world. Compare your description of the world with other people's descriptions and you'll begin to catch on to different realities.

TRUE EMPATHY

Grasp the insight of different realities and you'll be fair with people. You'll be tolerant, accepting, and kind. One of the many paradoxes of higher states is that, the more nonattached you are to someone (as opposed to noninvolved), the greater your sense of connectedness. You'll feel more bonded once you realize others live in their own separate realities. When you're in a restaurant or out in a crowd, you will naturally replace contempt for strangers with respect.

Once you understand different realities, you'll no longer try to fuse with others or need to distance yourself to avoid feeling bad. Instead, find a good feeling and move to a higher level of understanding. From this higher perspective, you easily reconcile conflicts ("You're right from your perspective and I'm right from mine. . . . How can we both get what we want?"). From this perspective, you are alone and together at the same time; you realize you live in a different reality, and yet you feel connected, one human being to another.

THREE FORCES AND SOCIAL ROLES

Once you understand separate realities, you can decide which force you want to bring to any situation. You can be a first force that initiates action, a second force that resists others, or a third force that brings two opposing parties together.

When you're the third-force spark, you can transform a diverse group of separate realities into a unifying cause. You can become like Eisenhower, who was commander of the Allied forces in World War II not because of his brilliance, but because he could bring all of the strong generals together.

With conflicting parties, you can become the impartial, reconciling third force that straightens out misunderstanding between the different realities. All you have to do is raise your state of mind, have good will, and stay impersonal and nonjudgmental—key elements in the third force.

COOPERATION

A good feeling gives you the means to span the gulf between yourself and others. Your deeper logic and greater understanding allow you to deal effectively with all people. Because of your greater insight into how people work, you can gain greater cooperation from others.

If you want to get along with a difficult person at work, you can use your greater maturity and greater inner authority to reconcile the differences between you. Because you realize difficult people are suffering and starved for understanding and friendship, you can see that their points of view come from their separate realities, and reflect your understanding back to them.

A conflict arose between a couple over whether New York or Los Angeles was the worse city. Neither would back down from his or her position. The topic eventually shifted to whether they were having a discussion or a fight over the matter. They spent the rest of the night debating whether they were having an argument or a discussion. Once you understand that it is impossible to force others to see the world through your eyes, you no longer need to convince other people that you are right and they are wrong.

On a superficial level, different realities mean that everyone interprets life differently. On a deeper level, people take on new meaning. For the first time, you see and appreciate others as individuals. You are grateful for people's positive sides and accept their negative sides—people in your life become wonderful and distinct beings.

LOVE

Ongoing love is all you need to make any relationship work. To keep love alive indefinitely, refuse to freeze the other person with your thoughts ("You're always like this"). When you start a relationship, you experience the other person as unique and vibrant. With wisdom, you continue to see the person as whole and dynamic.

Thoughts can destroy love. Fixated thoughts are dangerous, because they kill off the real person in front of you. Good feelings, in contrast, give life. When you feel good, you experience others multidimensionally. You're able to take another person inside you, and you're able to be open and give yourself to the other.

Move to a level where you can be aware of yourself and the other person at the same time. Divide your focus and allow yourself to be in the other person and the other person to be in you. Experience your own feelings of love; experience the person you're loving at the same time.

To keep this chemistry going, disregard all thoughts that freeze the person in your mind. See the other person directly instead of the character you've created in your mind. Because everyone is constantly changing, every meeting is a meeting with a stranger. Remember to take a fresh look at the person each moment. George Bernard Shaw said, "The only man who behaves sensibly is my tailor; he takes my measure anew each time he sees me, whilst all the rest go on with their old measurements and expect them to fit me."

RISE TO THE OCCASION

Have the eyes of an anthropologist and make the conscious choice to see each person as a separate culture. Allow others their values, rituals, and customs, and make your own choices about what *you* want. Life becomes endlessly fascinating as you see how the moods and thinking of your friends and co-workers lead to their different realities.

By living in good feelings, you open yourself to new ideas and new perspectives on people. From the third-force perspective, you see each person with a balance of first-force goodwill and second-force acceptance. Move to a higher way of living and you'll see people and yourself completely differently. Rather than be led astray by others' first force or blocked by their resistance, move to a higher plane and see that everything is a manifestation of different realities; once you have this insight, your difficulties start to disappear.

ILLUSION OF FUSION

Your style may be conservative—you may want to stash all of your money under the mattress. Your partner may have a Monte Carlo style and want to invest it all in the commodities market. You may think, "We're not compatible. . . . We should separate." Compatibility is a myth: you always live in your reality, and your partner lives in his or her reality.

Once you transcend the illusion that you must fuse with someone before you can be happily together, you can create a good relationship and reconcile your differences.

No matter how well you know someone, you can still find infinite distance between you.

From the vantage of a higher state of mind, you love the differences between you rather than try to ignore or eliminate them. Once you connect and form a third-force bond, you will love and respect the other person for being complete and separate.

APPRECIATION

If you can see the other person fully, you're thankful for his or her distinctive being. You look *at* the other person and stop wanting to see yourself mirrored back.

You go to great expense and trouble to take a vacation. Does it make any sense to complain because the people are different? Look at your relationships in the same way. You go to a great deal of trouble to form a relationship. Disregard the urge to call the complaint department because the other person likes country music and you like classical.

While others are different from you, they are also the same. Be honest about how inconsistent you are and you'll accept others' inconsistencies. Accept your multiple personalities and you'll accept the twelve faces of your husband or wife.

HERD REALITY

With insight into different realities, you become more direct and more sensitive. You treat people as *they* want to be treated.

You understand that one friend would love a surprise party but another would rather be shot at dawn; you sense that your aunt likes to be visited and sent flowers when she is ill, but your uncle wants to be left completely alone when he is laid up.

In lower states, you think reality is one big game that everyone is in on but you. Realize that such a herd reality is an illusion: everyone lives in a separate version of reality. You experience a company picnic one way, your boss experiences it another. Though there are obvious overlaps and shared perceptions, every group you enter into is a composite of individual realities.

NONE OF YOUR BUSINESS

As you become wiser, you stop being thrown by others' low states. You know it takes two to quarrel. If your partner is in a bad mood, see it as your partner's reality—not yours. If you do have a physical reaction, feel it through rather than act on it. After your partner is through feeling bad, *forget about it*. Why go over it and relive it?

Other people's lives are their business. With insight, you can develop the wisdom of the five-year-old boy who responded to gossip with, "That's really none of our business, is it?"

The less time you spend going through others' medicine cabinets, the better; and the less time you spend worrying about others' problems, the better. You're unable to feed the starving world by refusing to eat, and you're unable to help others by ruminating about their problems.

FORGET ABOUT IT

Once you truly grasp different realities, you will be more forgiving. You can drop your general policy—"I never hold a grudge for more than five years"—and stop forming grudges and planning revenge. Keep in mind that all people react as they do because of how they are seeing the world at the moment.

If you need to talk about it, wait until you're both feeling better. A famous haiku can be translated roughly as: "Whatever happens, not talking about it makes for peace." To help you tolerate others' unpleasant behaviors, see how you do the very same behaviors yourself. To help correct your reactiveness when someone slips into a negative pattern, remember one of *your* negative patterns. To cancel out your upset feelings when someone is rude to you, recall a time you were rude in the same way. Turn a negative into a positive. Let others' negative behavior be *a cue to be more conscious of your own shortcomings.*

When you criticize another, you're usually projecting your flaws onto the other person. If you catch yourself about to correct another person, let your attitude be, "I know what *you* are, but what am *I*?"

CLARIFICATION

Remember, the guiding principle is further clarification of reality. As you talk to others, translate what they are saying into pictures in your mind. If the person says, "I drove out to the country on Saturday," picture in your mind the person driving out to the country. Ask questions to fill in gaps in the picture ("Where in the country did you go? Who went with you?"). Your natural curiosity will guide you.

Picture the person's reality as clearly and as vividly as you can, and then feed the picture back to the person to see if you understand ("You went to the Pine Barrens with your son on Saturday morning").

When someone thinks you live in his or her reality, speak up about how you feel. Clarify your own reality. Make your different realities clear and you'll avoid rifts with people. Be objective about your subjective reality: tell others how you feel ("I'm feeling upset right now, but I'll feel better later").

When you never clarify your position, others assume you share their points of view. If you are starting a new job and you are unclear about what's expected, keep asking questions (even if you look like a fool) until you understand your boss—and your boss understands you. By telling the truth, you raise your level of functioning.

FRIENDLINESS

At times you will feel some discomfort or distance from others. Find out what is going on with you. What bodily sensations do you have? Where are they located? Be willing to endure the discomfort to clarify your own second-force reality.

After you experience and clarify your uncomfortable feelings, look for a friendly feeling. With spiritual intelligence you come to see that *friendly feelings are the secret of all good relationships*. Evoke and promote positive feelings toward others and you create positive rapport.

If you want to give a good speech, feel friendly toward your audience. If you want to have a good interview, feel friendly toward the person you'll be talking with. If you want to get along with your kids, feel friendly toward them. Aim to be friendly and you can always find common ground with another person.

When you feel good, you feel closer to everything and everyone. Friendly feelings are the relating force. You have a sense of merging with what you feel good about.

Decide to have an *inner* good feeling toward another person and you create a bridge that brings you together. Simply choose to have goodwill toward the person and be willing to do whatever it takes to earn his or her goodwill.

TO UNDERSTAND IS TO LOVE

Above all, people want to be seen and understood for who they really are. Refuse to take others for granted. Aim to experience others directly. Get to know others without prejudice or value judgments. Honor the process of directly knowing and understanding for its own sake.

Look at, listen to, and appreciate people as works of art and you'll become genuinely interested in them. Good feelings toward someone are a portal to the third force and come from the gratitude you have for being with that person. No matter how well you know friends or family, you can always learn more. How do their clothes relate to their world views? What words do they choose? What types of images do they use? Watch their body language and relate this to how they are seeing the world.

When you are in love, you want to know about your beloved's favorite foods, movies, childhood memories, and past adventures. The more you discover, the more love you feel.

Many cultures have a version of the saying "The foolish talk, the wise listen." Seeing and listening are third forces. The more you emotionally tune in, the clearer and sharper the person comes into focus. No matter how intimately you've been involved with someone in the past, you can know him or her at an even deeper level.

You can get an emotional high from looking at paintings in a museum: you get a contact high from the artist's high. Listen to what other people are really saying and you'll find, as you take in more reality about them, that you start to feel good in the moment. The more deeply you tune in to people, the higher your state of mind goes—and the higher their states of mind go.

4

PRINCIPLE TWO:
YOU CAN CREATE
YOUR STATE OF MIND

I n higher states of mind, your ability to choose what you think and to direct your focus is multiplied tenfold. As your understanding rises, your true self appears and you're able to create the experiences you want out of thin air.

To raise your level of functioning, understand the hierarchy of your moods (see the "Mood Ladder" chart) and realize you can guide yourself to higher states of mind by focusing on good feelings.

You can cycle through different states of mind in a matter of moments ("Why did I lose this sale? . . . I'll never make another one. . . . I'm mad about this. . . . What a drag. . . . Maybe it's okay. . . . Maybe it's even a blessing in disguise"), or you may cycle through them each week (depressed on Monday, anxious on Tuesday, angry on Wednesday, excited on Friday, bored on Sunday).

Learn to read your moods the way a ship's navigator reads instruments. In stormy weather, you may think you are going north

MOOD LADDER

	Serenity
HIGHER STATES OF	Joy
MIND	Happiness
	Enthusiasm
	Interest
NEUTRAL --------------------	
	Boredom
	Excitement
LOWER STATES OF MIND	Anger
	Anxiety
	Depression

when you are really going south. Ignore your thoughts, which give you a false reading, and trust the hierarchy of your moods.

First-force *excitement*, for example, is below *interest* and above *anger*. To raise your state of mind, become familiar with your mood levels. When you drop below the line, accept your uncomfortable bodily sensations and focus on gentle, positive feelings. No matter what your current state, you can always focus on subtler and higher feelings.

PSYCHOLOGICAL

Your feelings are gauges of your psychological functioning. Your feelings, like all reality, are in constant motion. Learn to read them and you'll gain greater self-understanding. Just as you would wait until the weather warms up and the ground thaws before relandscaping your backyard, wait until you feel better before you make big decisions. Wait until you're no longer angry before you decide to quit your job, and wait until you're calmer before you decide to buy a Great Dane puppy.

Your psychological thermostat has a set point. If you drop below the set point ("I feel awful"), the furnace goes on, warms you up, and raises you back to your normal state. If you get too far above your set point ("I feel too good"), the air conditioner goes on and cools off your good feelings.

53

To raise your set point, dismiss your killjoy thoughts and allow yourself to feel happy in the moment. If you continue to look for good feelings and stay with them long enough, you can reset your thermostat to a higher level.

CHANGING STATES

Realize that at one moment you're in a low state, grumbling about your job, and at the next you're singing while you work. In a first-force state of mind, you're full speed ahead, damn the torpedoes; then reality throws a cold bucket of water, and all of your desires vanish.

Through repeated observations, you'll learn not to be fooled by your states of mind any longer. You realize that the world stays the same; it's your shifting mood that determines your points of view.

Develop a taste for your shifting states of mind; tune in the helpful ones and tune out the others. When you feel low, dismiss malcontented states of mind as you would dismiss a troublesome employee ("I don't know how we'll manage without you, but we'll find out") and look for a good feeling to raise your state of mind.

Refuse to take your lower states of mind seriously. Realize that, just as another bus will be by in a few minutes, another state of mind will be here shortly to take you to higher ground.

QUESTION YOUR LEVEL OF THINKING

Before an eye exam, you think everyone sees as you do. Only after your eyesight is corrected can you see that your vision was off. In the same way, when your state of mind drops, you think everyone sees the world the way you do. Projecting your ideas onto reality, you think others dislike you as much as you dislike yourself. Only after your mood rises do you realize how off base you were.

The big fact: *you can't think your way out of a low state*. The more you try to dig your way out of a hole with self-talk, the deeper you dig yourself in. When you feel yourself in an emotional hole, quit thinking—allow your state of mind to rise before you look at the situation.

SMARTER

When you are in a low state, the bright light of truth can be too painful. Use good feelings as a sunscreen. Once your state of mind rises, you can look directly at the facts without getting burned.

Research has found that you gain the equivalent of twenty or twenty-five IQ points when you move from a low to a high state of mind. When you're down you waste your time trying to get answers from yourself ("Why did this happen?"; "What if that happens?"). Wait until you are feeling better and the answers will come to you naturally.

No matter how out of touch with reality the patients in mental hospitals become, they never break the television set. Even when you're in your lowest state, you still maintain a kernel of wisdom and common sense. In a lower state, use this kernel of understanding to remember you are dealing with your distorted thoughts about reality—the source of the problem—and not directly with the experience of reality. Remember that, when you believe you are putting your problems to bed by thinking about them, you're actually keeping them awake.

Understanding and insight come from a high state. If you have a real problem (as opposed to a pseudo-problem), the solution will appear naturally and spontaneously once you find a good feeling and raise your level of functioning.

SEEING VERSUS THINKING

Your subtle feelings lead to subtle thinking. Clear your mind of your ruminating thoughts and subtle insights will start to appear. Insights come from seeing a higher order of reality; you're able to align your observations correctly with what's really going on.

Insight can come at any time—and can come via the positive or the negative. You may get a good feeling and all of a sudden find your confusion cleared up. On the other hand, you may be angry at the world, but realize, when you have quieted your mind down, that you're really upset with yourself. One insight leads to another: you may come to see you are innocent because you can only function at your level of understanding.

The evolutionary process is toward higher levels of awareness. Good feelings are always at the top of your current level of awareness. This is nature's carrot or motivation for you to go to the next higher rung of awareness (just as bad feelings are nature's stick to motivate you to get smarter). Each step upward allows you to see reality more clearly. When you have an insight, your mind rewards you with a surge of energy—an increased sense of well-being. With each new connection, reality becomes bigger, clearer, more coherent, and more understandable.

In moments of insight, the good feeling you experience is your mind's gratitude for seeing how life fits together. You feel happy because you see you belong; you realize you have a place in the overall scheme of life.

ATTRACTION

Move to a higher psychological neighborhood and you'll stop attracting unsavory thoughts and feelings; you'll become a magnet for creative and inspiring thoughts and feelings.

As you feel better, your state of mind expands and you connect with a larger intelligence. You become like the artists and inventors who report that inspiration seems to come from out of the blue.

Your state of mind, which you experience as a feeling, attracts your life circumstances. Just as a restaurant owner sets a tone or an ambience to attract customers, your feelings or state of mind attracts your life experiences. If you dislike the people and experiences in your life, remodel your interior. Replace your unattractive interior with nicer, warmer, and more attractive decor.

Out in public, you'll attract smiles with a smile. If you're a teacher and can stay in a high state of mind, you'll bring out the best in your students. If you're a salesperson and can stay in a high level, you'll generate more leads and more business.

As you become happier and healthier, healthier people will gravitate toward you. Some people may be turned off by your good feelings, but you'll draw new friends, who live at higher levels.

FIRST STEP

If you want a new job, before you rush around, printing a new résumé and looking for job leads, first find a good feeling toward acquiring a new job and raise your state of mind. The job opportunities and the hunches about where to send your résumé will start to appear naturally.

If you want a new relationship, before you place an advertisement or look for a singles club, drop your bitterness and find a good feeling toward people in general. Just as you're more likely to find a parking place when you feel happy, you're more likely to meet and connect with someone when you're in a good frame of mind.

In a high state, when you hear opportunity knocking at your front door, you open the door and see who is there. Because you're open and positive, unexpected coincidences start to happen—you find yourself in the right place at the right time. The reason is not a mystery. You become receptive to possibilities you might otherwise ignore. Because you say "yes" to life, you put yourself in situations where lucky coincidences are likely to happen.

PEAK TIMES

You wear different hats throughout the day. Your state of mind or level of being fluctuates across time and place.

A schoolteacher's level of being soars when she's with people. Around people, she surrenders herself fully to the moment and has an inner feeling of warmth and closeness.

One computer engineer said his level rose when he was out on a basketball or tennis court. Time slowed down, and he saw all of the action in rich detail and great depth. He had an exquisite sense of being alive and in touch with his experiences.

A sense of bliss arose when a young mathematician engaged in intellectual pursuits. He experienced a sense of reverie when he read a new book or found a new theory. He felt in communion with the author and able to synthesize and savor the intellectual insights and connections.

The highest states of mind for a machinist came when he was working. If he was calculating an exact measurement, he was in full rapport with the task. He participated on all levels of his being and found order, beauty, and meaning in what he was doing.

A doctor's highest states came when she was with her family. She moved into a feeling of flow and childlike innocence simply by being with those she loved. She felt cozy, secure, bonded, and deeply grateful and blessed for being part of her family.

For one video director, her awareness was heightened when she was in touch with beauty. When she read a poem, looked at a painting, or listened to music, she had a sense of homecoming, of undifferentiated merging. She lost her separateness and became part of something much larger.

When a chemist was out in nature, hiking in the mountains or strolling on a beach, he dropped all his concerns and became a spirit without a body. As he united with nature, he had an overpowering sense of equanimity and deep contentment.

Realize that, although your higher states are triggered by outside circumstances, they come from within you. Rather than limiting your high states to one special time and place, you can learn gradually to expand this feeling and state of mind to all areas of your life.

STAYING ABOVE WATER

When you first-force desires hit the second-force resistance, why sink into a sea of despair? Why drive off the pier? Lighten up when you encounter resistance. Third-force feelings keep you buoyant and prevent first- or second-force riptides from dragging you under.

You only have to raise your feelings a little to transcend the lower forces. Next to a two-year-old, a five-year-old seems to have the wisdom of Solomon. With insight, you refuse to let a two-year-old's state of mind drive you off the deep end.

Verify for yourself the value of good moods. You'll find that when you feel good you are more generous and helpful. Your judgment, creativity, and physical skills improve—you walk better, see better, hear better, look better, and breathe better.

As you leave your dark moods and move close to the light, you enter into a sparkling, vivid paradise. The higher you go, the clearer the world looks. Your take on reality becomes crisper: colors become brighter and you see more of nature's detail.

You experience the first and second forces in your body—you tighten up and breathe more rapidly. When you start to feel too excited or too down, breathe deeply and rhythmically and you'll start to feel better. Calm your breathing down and you'll calm your mind down; you'll shift the momentum from your negative self to your positive self. As you relax your body, you'll find it easier to let go of your heavy, serious thoughts.

DISSOLVING PROBLEMS

All of your low moods and problems come from making something too important. Going over your problems anchors you to them and sinks your mood. Make living lighter rather than heavier. Disregard your heavy thoughts about money and you'll lighten up and have fewer problems with money. Disregard your serious thoughts about becoming ill and you'll be healthier. Disregard your heavy thoughts about life and you'll soon be able to laugh at what you once saw as life or death.

Your thoughts are puny gnats, small irritants of little importance. No need to take extraordinary measures with your thoughts—no need to control or call out the army—simply have the courage to let go of them and move into a sea of happiness.

AUTHENTIC VERSUS SERIOUS

With insight, you discover that your thoughts alone make life heavy. This applies to whether you think about a broken fingernail or getting cancer. "Breaking up is hard to do" because you *think* it's hard to do. Thoughts are not subpoenas you must respond to. You can simply toss them away, as you would junk mail.

Your intellect wants to convince you life is serious business. Your intellect bombards you with survival thoughts. With insight, you'll see that you alone make something serious, by thinking it is serious. Sickness, death, and old age are only serious if you think they are.

Drop your seriousness but keep your integrity. Authenticity

about who you are and what you want is as different from seriousness as air is from water. When you are authentic, your
thoughts, feelings, and actions are congruent—you say what you
mean and you mean what you say.

You're naturally weighted toward feeling good. If you are willing to drop the heavy thoughts that keep you down, your feelings
will automatically take you to a higher level of being. You can learn
to soar if you take more of life lightly. You'll find your spirits rise
when you stop going over your worries and regrets. Good feelings
take you to higher levels. Drop your thoughts and free yourself
from negativity. You'll shift the momentum toward good feelings
and higher levels of functioning.

LIGHTENING UP

Once you accept what is wrong and focus on what is right,
you're no longer the Creature from Twenty Thousand Leagues
Beneath the Sea. With patience, you can learn to rise above your
emotional depths. Even though initially you may feel like a fish
out of water, keep in mind you can get used to anything, even
being happy.

Understand that when your mood goes up you may initially
feel insecure, because you are in open seas. Bad feelings give you
an excuse to hide from life; you may think "being happy means I
must perform and make up for lost time." Relax—when you have
mental health, you know you don't have to do anything, or prove
anything.

UPS AND DOWNS

Be philosophical about your occasional low moods. Even saints
have their bad days. Be patient, and remember you'll always resurface. The contrast between bad and good moods can be highly
enlightening. Feeling bad becomes an asset when you allow it to
add to your insight into how you function.

Refuse to complain. Voicing your complaints can torpedo and
sink others. Instead, consider others' feelings and refuse to burden
them with your temporary insanity.

Because your intellect wants to accentuate the negative (to help you survive), a twenty-minute bad mood may make it seem as though you've ruined the whole weekend. Rather than berate yourself for your low moods, appreciate them. Your occasional dips prove that you're naturally buoyant and will always resurface.

BEYOND PROBLEM-SOLVING

The secret to mental health is that *you must first make room for good feelings.* Inwardly separate yourself from your thoughts and negativity. Throw overboard the idea that you must solve all your problems before you can be happy. Trying to solve all of your problems is like trying to bail out a leaky boat. Living is only a series of problems if you *think* problems are what life's all about.

Look back over what you were stuck on in the past (a business failure, a flaw in your appearance, rejection by a boyfriend or girlfriend) and you'll find that, rather than solve your problems, you transcended them.

You may think your problems are ghosts that will haunt you forever it you forget them, even for a moment. The opposite is true. Repeating your fish stories keeps you in a sea of despair. To resolve your problems, you first need to find a good feeling and rise above them.

As you feel better and shed the light of reality on what is going on, your problems start to evaporate on their own. You'll realize that your reasoning was all wet ("My headache didn't mean I had a brain tumor"). You'll find that much of what you imagine to be a problem (your cat is sick; your boss is angry at you; your competition at work is about to be promoted over you) is simply the way life is at the moment.

DISREGARD YOUR EGO

The bigger you make yourself, the heavier you feel and the deeper you sink. As your ego—your thought that you are special—grows, your state of mind sinks. Your ego has a vested interest in fighting happiness: when you're happy, your ego fades from the picture.

Your ego's essence is "I think, therefore I am." Disregard your thoughts of self-importance ("No one suffers like me") and your ego vanishes. When your spirits rise, your ego disappears. When you're in a high state of mind, you're not thinking, "I'm great"; you forget about yourself. You're too busy living in the moment to focus on yourself.

Your ego acts as if you are inadequate but at the same time as if you're the center of the universe ("What I said was so stupid. . . . Everyone was looking at me"). From a higher state of mind, you free yourself from responsibility for how the planets rotate; you'll find it's a great relief not to think any longer that the world revolves around your every move.

THIRD-FORCE UNDERSTANDING

Thinking about your problem in a low state is like trying to figure out how many gallons of water are in the Pacific Ocean: you only increase your sense of being overwhelmed. After you move to a higher state, you know that the size of the Pacific Ocean is irrelevant to your happiness.

Build an ark of understanding that allows you to ride above the inevitable turmoils of life. With understanding, you float above difficulties that previously pulled you under.

Letting go and forgetting about controlling life is the secret to good feelings. To move to a state of mental health, let go of your need to control the past ("Why did this have to happen?"), the present ("What am I going to do?"), and the future ("What if this happens?").

TRANSCEND THE PAST

In nearly every scary movie, a person decides to take a flashlight into the dark basement and see what all that groaning is about. Anyone with common sense would stay upstairs or leave the house.

Your memory is a treasure chest of bogeymen, complexes, and assorted craziness. In a lifetime, researchers estimate you have over 280,000,000,000,000,000,000,000,000,000 memories. Trying to get to the root of the problem *is* the problem. The more you dig into the past, the worse you'll feel.

Trying to find satisfaction through thinking about the past is like trying to quench your thirst by drinking seawater. The more you think about the past, the less satisfied you become.

Luckily, you have a free mind. No need to be lobotomized or go in for electric shock to avoid thinking about the past. You can simply decide to quit rummaging around the basement and instead look for a good feeling in the present. The real treasure is when you discover, "Thank God, none of that has anything to do with my being happy right now."

SHIP OF FOOLS

If you are waiting for your ship to come in before you can be happy, you'll miss the boat. Instead of waiting to be happy in the future, decide to raise your state of mind right now. When asked the time, Yogi Berra said, "You mean now?" Now is the only real time you ever have.

Even if your ship does come in (you get married, you inherit money) your happiness will be fleeting: *nothing stays wonderful for long.* You quickly adapt to what you longed for, just as you quickly adapt to loud music at a rock concert. Instead of hoping your cargo will arrive on the next ship, realize that happiness is always with you, ready to be acknowledged and used.

When you feel good, you are free from needing others to blow wind in your sails. You become self-motivated and no longer need to have others rescue you. Learn to restart your own mood and, if you slip, rescue yourself.

VALUE GOOD FEELINGS

When you feel good, people treat you better. If a shark or a school of fish does attack you, you can dismiss it offhandedly. You see through others' antics and their attempts to bring you down to their levels.

With insight, new options open and you're able to transcend everyday hassles. As long as you feel good, you stay above your current circumstances. You're impervious to life's ups and downs and are able to live above your everyday gains and losses.

Just as you can increase your hearing sensitivity by wearing a blindfold, you can increase your sensitivity to the good feelings of the moment by quieting your thinking and focusing on positive feelings. As long as you feel good, you are above your current circumstances.

At first you may feel awkward and unnatural living in good feelings. But, with patience, it becomes a new habit, and you learn to live naturally at a higher level of functioning.

5

FOCUS CREATES
ENERGY

hen the first force is active, you excitedly rush toward what you picture happening. When what you want fails to materialize right away, the momentum shifts and the denying force comes into play.

Your mind creates your outer reality by taking an inner picture of what you want and then letting it develop naturally. At first your photos are too bright, because you're shooting into the first-force sun; later they are too dark, because you're trapped in second-force shadows.

Your mind is your ability to direct your focus and create the experiences you want. The good feelings of the third-force focus even out the bright light of the first force and illuminate the dark, shadowy second force. Learn to use your good feelings as a third-force focus and you'll begin to bring into reality the pictures you want.

As you understand the power of good feelings, you raise your focus above the furious pursuit of success and the crippling fear of failure. Feeling good in the moment brings you to a point of awareness from which your perspective becomes fresh, clear, and alive: you naturally act from your own best interest.

To create your own third force, realize that *you reinforce, strengthen, and increase what you focus on.* Imagine you are in a cabin in a vast desert. Next to the cabin is a TV satellite dish. Focus on being isolated and you will be, even though there are hundreds of radio and television signals bouncing overhead. Learn to direct the satellite dish and you can connect with the outside world.

Your mind's ability to direct your focus is more subtle and powerful than thoughts, feelings, and actions. At any moment you can choose to focus on any thought, feeling, or action.

MENU OF CHOICES

You fill your awareness, an empty container, with what your mind focuses on. You can fill it with joy or sorrow. Be mindful of all you have and you feel happy. Focus on your troubles and you create a troubled mind. Focus on harmony and you create peace of mind.

Focus on feeling thankful for your family and you'll want to express your feelings of gratitude. You may start buying small gifts or being more considerate to your family. Keep focusing on being thankful and your gratitude will increase until you are grateful for feeling grateful.

Through the law of use and disuse, you become what you focus on. Your focus becomes a habit. Focus on living and you become full of life. Focus on your aches and pains and you become a pain to yourself and others. Focus on money and you become as cold and lifeless as paper currency.

MULTITALENTED

You can only think one thought at a time, but you can focus in eight or nine different directions at once. Driving to work in the morning, you're like a one-person band—you can steer, watch for oncoming traffic, work the pedals, listen to a song on the radio, balance a cup of coffee, and carry on a conversation with someone in the back seat.

Use your ability to split your focus to your advantage. To get what you want, be both a realist and a visionary: balance your focus between first-force desire and second-force reality. Focus simultaneously on what you want and on the present and you can orchestrate your life.

From a high state of mind, you can see your past, present, and future. You can tune in to a vast array of choices at will—good, bad, or indifferent. When you feel good, you know intuitively what to focus on. You are able to balance your focus between vision for the future and action in the present.

SWITCH RATHER THAN FIGHT

If you dislike the violence on Channel 4, or the video shopping program on Channel 31, remember that the remote control is in *your* hand: simply zap to another channel.

No need to subscribe to a television guide. Your feelings let you know when you need to change channels. Are you too caught up in self-dramatizations? Switch from "General Hospital" to "M*A*S*H" reruns. If you're getting too excited, switch from "Fantasy Island" to the nightly news.

WHAT YOU SEE IS WHAT YOU GET

Everything in life has its price. You get what you pay for. If you want health, happiness, a stable relationship, or a well-paying job, you have to pay attention to it.

You are born with an inheritance worth more than gold—your ability to focus your attention. You can squander your inheritance or you can lead the life of Riley. As you walk through Central Park, you can pay attention to the trash or to the beauty. A dying millionaire would gladly trade all his money—all the money in the world—for one more chance to look at and focus on life.

Like compound interest, what you focus on multiplies. Focus on good feelings and you'll find more to feel good about. Focus on being free and you'll amplify your sense of freedom. Focus on compassion and you'll have empathy and sympathy for others.

Invest your focus wisely and you'll create high dividends. The sounder your investment, the greater the yield. Look at your life. It is the sum total of your focus. Are your investments paying off? Are you in the red or in the black?

PATTERNS

Your predominant failure and success patterns, which were developed in your childhood or adolescence, revolve around where you place your focus.

Just as there is a structure and a pattern in how you get up and get ready for work each morning, start to see the structure and pattern in your failures. The contents vary, but the steps are the same. You may take twenty years to go through one cycle of the pattern, or you can go through it in a matter of minutes.

The initial phase is all first force. What you want is contaminated by your ego: you focus on something to prove your importance. You may jump in right away with a furious first force ("I'm head over heels in love after my first date") or you may let the first force build slowly ("After a year in class together, I think I'm in love").

In the middle phase, you run into resistance, the inevitable second force. In your failure pattern, you respond to the second force in one of three ways: you focus on how to control and overpower the resistance (which only increases it); you focus on trying to ignore the resistance and hope it goes away (which only causes it to go underground); or you focus on how you can quit.

The inevitable happens in the final phase of your failure pattern. Your low mood becomes a negative third force and you fail to get what you want.

SUCCESS PATTERN

Just as failure is a bad habit, success is a good habit. You succeed in a predictable way. In the initial phase of your success pattern, you focus on what you authentically want—your desire comes from your truest self.

Because you're true to yourself in the initial phase, you are willing to do whatever is necessary when you hit the resistance stage. In the middle phase, instead of fighting or ignoring reality, you focus on how to turn obstacles to your advantage. As you overcome resistance, you start to feel better, and this generates more success. The inevitable happens in the final phase of your success pattern. Your high mood becomes a positive third force and you get what you want.

ATTRACTION

What you focus on increases. Focus on good health and you'll naturally go to bed earlier, eat better, and exercise more. You attract what you focus on. Focus on telling the truth and others will be more honest with you.

If you focus on what you have, more will be given; if you focus on what you have not, more will be taken from you. Pay attention to what you have, be thankful, and you'll be given more.

Invest your focus on what you *want*, not on what you *don't want*. Focus on the long lines and expense while you're at an amusement park and you'll have a miserable time; focus on having fun with your family and you'll laugh, tell family stories, and enjoy watching people—no matter how long you wait in line.

Because what you focus on increases, you can increase your focus by focusing on it. Just as a woodchopper sharpens his ax before he chops wood, you can increase your focus or concentration power before you do a task. A good way is to focus on your breathing for fifteen minutes. Simply focus on the breath going in and out of your nose. Experience with concentrated awareness and even-mindedness the breath coming in the nostrils and the breath leaving. You'll find, if you practice, the investment in efficiency will pay off ten cents on the dollar—you'll get ten times the energy and time back.

Creative energy is concentrated focus. You would find it easier to write an essay on the history behind one tree in your hometown than on the whole town because your focus would be concentrated on awareness of the tree.

The two important creative skills are the abilities to concentrate your focus and to direct your focus to the end result you want.

How do you learn to direct your focus to what you want? Look at the ceiling—now look away from it. Learning to focus on what you want, rather than on your difficulties, is that easy.

SELF-CREATION

You validate your version of reality by automatically focusing on what proves your point of view. If you see the world as friendly, you'll find friendly people in the mall and out in traffic; if you see the world as dangerous, you'll find teenage gangs at the mall and crazed drivers on the road.

If you see yourself as a follower, you'll seek out a leader. If you see yourself as a leader, you'll seek out followers. If you think people like you, you'll act in ways that lead to being liked. If you think others dislike you, you will act in ways that lead to being disliked.

Your ability to bring about what you want by focusing on it is the greatest gift you have. Life is a huge catalogue—you can order anything you like. You can focus on being an underworld crime figure or on building a children's hospital in your community.

Do you have money but no friends, or friends but no money? What you have depends on what you are interested in. You can't have it all, but you *can* have what you get interested in and stay focused on.

UNDIVIDED ATTENTION

Direct your focus to what you want and you'll soon have it. The difference between success and failure is how steadily you hold your focus.

Get a clear picture, sharpen the definition of what you want, and hold the picture until it becomes reality. Keep your focus off of anything that would cloud or destroy your vision, and refuse to let yourself or others distract you from your purpose.

A clear picture of what you want is essential. You find it easier to repeat a success, because you already have a clear idea of what you want. Similarly, you'll find it easier to get a clear picture if you have a role model.

Start with approximations. If you're unable to picture yourself married, start by picturing yourself going with someone or living with someone. As you become successful in bringing about what you want, your thumbnail sketches evolve into masterpieces.

At first the picture of what you want may be vague and out of focus; the most important aspect is to have a *feeling* for what you want. As you get closer to your vision, you will see more light around it, and your vision will develop form and texture.

CURE FOR NEUROSIS

Being neurotic means you sabotage yourself. You're mean to someone you like; or, because you're mad at your boss, you throw up your hands and quit a good job.

Once you see that *your neurotic feelings come from your self-absorption*, you can stop a downward spiral. To put the brakes on a neurotic slide, find a good feeling and focus on something outside of yourself.

To be successful, you need to focus outside of yourself. Dwelling on yourself ("How do I feel? . . . How do I look? . . . How can I improve myself?") increases your sense of separateness and leads to feelings of isolation and loneliness. You can be so self-involved that when you're with people you're actually visiting yourself.

An empty stomach will eventually eat its own lining and cause an ulcer. Focus on something external and you'll feel fulfilled and stop eating at your own psychological lining. You'll become more psychologically healthy and more successful.

Your desires and the resistance you encounter are turned into good investments by outer forces. Refuse to let your focus get lost in a first-force psychological spending spree or a second-force emotional bankruptcy.

OUTER FOCUS

A television satellite dish turned on itself picks up only the sound of its own motor running. Your desires and the resistance you encounter become a problem only when you're stuck in the first person ("I," "me," "we"). Shift to a third-person focus ("he," "she," "they," or "it") and you'll find a good feeling and move to a higher level of functioning.

Use the few minutes of warning before a first- or second-force storm to get interested in something other than thoughts about yourself. Put your focus on the rug in your office, the clouds in the sky, or your body sensations. You can focus on nature or on your breath—it doesn't matter. Do something physical to shift your focus. Organize a drawer or take a walk. Whatever it is, pay attention to it.

The more attention you pay to your awareness of reality, the more reality you'll see and the better you'll feel. When you take a walk, your mood will go up if you swing your arms, take long strides, look around you as you walk.

As you turn your focus out, you expand and you feel better. You see the scenery vividly and hear the sounds clearly; you feel strong, and the future looks big and bright. Your hopelessness is replaced by a sense of mastery and gratitude.

The mere act of choosing to switch your focus raises your state of mind. When you take any active role in your life, your spirits, our of this sense of mastery and gratitude, soar.

VISION VERSUS FANTASY

First-force fantasies cause you to focus inward on thoughts of self and ultimately to defeat yourself. Your fantasies or daydreams are "show business"—you need to show your parents, friends, and co-workers how important you are.

In your fantasy, you are adored as a rock star, Nobel laureate, wife of Mr. Success, or boyfriend of Miss America. Fantasies are private playgrounds where you can escape from the real world.

Unlike visions, which may be vague and sketchy at first, fantasies are Technicolor Hollywood productions in exacting detail and airbrushed perfection.

You may try to act your fantasies out. You daydream about being a tycoon, so you invest all your savings in the stock market. Reality eventually shocks you awake; as you look at your portfolio, you discover you're no Donald Trump. You may fantasize about being at the Indianapolis 500 but come back to reality when a highway patrol officer pulls you over for speeding.

EXPRESSION OF TRUE SELF

Trade in your fantasies for visions. Unlike fantasies, visions are authentic; they are something outside of you that you truly want to bring about—they become even more real as you move toward them.

Visions are blueprints for action; you lay them out clearly before you start construction. Visions are organic and alive; as you get closer to them, they may shift and change form until they become exactly right. Visions pull you forward and invite you to become a participant in bringing about what you most want.

Daydreamers give visionaries a bad name. Fantasies are frauds. In your heart of hearts you know you'll never do what it takes to bring them about. Fantasies are like plastic flowers. They are ultimately unsatisfying and leave you feeling more empty. They are false adornments for the ego—artificial ways to feel special without putting in the work.

Visions are a source of interest and aspiration—a call to action. You want to bring the vision about for its own sake, and you're willing to do whatever it requires. You serve the vision and let your ego gratification take a back seat.

Visions, expressions of your true desires, lead to willingness and eventually to accomplishments. Visions and fantasies are distinct and qualitatively different. Your fantasies are located in the back of your head; they are a cave you crawl into to escape from life. Visions are in the front of your head and project outward like headlights.

MASTERY

Much as you train your dog to chase a ball, you can train your focus to go where you want to send it. Stars in all fields shine because they have laser focus they can direct at will. Magic Johnson is a genius at basketball because he focuses on the game when it

73

counts. Einstein was a genius because he could focus on the big picture.

You find a good feeling by radically shifting your focus of attention. Balance excess first or second force by focusing on an opposing positive feeling. By balancing your burning desires with the feeling of patience, you'll avoid feeling fried later. If you're constantly turning the other cheek, focus on the feeling of courage. If you're constantly fighting, turn the other cheek and focus on feelings of peace and reconciliation.

FINDING A GOOD FEELING

Focus is the key to good feelings; to feel good, stop focusing on what makes you unhappy. *You can't be happy by focusing on what makes you unhappy.* Problem-solving leads to momentary relief, not happiness. Rather than seek after happiness, focus on being happy in the moment.

Good feelings are your birthright, your inheritance. Your natural state is happiness. Like money in the bank, good feelings are something you always have within you. All you have to do is write out the check by focusing on good feelings in the moment. Unlike money, the more good feelings you spend, the more you have.

Good feelings are always standing right outside the door. Your job is to open the door, put out the welcome mat, and make room for them by quieting your mind down. Set the right inner conditions and happiness will rush in.

Make an inner choice—decide to feel good. Show your thoughts the back door and put your heart into good feelings. Just as you can raise your arm at will, you can let good feelings in at will.

DIFFERENT OPTIONS

At times, taking action (going for a walk, phoning a friend) will get your focus off of your dismal thoughts and make room for good feelings.

At other times, you make room by *nondoing*, by taking passive action, by dropping the ballast of your negative thoughts. Dismiss your negative thoughts as you would dismiss any propaganda. Even if there is a kernel of truth in the propaganda, you're better off dismissing it until you have a more objective source.

Physical sensations are conduits to good feelings. Find and focus on a positive sensation in any part of your body, and gradually the current of good feelings will spread throughout your body. If you focus on positive sensations and good feelings, they will expand until they fill your whole mind and body.

You'll inevitably forget to feel good at times; however, when you remember your good feelings, they remember you and come back in full force. Happiness is inside you, at the core of your being. Good feelings are always within you; they aren't attached to or dependent on anything. Rather than try to bring happiness to yourself, you enter into it—a state of pure being.

Dedicate yourself to the cultivation of good feelings. Understand you only feel like yourself when you feel good. You're real only when you feel real. Good feelings bring you into the moment and put you in touch with your essence.

CREATING HAPPINESS

Focus exclusively on one view of the world and you'll homogenize all your experiences until everything looks and sounds the same. You can direct your focus anywhere you choose.

You always hold the key to your own happiness. Create a good day by focusing on the beauty and harmony around you. Enjoy your work by focusing on what you like about it. Enrich your life by focusing on your children, your family, and your friends.

Imagine you just spent the last twenty years in solitary confinement. Focus on the world as a gift and you'll connect with life and gain inner harmony. The more reality you focus on, the more you have to be thankful for. Get high from seeing the sky, leaves, and green grass—become intoxicated with the mundane, the ordinary, the everyday sights and sounds.

Unending gratitude is the correct response to the gift of life. With third-force balance, you no longer need the extraordinary to make you alive and happy—you become high from focusing on the wonder of the ordinary. Appreciate, cherish, and celebrate the ordinary. Be like new parents who are overwhelmed with gratitude as they see their new baby engage in the most ordinary activities.

6

WORLD
OF GOOD
FEELINGS

At any moment you can leave the cold, unreal city of thought (where concepts are like government enforcers who try to control you) and step into the vivid, alive world of good feelings.

You get your best first impressions from your direct good feelings of the moment; they give you a multidimensional focus and a truer take on reality. Good feelings are both a bond with reality and a subtle, deep perspective on reality.

To design a good life for yourself, let form follow function: first feel good and then let the form of your thoughts follow from your good feelings. Feelings give you a direct perspective on reality. Stanley Kubrick said, "The truth of a thing is in the feel of it, not in the think of it." Get the feel of a new city, new job, or new person before you make up your mind about what it means to you.

As you move to this "good-feelings-first" state, you become vibrant and expansive. You return to a childhood innocence, a state of love, where living is real and beautiful.

77

FEELING OF LOVE

When you're in love, you live in a world of good feelings. You experience the feeling or presence of the person you love, not your thoughts about the person or the reason you're in love. When you make love in a good-feelings-first state, you focus on the alive feelings of the moment. You're experience based rather than fantasy based. As long as you focus on the feelings of making love, sex never becomes mechanical.

Once you slip out of the world of good feelings, you start to be analytical and critical of the other person. Your thoughts dilute the real experience. The little quirks that you once felt were wonderful become intolerable. Rather than build a good relationship by developing a backlog of good feelings and goodwill, you start to work on issues and problems.

With insight, you'll realize you can move back into paradise simply by putting good feelings first. A feeling of love is a way to return to your childhood innocence—a way to deal firsthand with reality without the interference of your thoughts. To regain your love for anything or anyone, put good feelings back in first place. Feel the person or activity, instead of your thoughts. Rather than think about your job, your friends, and your home, feel good about them for their own sake. To stay in love indefinitely—with a person, a job, or a hobby—focus on good feelings and disregard thoughts that separate you from the other person.

ENTER THE THIRD DIMENSION

When you think of something without good feelings, what you perceive is uninteresting and two-dimensional. *When you add good feelings, you add the third dimension of depth.* Have good feelings about a person and the person becomes real and meaningful to you.

When your good feelings take the lead, your feelings and thinking work in tandem. You live in a world of bliss and innocence. You may revisit this world when on vacation or when you are out in nature. If you live on the mainland, you may go to Hawaii in search of feelings of bliss and innocence; if you live in Hawaii, you may come to the mainland.

You may believe you have to fall in love or spend a thousand dollars on a new wardrobe to get this good feeling. Just as your heart is always there, good feelings are always within you. Simply look for them and they will appear. Happiness is anticipating something good; bliss is living what is good. With insight and practice, you'll find you can effortlessly surrender to feelings of awe, wonder, and mystery and actually live in these good feelings every day.

PROCESS FEELINGS

Move to a feelings-first state and you quickly process *all* of your feelings. Put a feeling in front of your reactive emotions and your emotions fade away. You may momentarily feel frightened, but if you directly experience the feeling with openness, it will rise up and pass away. Fear is a flavor of feeling that comes from a perceived threat. To prevent fear from turning into anxiety, accept the feeling and stop building up the danger in your mind.

At times you will feel mad. You experience this sensation when your psychological or physical space has been intruded upon. To avoid escalating this feeling into anger, allow the feeling to go through your body and disregard your thoughts about unfairness and revenge. Once you have internally digested the experience, you will know how to skillfully handle the external situation. You may decide to express your feelings or you may decide not to.

You experience a feeling of sadness when you suffer a loss. With insight you stop this feeling from hardening into depression. As often as is needed, let this flavor or sensation of feeling rise up and pass through your body. Resist the temptation to go over what the loss means to you personally.

NATURAL ORDER

Feelings give a sense of reality. To move to a higher state of mind, stop *feeling your thoughts* ("I feel my thoughts are true; therefore they must be"). Instead, feel life. Get direct impressions of reality from your senses and good feelings.

The feeling center in the brain (the limbic system) developed millions of years before the thinking center (the neocortex). The natural order is to feel reality directly in the moment and then expand on this through your thoughts.

To feel happy, make your good feelings the master and your thoughts helpful servants—let your thoughts express whatever your good feelings are showing you at the moment.

Realize that, when your good feelings are in first place, your experiences, instead of coming from your memory and intellect, come from what is going on in the present. If you're at the beach, feel you're at the beach; if you're at home, feel you're at home. Put your good feelings first and you'll have a direct line to reality: you will sense the impulse of what to do next intuitively, out of the moment.

RETURN TO DIRECT LEARNING

As a baby, you were all feelings and little thought; then, as an adult, you became all thought and little feeling. As a child, you soaked up information because you operated from feelings first. You'll find, as you return your exiled feelings to their rightful throne, that your ability to learn directly from life returns. Like small children who get pure joy from seeing how their hands and feet move, or are in awe as they walk down a grocery-store aisle, you'll be constantly delighted and surprised by what life offers.

To make contact with the world of your childhood, stop labeling reality and then reacting to your labels as if they were real ("He's a police officer"; "She's a woman"; "They're students"). Instead of subdividing life, make it a seamless production—aim to experience life in a fresh and direct way.

WISDOM

You become wiser as you return to the world of feelings. You hear something you've heard a thousand times, such as "The truth shall make you free," and for the first time you really understand what it means.

Understanding and good feelings are different sides of the same coin. When you understand what is going on in the moment, you feel good. And when you find a good feeling, you are intuitively led to a deeper understanding of reality.

The more you put good feelings first, the more insights and essential connections you make. You get in touch with a deeper intelligence; you are smarter and more effective all around—you're able to put into practice what you already know. You'll treat others and yourself better. You'll pay more attention to your work and your family and you'll do more of what you really want to do and less of what you think you should do.

Keep in mind that your thoughts capture only a small piece of reality; your good feelings give you a deeper and more complete picture. With good feelings, you discover new orders and new connections—life becomes coherent and full of possibilities.

HOW TO BE CREATIVE

When you have a good feeling, you sense you're part of all existence. New ideas and insights start to emerge out of this realization. Like a poet or a mathematician, first you feel what is true and then you express it creatively or logically.

In a high state of mind, such as when you first fall in love, visions and ideas that are beyond your normal cause-and-effect thinking start to appear. You are never more creative and imaginative than when you're in love. In this pure good-feeling-first state, you're filled with plans and ideas for your future together.

When you have good feelings, you spontaneously create what you want. If you stay in love, your plans turn into reality. Like a jazz musician, you improvise and create what the moment calls for.

Because your good feelings come out of the freshness of the moment, new forms spontaneously appear. Your joy puts you in accord with the truth and allows you to take in reality directly. Reality is no longer a movie screen you project your thoughts onto.

You see past the wall your thoughts put between you and reality. Impersonally and clearly, you see what is going on, and your higher state of awareness becomes the means to new experiences and new insights.

81

FROM THE BOOK

Thinking about what will happen next is like teaching from a book—you may feel in control, but nothing new or exciting happens. A good teacher first loves the material. From this love comes a good feeling for what to say or do—then the teacher acts from the inspiration. In the same way, trust the insightful thoughts that spontaneously come from good feelings and you will intuitively know what to do next.

With wisdom, you no longer try to use your thoughts to control reality. You realize that it's futile to try to control a complex and multivariable world through simplistic, horizontal thinking. Instead of endlessly grinding out cause-and-effect theories, you look for good feelings and give inspiration a chance to work.

BECOME FREE

What you bring to any situation is what you take out of it. Look for good feelings after you are with your friends or customers and you'll find your conversation unfolds naturally and organically. Allow good feelings toward the report you're writing to arise, and the report writes itself.

Bring good feelings to what you do and you'll have no need for cookbook solutions. What you need to do next comes before you ask—you have intuitive flashes and hunches about what to do.

Rather than try to preempt and control life, aim for a good feeling and become one with whatever you are doing. Move out of the artificial and mechanical world of thought and into the organic world of good feelings. If you collaborate with circumstances instead of trying to escape or control them, living becomes a joy rather than an unending series of problems to be solved.

MASTERY AND GOOD FEELINGS

You're most successful when you operate from a good-feelings-first state. The jobs you excel at, the people you click with, and the classes you shine at, all come from the good feelings you have toward each person or activity.

Mastery is a feelings-first state. When you learned to drive, you were in the beginner's mode—the world of thought. You actively talked to yourself about how to steer, shift, and watch for traffic. Later you developed a feeling for how to drive and stopped talking to yourself about it.

Become like athletes who train to operate from a good feeling toward their sport. Aim for a good feeling and you'll move into a state of grace, where you can do no wrong. The better you feel toward any activity, the better you'll be at it. You'll be like basketball star Michael Jordan, who said, "When I have the feeling, the hoop becomes as big as Lake Michigan." To avoid slumps, rather than think about how to throw the ball, look for a good feeling in the moment.

Stop going over your concerns and stop rehearsing your fears and you'll find living becomes smooth and easy. Experiment and learn for yourself that you can disregard your self-talk and trust yourself, and the details of living will take care of themselves.

DEVELOP TRUST

To step into this higher state, simply *dismiss your negative thoughts about the past and future and allow good feelings to emerge in the present and envelop you.* You still think, but this is secondary to your primary experience of good feelings. The beauty of good-feelings-first is in its simplicity—as a child you did it without even trying.

GENTLE MOTIVATION

Become motivated by good feelings instead of by self-coercion or self-manipulation. Tom Sawyer understood that the best way to motivate people is with good feelings. If you feel good toward whitewashing the fence, you'll gladly do it. Start with a good feeling and you naturally and spontaneously do what needs to be done. You'll no longer have to manipulate yourself ("I have to do it") to overcome your resistance to everyday jobs—because you'll have no resistance to overcome.

Move into a state of good-feelings-first and you'll no longer have to repeat to yourself endlessly what you have to do. If you're driving down the street and need gas, you pull in and get gas because you feel good knowing the tank is full. If you need to call someone, you pick up a phone because you feel good about making the call.

Refuse to think about your mental "to-do" list. You may miss a few opportunities, but the good feelings you experience in exchange for the mental grinding more than compensate for the loss.

SOUL FOOD

Just as you need fresh air and fresh food to be physically healthy, you need fresh impressions to move into a good-feelings-first state. Fresh impressions are third-force food. You're as good as your last direct impression of reality. To be in a good-feelings-first state, make yourself receptive to life's images. Good feelings come from feeling the good in life. Throughout your day, slow down and look for what is real, true, and beautiful.

The third force is the relating force. To feel real and balanced, bond with current reality. Become like Greek islanders who measure distances by how many cigarettes they smoke while walking to their destination; or like Native Americans who measure life by how many sleeps, moons, or winters they live through.

Sit quietly for a moment and you'll discover how long a moment is. Your day is made up of thousands of moments. Within any one moment you can take in new impressions that bring on good feelings.

Connect with your everyday experiences and directly see, smell, hear, and touch life. Take in a balanced diet of impressions: counterbalance active first-force impressions with passive second-force impressions. When you're getting too active, take in a serene impression—sit in your garden and look at the sky. If you're too passive, listen to lively music or go for a bike ride.

Just as you order what you like on a menu, consciously choose the impressions you want to have. Take in the highest and best impressions you can at any moment. If you want to be in a good relationship, look at happy couples. If you want to have peace of mind, look at sights or listen to music that gives you peaceful impressions.

LIVING MUSEUM

Look at your surroundings as the masterpiece they are. Just as you forget yourself and wonder what Mona Lisa is thinking, lose yourself in the images you take in daily. Instead of seeing the beautiful sky in a painting, see the painting in the beautiful sky. Lose yourself in the details, the subtle colors, and the movement of this picture.

To find a good feeling, be a third force and bring together opposites in your current surroundings. Notice movement and rest; animate and inanimate objects; warmth and cold; smooth and rough, soft and hard textures; sameness and difference.

To take in first impressions that will nourish and feed you, quiet down and pay attention to reality. Good feelings come from seeing in depth. Imagine putting on 3-D glasses and you'll see the depth of your surroundings—you'll immediately add a feeling dimension and transcend the flat two dimensions of a lower state of mind.

Look around and note to yourself whether you are seeing "objects" or "space." Gradually drop the noting and keep refocusing on the space between objects you normally don't see. As you get used to observing more space, start to note "movement" and "stability" in your screen of awareness.

By making finer distinctions in your visual field, you increase your resolution power and raise your level of awareness to where you can see into the nature of nature. You discover the impermanence of all things, including your sense of self.

As you transcend concepts of self, time, and space, you move fully into the moment. Emptiness of thought allows you to experience the fullness of life. You become a pure spirit that moves through time and space without resistance, as if you were swimming in a waterless pool.

THE NOVELTY OF TRAVEL

You feel good when you travel because you take in new impressions. You can take in new impressions in your own backyard. Look at your surroundings as if seeing them for the first time and new impressions will flood in.

If you could look back over your life, you would discover not that you did anything so bad, but that you failed to appreciate everyday wonders.

Nostalgia is a desire to take in more deeply good impressions from your past life. Imagine it is thirty years from today and you have returned to re-experience this day. You are delighted to see your children, your friends, and your family. You are filled with gratitude as you look at your young face in the mirror. You are filled with joy, energy, and vitality as you look at the buildings, hairstyles, clothes, restaurants, and television shows.

Why wait thirty years to feel delight, gratitude, joy, and love for today? Be grateful and joyful today and you'll avoid later remorse over having failed to have fully appreciated your life.

Remember when you were in love and open to fresh impressions? Look for first impressions that feed your feelings of love. To love music, listen to it as if for the first time. Allow yourself to be astonished by the moment. To love your grandparents, see them anew each time you're with them.

IMMEDIACY AND PASSION

In high states, you have great equanimity and even-mindedness. Make all your impressions of equal value and all of your experiences will become colorful and meaningful. When everything is wonderful, a moment with one person or one event is equal to the next.

Disregard thoughts that compartmentalize and close off reality and destroy first impressions ("This could be more fun with chilled wine"). Drop evaluating thoughts, find a good feeling, and you can unite with reality. When you love someone, you love the person as a whole—you have no need to pick the person apart.

Open your heart, feel reality, and new, bright, glittering impressions will pour in. With practice, you sharpen your ability to feel the inherent goodness of each moment. You can vividly feel people, objects, and surroundings. Just as you can sense when a house has been empty for a while, you can feel any situation. You can feel someone's sexuality or lack of sexuality. You can feel when someone is telling the truth and when someone is lying.

RISK

To feel more secure, live more dangerously. Let go of the thoughts that give you the illusion of certainty and control. Feel good and you'll experience the world as being safe and friendly.

Once you're willing to live without the protection of your thoughts, your illusionary fears start to disappear. Good feelings dispel fear and insecurity. Bring a good feeling to the freeways and you'll feel safe driving on them. Create a good feeling toward people you want to meet and you'll feel comfortable talking to them.

GOOD FEELINGS AND SUCCESS

Good feelings give birth to success. Love your work and you'll put in the extra effort that leads to financial success. Feel good about your body and you will treat your body with respect. Cultivate good feelings toward others and you'll automatically be kind and considerate of them; and they in turn will likely be kind and considerate of you.

In the world of good feelings, you see reality more clearly, and life becomes one surprise after another. You'll find that nothing in reality is ever created the same way twice. To enter the world of good feelings, lighten your load: give up your past formulas, leave your defenses behind, and disregard your need to be important and your desire to gain reward and avoid punishment.

7

PRINCIPLE OF GOOD FEELINGS

Joseph Conrad wrote, "Words, as is well known, are great foes of reality." In the lower world of thought, you live under the influence of words and thoughts. Move to a higher state of mind and you come under the principle of good feelings.

The world of thought is based on the premise, "My well-being depends on past, present, and future circumstances." Under this assumption, you try to control and outwit circumstances through cause-and-effect thinking ("If I work hard, I'll be successful," or "If I get people to like me, everything will be okay").

The principle of good feelings is based on observable fact: "In high states of mind, I can transcend past, present, and future circumstances." Once you drop cause-and-effect theories and formulas, your life opens up—you become free of your conditioned thinking.

WIDE ANGLE

Reality is too big to be captured by linear cause-and-effect thinking. Positive and negative expectations about the future are futile: the future is unknown. Your expectations, which come from the world of thought, are based on the false assumption that you can predict and control the future.

Under the influence of the third-force principle of good feelings, you stop looking for situations where you can justify your first-force desires or find something to blame your second-force obstacles on. Start to see how blame and self-justification come from the lower, illusionary world of cause-and-effect thinking. Even a broken shoelace is too complex to blame on one cause or one person.

Use the principle of good feelings and you see you have no need for causes, excuses, or reasons to feel good and successful ("I've worked so hard, I deserve a vacation"). Feel good simply because you *want* to feel good. You may have behaved terribly five minutes ago, but so what? Whether you deserve to be happy or successful is irrelevant. You may *not* deserve to be happy or successful, but under the principle of good feelings, you rise above cause-and-effect thinking.

BEYOND PAST AND FUTURE CAUSES

With insight, you no longer live on the installment plan. You take ownership of the present moment and transcend past concerns and future worries. Your history and your past conditioning become irrelevant. You have no need to be your own judge, jury, and executioner, or any need to punish yourself for past errors.

Future circumstances are equally irrelevant. Once you realize you can never control the future through your thoughts anyway, you stop worrying about what might happen.

DIFFERENT WORLDS

The world of good feelings is beyond the physical world of matter, space, and time. To feel good, remember you have all the necessary ingredients. You don't have to add anything or do anything. Good feelings come from the absence of thought about what you need to be happy.

Nothing external or physical needs to change for you to move to the world of good feelings. Because your psychological world is completely separate (none of the old rules apply any longer), you can feel good anytime.

Good feelings come from being fully in the present. You can create good feelings by working backward—link with the moment and a good feeling will appear. At any time, simply decide to enjoy whatever you are doing for its own sake. If you are with someone with whom you are nervous or having problems, instead of focusing on what you dislike about the person, focus on being fully with the person.

When you live in the here and now, you are beyond space-time limitations. Because you're in the real universe, not the universe of thought, you can relax, be yourself, and allow outside forces to work in your favor.

Cause-and-effect logic explains, in a limited way, the physical world. However, even in the physical sciences, concepts such as "mutually determined events" are replacing the traditional cause-and-effect model.

What seem like paradoxes in the physical world ("We all are one," "More with less," "When you seek something you cannot find it") become self-evident truths in the good-feelings-first world. The psychological world works in the opposite way from how the physical world is thought to behave. If something you hear about your psychology doesn't seem paradoxical or too simple, it's probably untrue or unimportant.

Words tend to obscure rather than clarify psychological reality. Language was developed to help understand the physical world. When the same static words are applied to the dynamic psychological realm, they seem contradictory. The insight "You need to lose yourself to find yourself" is one example. This means you need to let go of the concept that your "self" exists as a physical thing or object. The discovery of your real self is a process that arises and passes away each moment.

RISE ABOVE CIRCUMSTANCES

Make the joyful leap to the world of being in the moment and you'll no longer be the servant of past causes and future events. You come under an influence of a higher order, where nothing can disturb or distract you. Junk your Rube Goldberg schemes and formulas and a new world of possibilities opens. When you encounter a first- and second-force clash, find a good feeling and rise above outside causes. If you get a divorce, are laid off from your job, or come down with an illness, you can still have peace of mind, and you can still move toward what you want in life.

HIGHER DESTINY

Move to the higher state of good feelings and you'll be able to bring about what you truly want. Under the principle of good feelings, your life is no longer determined by circumstances and accidents. You are intuitively led to the means for getting what you truly want.

You're able to fulfill your highest purpose and bring forth your greatest gifts and talents. You start to encounter people and circumstances that help you bring about life experiences you want. Your deeper feelings create an invisible catalyst—illogical impulses and serendipitous meetings move you toward your destination.

QUIET MIND

When you are in good physical condition, you are unaware of your physical functioning. Similarly, when you're under the influence of good feelings and are in good mental condition, your thoughts are so subtle that you are largely unaware that you're thinking.

Just as a racing pulse is a sign of a physical maladjustment, a racing mind is a signal to make a psychological adjustment. Assign your thoughts to the back seat and your good feelings to the front seat and, like your pulse, your thoughts will become slow, stable, and unnoticeable.

ZERO-SUM GAME

Your thoughts are parasites that drain your life force. A racing mind quickly wears you out and gets you nowhere. Keep track of the thoughts that come from a low state of mind and you'll find that *your thoughts add up to zero.*

Cause-and-effect thinking is like driving your car back and forth in your driveway—you waste your gas and never get anywhere. Each thought is canceled by its opposite. Your positive thoughts are canceled by negative thoughts. Your self-reassuring thoughts are canceled by your self-doubts; your self-praising thoughts are canceled by self-condemning thoughts.

Your cause-and-effect thoughts are symptoms of an insecure state of mind. Realize that *you'll never get rid of a thought by thinking about it.* When you encounter the second force, shift your focus of attention off of your insecurity. You'll find that your state of mind will rise and your insecurity symptoms will disappear on their own.

REFOCUS

The means are simple. To raise your awareness, set your thoughts aside. Shift your focus directly onto being in the present. Don't try to stop your thoughts when they come in; just note them and let them go. Remember that most of your thoughts are automatic and will come in no matter what you do. The idea isn't to eliminate thinking, but to see that your thoughts are a poor way to perceive reality—they narrow and distort perception. It's a waste of time to chase down and fight with every driver that honks at you or gives you a dirty look, and it's a waste of time to chase down and fight every thought that appears to you.

Trying *not* to think a thought is like trying not to notice the phone is ringing. All you can think about is the phone ringing. Try to deny or fight a thought and you empower it. Your intellect reasons, "My thought must be pretty serious. Why else would I fight it?" Your thought system concludes, "This call is too important to miss," and the thought keeps ringing through. Give your self the opposite message. Acknowledge the thought, realize it's a wrong number, and move on.

BEHAVIOR MODIFICATION

In a low state, your insecure thoughts, like little children, climb all over you and yell in your ear. When your thoughts get too loud and rowdy, send them to their room for quiet time. Note the thought and let it go. Remember that a thought that disturbs your peace of mind can be easily disregarded—you can drop it or you disregard it as just a thought.

In higher states of mind, you become a superadult: you modify your inner state the same way you modify the behavior of undisciplined children—attend to and reinforce what you want, and stop attending to and reinforcing what you don't want. Focus on good feelings and ignore cause-and-effect thoughts.

Aim for self-understanding rather than self-calming. When you talk back to your thoughts, *you initially feel calmer, but then you feel worse.* You feel relieved for the moment, but you reinforce your insecure thoughts, so they return louder than ever. If you stop attending to your thoughts, you may initially feel worse before you feel better; however, ignore the thoughts and they will disappear and drop away. Continue to shift your focus away from your insecure thoughts; your intellect will get the message "The thoughts are unneeded" and stop sending them.

THOUGHT PASSAGE

With understanding, you use *thought passage*—you let the thoughts float on by—instead of *thought replacement*. If an insecure thought comes down the stream, no need to fish it out and correct it. Simply let it pass by unattended.

Thoughts have no sustaining power of their own. Any thought can come into your head. You have little say over what thoughts are sent out, but you have total say over what thoughts you tune in and listen to.

CREATING POSITIVE SENSATIONS

Just as the starter for sourdough bread is sourdough, the starter for good feelings is a physical memory of good feelings. Good

93

feelings are always within you. As you become more sensitive to them and allow them to emerge, more will appear. After you've felt good for a while, you will carry the starter for good feelings within you. Keep in mind that you can train your physiology to produce more good feelings. Focusing on physical sensations is the means to good feelings. When you lose your good feelings, focus on the physical sensation of positive feeling in your body and the feeling will start to increase.

When you wake up in the morning (and throughout the day), you can create a good feeling by shifting your attention to pleasant sensations in the body. If you simply focus on positive sensations in your body, you'll find that good feelings will start to appear. Throughout the day, you can go back and reconnect with your good feelings through positive physical sensations.

As you build memories of good feelings and positive sensations in your body, you'll find it easier to call up good feelings intentionally.

As with any other skill, the more you practice recognizing and feeling your good feelings, the better you become at it. Every time you remember to look for a good feeling in your body, you deepen the skill and retrain your physiology.

SUCCESS IS FEELING GOOD

Good feelings allow your true self to appear and lead to your real purpose—to enjoy life and bring about what you truly want. When you value good feelings sufficiently, you focus on good feelings throughout the day. Find time each day to feel good. Use the time you spend waiting in lines and for others as a chance to focus on good feelings.

Move from the thinking center to the higher-feeling center. You can stay in a high state of functioning by tuning in to good feelings four or five times a day. Rather than think about something in the past or future that makes you feel good, go directly for a good feeling in the present.

You magnify good feelings, by focusing on them. Focus on the warm, vivid feelings you have around special holidays and the times you've noticed the diamondlike sparkle on the ocean waves or seen the golden gleam on falling leaves. Look for feelings of aliveness—

the noncontingent, peaceful feelings you have while walking on the beach or watching children play.

INTERNAL COMMUNICATION

You make room for good feelings by internally separating from your negative thoughts. Realize that real liberation is freedom from your overlearned, conditioned thoughts. Your brain is a large switchboard with thousands of calls coming in each day.

You may hear a story about hostages on the news and have the thought "What if I get taken hostage?" Immediately you disregard the thought, because you realize it's a wrong number. However, if you're insecure about being a hostage, you may think, "That call's for me." You may even repeat the thought all day long.

Remember, *just because the phone rings, you don't have to answer it.* Disturbing thoughts are crank calls. Rather than talk to and encourage them, let the wrong numbers go unanswered.

You may have to ignore a line of thinking a dozen times before it stops calling. Even then, it may wait some time and call back to reeengage you in a conversation. Once you recognize its voice, hang up.

Accept that, even if you hang up on an insecure thought, your ears may burn. Your thoughts can have a lingering physical effect on your body. Disregard your resistance ("I can't stand this"; "I have to do something") to the pain. Accept the discomfort and be impartial to it; *will the pain to be* and get in accord with the sensation and it will soon pass and fade away and make room for a nicer, lighter feeling.

NOT WHAT YOU THINK

Your second thought is usually "What if my first thought is correct? What if the call *is* for me? What if this is the dreaded call in the middle of the night that I've always feared?"

Reality is always bigger, more complex, and more dynamic than any thought about reality. Whatever you think reality is, it's not. Your thoughts arbitrarily qualify, limit, and box in reality. You may have had some earlier thoughts about what you're going to be doing now. But tune in to the internal and external present and you'll see that the reality of this moment is much bigger and grander than anything you could have possibly imagined.

Ideas and beliefs are at best sketchy outlines of reality. Like road signs, they can point you toward reality, but they are never reality. No matter how well worked out and detailed your thoughts, they are always removed from reality in some degree—they are always smaller and less alive than reality.

All you can know for sure is that you are here and it is now. Because reality is constantly changing, your thoughts are always out of date. A snapshot of a moving freight train is not the moving train, or even a full representation of the train—the train is always more than what you think about it.

PAST CONDITIONS

Under the principle of good feelings, you transcend your past conditioning—your inherited and acquired memories. You have many systematic biases and prejudices about yourself and the world. To try to change or unlearn them all would be an unending, thankless job. As fast as you can pull the calls off the switchboard, your intellect is putting through new ones.

Under the principle of good feelings, you can transcend any thought simply by seeing it's a thought and deciding to disregard it. Note, "It's just a thought," and refuse to respond to it. Let the phone ring unanswered, and go about enjoying and appreciating your day.

OTHER-CONSIDERING

To use the principle of good feelings, refuse to be concerned with what people think of you. Make a general policy to immediately replace *self-considering* ("What do others think of me?") with *other-considering* ("What can I do for others to help them and make their lives easier?").

Above all, stay away from identifying with a thought or from believing you are equal to a thought. Detach yourself and remember, "I'm always more than the contents of any thoughts I have."

True freedom is not caring what people think—*starting with yourself.* If you're impartial to what you think, you'll be impartial to what others think. If you're unruffled by your own critical thoughts, why would you care what the neighbors think?

INTERNAL ADJUSTMENTS

With wisdom, you make good feelings your utmost priority. You know that, if you rest, exercise, drink enough water, and eat healthy food, you'll find it easier to stay in the third-force world of good feelings.

Just as you keep your blood-sugar level up by having an apple or a glass of milk, you can learn to keep your good feelings up. Once you enter into a good state, your feelings will largely take care of themselves. You need only to make an occasional adjustment when your mood drops or when your cause-and-effect thinking starts up.

ALLOWING

Finding a good feeling in the moment is more "allowing" than "doing." Value good feelings more than you value your thoughts. Once you appreciate good feelings sufficiently, you naturally allow them to develop throughout your body.

The general rule is: make your thoughts passive and your good feelings active. As quickly as you can, dismiss your cause-and-effect thoughts ("What did I do wrong?"; "What should I say?"; "I don't want to look stupid"; "How can I get them to like me?") and look for a good feeling in your body.

GOOD FEELINGS: THE PASSKEY

Moving into a state of good feelings is easier to do than to explain. Finding and focusing on a good feeling is an inner gesture, like opening and closing your hand. Realize that good feelings are the key that fits all psychological locks—the key is always in your pocket. When you're locked out in the cold, rather than frantically rush around trying to get in, calm down and look for a good feeling.

Throughout the day, switch from descending first- and second-force thoughts to ascending third-force feelings. Learn to soar like a seagull and let the air currents naturally lift you to a higher level of being. Look for a pleasant updraft of good feelings and ride that to the top. If your mood falls, just catch the next updraft and you'll be carried to a higher place.

Under the principle of good feelings, you are liberated from the prison of your past conditioning and free to be your real self. Feeling good is stacked in your favor: it feels good to feel good. All you have to remember is that good feelings lead to wisdom, understanding, and greater clarification of reality.

8

BELONGING:
THE PATH
TO HAPPINESS

Realize that, just as happiness comes from belonging in the moment, unhappiness comes from seeking happiness in the present, past, or future. For every action there is an equal and opposite reaction. Your first-force desire ("I need to be happy") creates an equal and opposite second-force reaction ("I can't be happy").

Your first-force desires and your second-force resistance are directly related—*the greater your desires, the greater your resistance*. The quicker you want to get home, the slower the traffic will be; the slower you want to go, the more the drivers behind will push you to speed up.

Equal to the heat you're generating through desire is the chill in the corners of the room. If you're hot to find a date, somehow the possibilities cool off. If you're burning to make a sale, you start to sweat and others move away from you.

Your difficulties ease up once you reduce the intensity of your desire. The less important you make your desire, the less resistance you'll encounter. If you take the importance off of finding your car keys, you'll stop rushing around and be able to find them easily. If you make getting a job more casual, you'll stop freezing up and stumbling over your words at interviews. If you make being in a relationship less crucial, you'll no longer drive off potential lovers.

HOSPITALITY

Eric Hoffer said, "The search for happiness is one of the chief sources of unhappiness." The fewer demands to be happy, the happier you'll be. Less desire for happiness creates less second-force resistance to being happy.

Learning to be happy is like training a bird to sit on your shoulder. You have to let happiness come to you rather than chase after it. With wisdom, you know that surrendering your need to change circumstances is the shortest route to happiness. Happiness is always in the moment—never in the future. The less you run after happiness, the more happiness will seek you out—whether you want to be happy or not.

CONNECTING

All happiness comes from being united with reality—and searching keeps you separated from the reality of the moment. *Happiness is a discovery without a search.* Follow William Blake's advice: "Arise and drink your bliss! For everything that lives is holy." To be happy, connect and merge with the wonder of the present moment.

Behind your feelings and just below the threshold of your conscious awareness are positive and negative subliminal thoughts. In the psychological world, subtle is significant—subtle thoughts and feelings bring you down or lift you up. The subliminal thought "I belong here" creates a feeling of belonging. To find the feeling of belonging or happiness, first quiet your mind down and find whatever feeling is within you. Unite with whatever feeling you have. When you feel you belong here and now, you provide a quiet, steady, secure perch for happiness to land on. Feeling you belong is the relating third force that reconciles you with life.

When you are connected to anything or anyone, feelings of

BELONGING

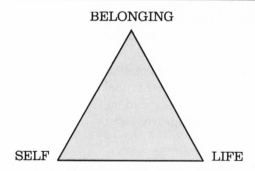

SELF   LIFE

happiness rush in. You may be cleaning up after dinner and be engulfed by a feeling of joy. You may be helping to buckle your daughter into her car seat and find that a feeling of bliss wells up. You may be drinking a cup of tea with a co-worker when happiness spontaneously and unexpectedly appears.

Happiness, a completely free spirit, works through the principle of attraction rather than promotion. Happiness comes to you when you create a warm, cozy haven for it. At first happiness may stay around for only a few moments. With practice and patience, the good feelings will stay with you, even during rough patches.

BLISS OF BELONGING

Form a third-force union with whatever you are and with whatever you're doing—feel you belong to the special events as well as to the simple, small pleasures of everyday life.

The secret to happiness is to feel congruent with your immediate surroundings. When you feel close to reality, you feel good. When you have a complete sense of merging with reality, you experience bliss: the world is in you, and you're in the world, and you know you're part of all existence.

Feel you belong, and you trust people and life. Small irritations roll off you; you feel comfortable and accepting of wherever you are at the moment. You're free from isolating thoughts ("I don't belong here. . . . How am I coming across?"). When you belong, you bring inner resources and inner strength to any situation in which you find yourself—you know that you can handle whatever comes up.

When you're bogged down in a conflict between the first and second forces, look for a good feeling of belonging as the third-force means to lift you above your resistance. Rise above the brown haze and you can think and act skillfully. Aim to *feel* good here and now instead of to *do* good to feel better later. When you feel good, you rise above the smog and pollution and see clearly. When you *feel* clearly, you *see* clearly and then you can *act* clearly.

NOTE AND DROP YOUR EGO

You have two types of belonging—contingency belonging, where you feel you belong when others accept you, and noncontingency belonging, where you feel you belong no matter what the circumstances. Real belonging starts with you. Make your first sense of belonging noncontingent on circumstances.

To get an unconditional feeling of belonging, drop your ego involvement ("I have to prove I'm special before I can belong"). Let go of your self-talk and become whole and congruent in the moment. Refuse to put people either on a pedestal or beneath you. Allow the good feelings of belonging to trump the lower-level urges to be accepted and approved.

The third force is the neutralizing principle. Rather than engage in constant skirmishes, emulate neutral Switzerland. While Rambo crawls cold and dirty through the jungle, the Swiss sit high in the Alps, eating cheese, counting money, and making pocket knives.

See that, because everyone has different realities, everyone is equal. To keep a sense of belonging, you need to have the equanimity to live and let live. Be impartial toward others' separate realities. Follow T. S. Eliot's advice: "Teach us to care and not care, teach us to sit still." Love to have others accept you, but don't take personally whether they do or not—this is out of your hands. Refuse to throw people out of your heart because they are not accepting you at the moment.

BE REAL

The more you drop your pretensions, the higher your spirits will go—and the more others will be attracted to you for who you really are. *Be real with yourself, and others will be real with you.* The more human you're willing to be, the more you'll feel you belong ("I'm one of the group"). People will be attracted to your sense of realness and down-to-earth presence.

Paradoxically, the more you can relax and accept your own shortcomings, the less inferior you'll feel around others. The feeling of inferiority falls away once you stop trying to boost your feelings of superiority.

To feel connected, allow others to experience the world in their unique ways, and allow yourself to experience the world in your own unique way. The more separate and different you allow others to be, the more connected you feel to them. Let the differences between you complement one another and form a third-force bridge.

BODY FEELING

To create a sense of belonging, first find a good feeling within yourself. Choose to feel good in the moment, and let the means to feel good develop naturally. When you find a good feeling, your body relaxes and becomes more flexible and light. Your body language signals others. The Buddhists say, "Preach with your body." When you feel good, others feel better around you—often without even knowing why they feel better.

Above all, realize that the state of your being has a profound effect on others. Whether or not they put it into words, people sense your level of being. Enter a room with a feeling of belonging and others will start to develop a sense of mutual belonging.

Aim to connect emotionally before you communicate. If you encounter a group of strangers at a party or a meeting, stand next to them until they make room for you to enter the circle. Before you say anything, quiet your mind down and find a good feeling toward them (remember: the higher your state of mind, the closer you'll feel toward people). Then, if you spontaneously feel an urge to talk, let what you say come naturally from within you.

BOOMERANG

You get back what you give at the level you give. If you give only at the physical level (you give money to your family but you don't give yourself), you'll be treated like a physical object by your family. If you give only at an intellectual level, you'll only belong and be accepted intellectually: people will relate to your ideas but not to your real essence.

To belong fully at the physical, intellectual, and emotional levels, physically extend your hand and emotionally and intellectually extend yourself. Let go, relax, and allow yourself to belong. Reach out. Surrender your sense of separateness and you'll find others will reach out to you. Realize that, like an echo, the feelings you send out come back. The good feelings that come back to you are always the good feelings *you* send *yourself*. With wisdom, you send out warm, positive feelings and are receptive to the warm, positive feelings that come back.

PARTICIPATION

A feeling of belonging comes from participating in life. Vote and you feel part of the political process; buy stock and you feel you are part of the economic game; willingly go to family gatherings and you feel you belong to your family; take a risk and introduce yourself to other participants and you feel you belong at the conference.

To create a sense of belonging, remember: *you care about what you take care of*; and *you belong to what belongs to you*. Belonging is always mutual. Talk and listen to your family and your friends and you'll feel you belong to them and they belong to you. Listen to life and you'll feel life belongs to you and you belong to life.

Realize that, the more you embrace your daily experiences, the more feeling of mutual belonging you generate. Take care of your home, your car, your work, your friends, and your family and you feel a mutual belonging. Walk in your neighborhood and smile at your neighbors and you feel you belong there.

Throughout the day, you have choice points. You can react to your isolating thoughts, or you can consciously choose to experience a feeling of belonging. You can choose to get up and do the house-work that needs to be done to make the house belong to you, or you can stay in bed. When you travel, you can choose to wall yourself off by avoiding eye contact or reading, or you can be open to the person next to you. At work, you can choose to hide in your office, or you can choose to walk around and talk to others.

WILLINGNESS

The key to belonging is the desire and willingness to belong. You have first to decide whether you want to belong. After you make the decision to give yourself over, take concrete steps: choose the simple over the complicated (write a short note instead of a five-page letter), the slow over the fast (take the slow lane home rather than the fast lane), the ordinary over the extraordinary (go to lunch with co-workers rather than plan a dinner for twenty).

You need little effort to belong and a little belonging goes a long way. Simply make choices that lead to a good relationship with your everyday experiences. Treat each moment like a first date. You have no way of knowing what the moment will offer, but be willing to give yourself over to whatever happens.

RELATE TO REALITY

A sense of belonging, rather than being the reward for reaching big goals, comes from an appreciation of the everyday details of life. Invest in small, daily good feelings of belonging rather than hoping to strike it rich.

Approach each experience out of choice, instead of duty or obligation. Remember that belonging is enjoying. As you wash your face, get the newspaper, have your breakfast, stop at the grocery store, or talk to a neighbor, experience a sense of privilege and gratitude for the opportunity to be alive and belong to life.

Go to bed with feelings of belonging to the moment; refuse to get out of bed in the morning until you have the good feeling of belonging to life. Refuse to go more than eight hours without experiencing a good feeling of belonging and your good feelings will stay warm, alive, and easily accessible.

Focus each day on belonging to life and the sum total will be a happy life. You only have so many days, hours, and minutes. You're not other people and other people are not you. Only you can experience your life. Each moment you consciously decide to feel you belong to others and the earth is a moment in which you move to the positive side of the ledger.

TRUE SELF

The common denominator in all feelings of belonging is that you *eliminate thoughts of being exclusive and unite with something larger than yourself.* Move beyond your illusion of separateness and you'll see the truth that you belong to something much bigger and much more profound than your small self.

Your true nature is part of all nature and appears when you drop your exclusive interest in yourself and focus on the world around you. Typically, you feel your true nature when you're walking on the beach, listening to music, getting lost in creative work, and when you're in love.

You have a sense of pure experience without mind or body. As you merge with a larger reality, you experience no interrupting thoughts, irritating emotions, or uncomfortable physical sensations. Your true nature appears in moments when you see with perfect clarity, "This is where I really belong."

To move into this true state of belonging, focus outside your small concerns; be willing to hold a door open for a stranger and let a car cut in front of you; be willing to cook a meal for friends, listen to your child laugh, and volunteer your time to help others.

Replace illusionary self-importance with the real importance of belonging to all of life. Be willing to lose your separate self and you find your real self: you feel spontaneous, natural, and unified. You feel the importance of belonging to the planet, to your family and friends, and to the work you do.

FIDELITY TO CURRENT REALITY

Happiness and love of life mean living in a state of total acceptance, contentment, and equanimity. The commonality in all forms of love is belonging. Once you value and love life, you have the two necessary ingredients for happiness: you love life and you take life for better or worse.

Decide to commit to and belong to reality, to the present moment. Take each day's good and bad experiences with a mixture of even-mindedness and appreciation. Be faithful to each day and your life will no longer seem like a life sentence; you'll discover that each day is made up of a series of separate, impermanent experiences that will never occur again.

Decide to commit to whatever you're doing and refuse to go through the motions while thinking, "I'll get it right next time." The third force, which reconciles you with your life, is a love of being alive—a sense of mutual belonging between you and your daily experiences.

INTERNAL ADJUSTMENTS

If you lose your love of life, make an internal adjustment—admit you're wrong and have been unfaithful to the present moment; apologize and aim to reconcile with what is happening right now.

To be true to the present, you have to be willing to separate from the past and future. The feeling of belonging, like all reality, is in constant flux. To belong in the present, you have to let go of thoughts of belonging to the past or the future. To belong in your current city, you have to let go of thoughts of where you lived before and thoughts of where you might live in the future. To belong in your current relationship, you have to let go of clinging thoughts of past relationships or dreams of future ones.

You're unable to love what you make horrible and terrible—you're unable to feel at home in enemy territory. To feel you belong, you have to drop your hostile thoughts and replace them with third-force good feelings, which bond you with reality.

When you feel alienated from life, make a radical shift in how you're experiencing the moment. Clear your mind and allow the meaning of the present moment to rush in on waves of happiness—let the awesome reality of being alive be sufficient; be glad to be alive for the sake of being alive. Good or bad, enter into the glory of the present and allow yourself to belong fully to the here-and-now.

EXTERNAL ADJUSTMENTS

Remember that, although you always want to have an inner united feeling of belonging, you'll encounter many external places and situations where you'll be out of sync and out of harmony.

You want to focus first on unconditional feelings of belonging, but pay attention to circumstances as well. You'll never be able to stay comfortably in a place that's not right for you. By finding a good feeling and raising your state of mind, you'll instinctively know where you belong and where you don't.

WHAT'S GOING ON

To form a solid relationship with life, you have to be willing to know what is going on—good, bad, or indifferent. Be willing to look at and experience all relevant reality—good, bad, and indifferent. Be willing to belong to the denying second force and the affirming first force, as well as to the reconciling third force.

A common second force resistance to belonging (which comes from a first-force desire for perfection) is wanting to avoid experiencing unpleasant facts. With third-force understanding, you discover that your feeling of belonging will be strengthened by looking at all of reality.

Approach what you normally avoid. Be willing to belong to unpleasant as well as pleasant realities. Stay with the uncomfortable body sensations—feel them through. Be willing to step on the scale, make the doctor's appointment, look at your checking account, talk to your business partner, and look at yourself in the mirror.

LOVE ALL THE FORCES

From the third-force sense of belonging, you fully accept the first and second forces. You're inclusive and accept both forces as part of living. Instead of "I want my own business, *but* I don't have the money," you are matter-of-fact and let the first and second forces belong to you ("I want my own business *and* right now I don't have the money").

From the higher state of belonging, you see both the first and second forces as helpful information; rather than shoot the messenger or praise the messenger, you read the message. The first force lets you know what you care about and the second force is reality's report card ("You need to put a little more time in on this subject").

To connect the first and second forces and belong to all of life, you have to practice. At times, you'll regress and want to kill off your desires or isolate yourself from reality; but if you keep practicing, you'll spend more time in the higher state of belonging.

TRUST LIVING

To belong in life, let go of the past, and live in the present. As you let go and trust the process of living (even though you have no idea of what's going to happen next), you'll find life gets on your side. People are nicer and more cooperative. Everything fits into your suitcase; your phone calls are returned; your checkbook balances; and you hit a string of green lights on the drive home. When you feel you belong, everything from your immune system to your jokes works better.

"Belonging" is independent of "having" or "doing." With insight, you can enter the state of belonging at any moment. As you practice entering this state, you find that your sense of belonging grows bigger and more profound. Keep in mind you add to the world by developing a mutual belonging with the world and by becoming one more positive influence on the earth.

9

HAPPINESS
VERSUS
PLEASURE-SEEKING

Just as happiness leads to success, pleasure-seeking leads to pain and failure. Happiness is the third force that allows you to transcend first-force pleasure-seeking and the accompanying second-force pain.

HAPPINESS

PLEASURE-
SEEKING   PAIN

With understanding, you learn to make pleasure-seeking passive and your happiness active.

LOYALTY TO WHAT IS

Happiness comes from forming a union with reality. Happiness is escaping into reality—pleasure-seeking is escaping from reality. Pleasure-seeking is having an affair and cheating on reality ("Life doesn't excite me enough"; "I need more stimulation, more excitement than everyday reality can give me").

The fatal attraction of pleasure leads to a plus/minus experience. On a surface level, pleasure-seeking feels good; on a deeper level, you dislike your infidelity and know you're going against your best interests. You feel good when you buy expensive clothes you can't afford, but you feel worse when the bill comes; you feel a burst of energy when you eat cheese cake, but feel drained and bloated an hour later.

Pleasure-seeking drains your life force. The best way to create internal life force or power is to clarify the nature of pleasure-seeking. Once you can see into your pleasure drivenness, it starts to melt away. You naturally start to practice restraint and consequently feel more centered and more powerful.

FOOL'S GOLD

Pleasure-seeking teases you with promises of happiness but delivers disappointment. Kierkegaard said, "A life of self-indulgence is racked with emptiness, loneliness, self-hatred, and nostalgia." After a pleasure binge, you feel guilty and remorseful. In contrast, when you drop your pleasure-seeking thoughts and feel through, with awareness and equanimity, your physical cravings, you feel powerful and free.

With wisdom, you see that pleasure-seeking is a phony high, a false sense of well-being; you know the counterfeit high actually lowers your state of mind—you know cravings for sex, food, drugs, or other forms of pleasure-seeking will temporarily calm you but will never remove the second-force headaches of living. From a third-force perspective, you see pleasure-seeking as part of the problem, not the solution.

MOVE TOWARD REALITY

Unlike pleasure-seeking, happiness makes you more awake, aware, and alive. When you're stuck, to find a transcending third force, choose happiness over pleasure-seeking. Rather than stay in a warm bed, get up and do what needs to be done. Rather than pick up a spy novel, reach for the report that needs to be finished. Rather than go shopping, decide to balance your checkbook.

Notice how pleasure-seeking narrows your perspective and actually takes you away from life. Everything blurs as you focus on reducing your tension with pleasure-seeking. Happiness, in contrast, comes from being in harmony with life. Look for the ordinary. Happiness slows down time, turns your focus outward, and connects you with a more detailed, higher order of reality.

TRUE SELF

Pleasure-seeking, a search for outside excitement to stimulate your senses, distracts you from reality. Happiness comes from inside you—it is a feeling of exaltation toward life. Once you learn how to be happy, you're able to move beyond the drive for pleasure to what is highest within you. You transcend the thought "I'm excited; therefore, I exist." You feel alive without needing the electric shock of pleasure-seeking.

When you're happy, you're attracted to inner calm rather than crisis. You stop playing one pleasure distraction against the other. When on a diet, you have no need to compensate for the lack of pleasure by spending more money on entertainment. You transcend your need for constant drama and excitement; you no longer fantasize about winning the lottery or becoming rich and famous.

MOVE BEYOND YOUR EGO

Pleasure-seeking comes from your ego, a false friend, a Judas who tempts you away from reality. Ego gets you coming and going. Your ego pleads, "Have some ice cream, you deserve it," then backhands you ("You're pathetic, you have no willpower"). Happiness is your true friend and encourages you to make good choices.

If you do make a mistake, happiness encourages you ("Forget it and decide to do better next time").

Happiness leads to success. Because happiness comes from inside you, you have no need to go off on a tangent to keep your good feelings going. You can face and experience the pleasant and unpleasant and still be happy—you're free to look at the real costs and your real needs ("If I give in to the pleasure of complaining, I'll feel worse later").

HAPPINESS, THE THIRD FORCE

You'll always be tempted to relieve the conflict between the first and second forces by seeking pleasure. Instead, use your free mind to create a third-force good feeling in the moment: *foster an emotional bond of happiness between you and the reality you're resisting.* If you're having difficulties with someone, you can get pleasure from feeling angry or you can look for a good feeling and transcend your differences.

Happiness loosens you up and expands your state of being and awareness. Pleasure-seeking appears to expand you, but it really constricts you. You are seeking to reduce tension; however, in the end, you're even more tense.

A cup of coffee and a candy bar when you're tired can help you feel better immediately; but watch and you'll see that twenty minutes later you're tense, grumpy, and more fatigued than before. On the other hand, a brisk ten-minute walk when you're tired helps you feel calm, relaxed, and energetic for several hours.

EGO-DRIVEN

Pleasure-seeking comes from a need to be separate and special. The underlying assumption of your pleasure-seeking matches the bumper sticker that says, "Damn, I'm good!" When you seek pleasure, the spotlight is on you—your body's desires become the center of your attention.

Your ego tries to trick you into sabotaging yourself through seeking pleasure. Your ego's two major lieutenants are "Mr. Pain" and "Madame Pleasure," who attempt to train you with a primitive conditioning process. Your ego seduces you with the idea that you're special and then punishes you for being human.

Pleasure-seeking breeds ignorance and greed—the two biggest causes of loss. You need the pleasure of someone's company so much that you drive the person away, or you need the pleasure of money so much that you suspend reasoning, fall for get-rich-quick schemes, and end up broke and wondering, "Why did I do it?"

Live on the firm ground of happiness and you'll no longer be reactive to circumstances. Once you discover, "I can feel happy when I'm on top and when I'm not," you react impartially to successes and failures—you know one end of the stick comes with the other.

LONG-TERM GAINS

Your ego tries to convince you to settle for immediate gratification ("What you want is hopeless, so you might as well feel good now"). When you're feeling bad, you need to learn how to accept your uncomfortable body sensations and ignore your self-doubts and pleasure-striving thoughts.

When you're happy and in union with reality, you are naturally more optimistic and expansive. Instead of many little hopes ("I hope the person I met last night calls me") you have an overall optimism, a sense that you can bring about what you truly want. Once you're feeling better, you'll be better able to see what is going on. You'll collaborate with reality instead of wanting to escape it.

You never have a better opportunity to catch and drop your thoughts than when you're in the throes of a pleasure-seeking binge. Your ego, through justification and rationalization, tries to convince you that your reactive craving for pleasure, which comes from your mechanical thoughts, is really coming from your conscious choice ("This is what I really want to do"). This is a pseudo-choice; the real choice and real power are found in catching and dropping your pleasure-seeking thoughts and feeling through your physical cravings.

SALES RESISTANCE

You have a free mind with dominion over whatever thoughts and feelings appear. Detach yourself and refuse to listen to your ego's pleasure pitches, refuse to imagine owning what your ego is trying to sell you.

Realize that imagination is stronger than self-talk. It is rare that you can talk yourself out of some imagined pleasure. You need to stop yourself before you picture the pleasure. Focus on your purpose instead. Rather than picture how good ice cream would taste, focus on being happy, healthy, and true to your purpose.

Your pleasure-seeking thoughts and physical cravings obscure reality and will never allow you really to enjoy the present. Happiness comes from being in the here-and-now; it is a by-product of paying complete attention to what is. Drop your thoughts of future pleasure, allow your physical sensations to rise up and pass away, and move into the simplicity and richness of the moment.

POWER AND ENERGY

You can use pleasure-seeking to escape a poor relationship with reality temporarily, but later the pain returns stronger than ever. You can go to the racetrack to forget about your unpaid bills, but after the last race is run, your reentry into reality is all the more unpleasant.

Wordsworth said, "Getting and spending we lay waste our powers." You'll find that, the less of your life you spend pleasure-seeking, the richer you'll become. Power comes from seeing past your pleasure-seeking. The more you embrace here-and-now reality, the more powerful and effective you become.

Aim for happiness and you feel stronger and more energetic. You *feel* better as well as *get* better. You easily handle minor difficulties before they grow into insurmountable difficulties. Rather than try to beat reality, you join it. You pay your bills when they come due and avoid interest and late penalties.

BEYOND MATERIALISM

Pleasure-seeking comes from the physical world; happiness is beyond space and time. Happiness comes from an unknowingness, from a willingness to live in the ever-changing reality of the present moment. Rather than fight it, you welcome the mystery. You're naked and innocent, without any thoughts about "the way things are" to protect you.

Because pleasure-seeking and happiness are from different worlds, they are under different laws. Pleasure-seeking comes from exciting your senses; happiness comes from calming them down. As you quiet your senses down, including your brain (a major sense organ), you become more receptive to reality.

GETTING ADDICTED

Pleasure-seeking leads to addiction. After you smoke a cigarette, you go into withdrawal and have an urge for another cigarette; soon after a spending spree, you start to feel deprived, so you need to spend even more to treat your hangover.

The more pleasure you seek, the less you have. You often feel cheated, because pleasure is inflationary: you get decreasingly less pleasure for the money. You end up eating more, smoking more, spending more, and enjoying it less.

You need increasing doses of pleasure to ward off the pain. After the first few bites of ice cream, you no longer taste it, but you feel deprived if you're unable to finish the whole quart.

You're like a fly in a Venus flytrap—at first you're attracted to the succulent buds of the plant, but you soon become trapped and devoured.

POSITIVE ADDICTIONS

Positive addictions are still addictions. You become addicted to physical exercise, so you need to increase your exercise to get the same high. Eventually you're likely to burn out or injure yourself. You quickly become habituated to pleasure-seeking and need more. You build up a tolerance for pleasure-seeking, unlike happiness, and need bigger doses to escape your pain. To get the same high from working out you must spend ten hours instead of five. At some point, pleasure-seeking becomes all pain relief and little actual enjoyment. When your pleasure pipeline is cut, you experience increased pain and need another fix.

Pleasure-seeking comes from gratifying your senses with external stimuli; happiness comes from an intrinsic sense of well-being. To keep the center of gravity, look for good feelings inside yourself.

Only when you're unaware of how to be happy do you seek pleasure. With understanding, you see that pleasure-seeking is a party in a graveyard that eventually leads to more unhappiness. Rather than go on to a new avenue of escape when the old one wears out or becomes too painful, aim to understand and transcend the pleasure/pain cycle.

To avoid getting caught in the pleasure/pain cycle, become aware of how available pleasure-seeking is in a consumer-oriented society. In a matter of minutes, you can go to a corner convenience store—the local house of pleasure—and buy imported beer, *Playboy* magazines, and chocolate-chip cookies, and play video games. Within thirty minutes, you can be at the mall—the *palace* of pleasure—and use your credit cards to access immediate pleasure.

RETRAINING

You can stay happy indefinitely—all you have to do is remember to be happy. Pleasure-seeking is time-limited: you can only stay at the fair for so long before you get a stomachache. If you work long enough in an ice-cream parlor, you'll soon develop an aversion to ice cream.

The feeling of satiety causes you more real suffering than does deprivation. Pleasure-seeking is driven by your physical center. This is the primitive, earliest part of your brain, the part that moves toward what feels good and away from what feels bad. Because the reptilian brain is unpersuaded by intellectual arguments, you need to train it nonverbally, as you would train an animal, with direct experience.

Many addicts, from workaholics to drug addicts, spontaneously give up their addictions in their late thirties and early forties. The pain and hangover of the second force start to outweigh significantly the pleasure of the first force. The toll becomes too high. As the pleasure decreases and the pain increases, the nonverbal part of the brain starts to catch on that a little pleasure leads to a lot of pain. At this point, the alcohol or drugs become aversive.

You can use your third-force understanding to speed up this process. First, find a good feeling in your body as you pass by pleasure-seeking and go for happiness—let yourself experience how good it feels to refrain from pleasure-seeking. Second, after you do engage in pleasure-seeking, fully and nonjudgmentally feel with heightened awareness the specific discomfort in your body and pain of the second force. Spend five or ten minutes focusing on the unpleasant sensation. Do this as often as you can. Remember your self-downing thoughts destroy your awareness and prolong the learning curve. Shorten the time gap between first-force plea-sure-seeking and second-force suffering, and you'll naturally be done with what you are now addicted to. Through the principle of association, you want to nonverbally show your deep mind the relationship between pleasure-seeking and the resulting pain.

SOCIAL STATUS AND PLEASURE

Advertisers play up to your pleasure-seeking and try to ma-nipulate you into picturing in your mind the pleasure they are selling. The message of beer commercials is that you'd better drink beer if you want to have friends and fun. The message of cigarette ads is that if you want to relax and feel calm you'd better smoke. With insight, you can learn to sidestep the swamp of pleasure suggestions—billboards, television commercials, and newspaper advertisements.

When you're intelligent, you learn from your experiences; when you're wise, you learn from *others'* examples. The lives of Marilyn Monroe, Janis Joplin, Elvis Presley, and John Belushi are warnings—they are case studies of what happens when you try to build a life on the quicksands of pleasure.

Look and you'll discover you can never get enough pleasure to be happy. Instead of emulating pleasure-seekers, model yourself after those who seek the real goods—people like Walt Whitman,

William Blake, and Mother Teresa, who lead lives of ecstasy and exultation.

Refuse to buy into your ego's concern ("Will others be more impressed if I go on a cruise or if I go camping?"). Happiness is found in the ordinary—taking a walk in a park, watching children play, having a talk with a friend, and feeling cozy and snug.

REAL PLEASURE

Becoming an antipleasure crusader, such as joining a temperance or antipornography group, is a way to get perverted pleasure by being superior to others. The idea is not to give up pleasure but to observe and distinguish the difference between pleasure-seeking and fully experiencing real pleasure.

With understanding, you experience sensual pleasure from a higher perspective. You have your cake and eat it too. Rather than be driven by the urge to seek pleasure, you *enjoy* pleasure. You're already happy, so pleasure is a bonus, not a need. Experience true pleasure, which is increased awareness of the body sensations of pleasure, as opposed to pleasure-seeking. Real pleasure is a means to clarify reality further, a way to *tune in to more reality* instead of a way to escape reality.

Pleasure-seeking only leads to more pleasure-seeking. Knowing that you have more pleasure ahead of you gets in the way of the pleasure in front of you.

Notice that when you seek pleasure you try to get the experience over as quickly as possible so you can go on to the next experience. You eat rapidly, make love rapidly, talk rapidly, and drive rapidly. Pleasure used as a substitute for happiness is never fully satisfying.

With wisdom, instead of using pleasure-seeking as a stimulant or a distraction, you use real pleasure as a way to experience reality even more deeply—you slow down and heighten your awareness of everyday pleasure.

AVOID THE EXTREMES

To create happiness, go for balance and avoid the extremes. Too much of even healthy pleasure turns to aversion. Quit before you reach saturation. Similarly, too severe a diet or regimen of any kind leads to second-force deprivation and brings on a first-force binge. André Gide said, in effect, that the total secret of happiness is not to compare the present with the past, because you didn't enjoy it because you were thinking of the future.

When you're happy, you enjoy the small pleasures of living right now. You feel full, satisfied, and free of deprivation. When you're happy in the present, you have no need to make up for lost time. Because you enjoy the days, you have no need to create excitement on the weekend. You live for today, not for your vacations.

LEARN HOW TO BE HAPPY NOW

You can learn to create happiness at any time in your life. When you feel happy, you change your whole body chemistry. You reach a state of being where you're fully awake. Happiness, as opposed to pleasure-seeking, is a wordless experience. No longer distracted by the noise and images in your head, you walk in clarity and silence.

Even if you felt deprived of pleasure as a child or were over-indulged, you can learn to bring about authentic good feelings now. Start by being open to the possibility that there are higher, happier states you can move to.

Pleasure is skin-deep, but happiness goes all the way to the bone. Happiness is deeper, more valuable, and more profound. Happiness reaches your essence. Once you get a taste of real happiness, you realize pleasure-seeking is second-rate, an inferior substitute. Pleasure-seeking is a thirteen-inch portable television; happiness is a big-screen color stereophonic set.

DEVELOP PATIENCE

Anything worthwhile is worth waiting for. Pleasure-seeking promises immediate gratification; you may have to wait for good feelings to rise within you. To your ego, five minutes of pleasure in exchange for ten years of suffering sounds like an okay deal. For happiness to arise within, you need patience, faith, and understanding that happiness will come.

Happiness, bliss, ecstasy, and exultation are more subtle than pleasure-seeking: as with classical music, you have to develop an inner taste for happiness. You have to override your narcissistic urge for immediate pleasure. With insight, you put your desire for the subtle beauty of connecting with reality over your urge for pleasure-seeking.

Once you tune in to feelings of happiness, they appear more and more frequently. The happier you are, the more happiness comes to you. You'll be out with your friends, and spontaneous good feelings will engulf you.

BEYOND MORALS

When you're happy and true to yourself, you follow your own internal values—even if they go against what others or society prescribes. Your state of mind has a corresponding level of conscience. When your mood and state of mind rise, so does your desire to be true to the highest in you.

Choosing happiness over pleasure-seeking is a matter of practicality, not morals. If you go against your own values, you will experience a bad conscience. When you feel bad about yourself, you sabotage yourself. Exclude the world and focus only on your own pleasure and you'll feel guilty, because you know on some level that your pleasure-seeking is against your best interests.

In a lower state, you may even love forbidden pleasure. You feel a rush when you sneak food, drink alone, or have illicit sex— you feel the same excitement you did as a kid sneaking into a movie.

Your ego then usually gets back at you by having you wallow in your own pleasure. Pleasure-seeking becomes its own punishment. You overeat to punish yourself for overeating; you spend money as revenge for being in debt.

Much of your behavior depends on whom you modeled yourself after. The most important model is yourself. When you act from your own true essence, you become your own self-inspiring model.

When you're happy, you follow your true conscience. In your heart of hearts, you know that what you're doing is right—this causes you to feel even more uplifted and to act even more in line with your true interest.

HIGHER LEVEL

Pleasure-seeking comes from egocentricity; happiness comes from *giving* of yourself, from passing your good feelings on to others. Happiness is something you naturally and unconsciously want to give others. Happiness has nothing to do with you personally. You can enjoy everything, not just what relates to you as an individual.

Life is short but wide. In anything you do, you have a range of options—to be happy in the moment is always one of them.

10

PSYCHOLOGICAL REVERSAL

Like the lives of Jack the Ripper and William Shakespeare, your life consists of a moving force, an energy that makes up your experiences. Your energy can move forward or in reverse. Jack the Ripper's energy moved backward, toward destruction; William Shakespeare's energy moved forward, toward creativity.

NEGATIVE THIRD FORCE

Your first-force desire starts the forward cycle, but you eventually run into second-force resistance. If you resist the obstacles in your path, you become psychologically reversed; you drop into a survival mode and focus exclusively on the negative. Your focus is all on what you don't want, not on what you do want.

Just as good feelings are the positive third force that allows you to transcend the conflict between your desire and your resistance, bad feelings are the negative third force. With bad feel-

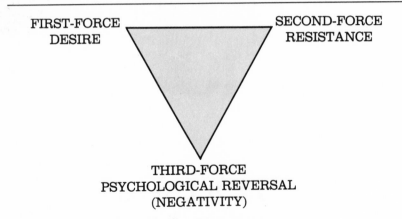

FIRST-FORCE
DESIRE

SECOND-FORCE
RESISTANCE

THIRD-FORCE
PSYCHOLOGICAL REVERSAL
(NEGATIVITY)

ings, you resolve the structural conflict between desire and resistance by becoming psychologically reversed and moving away from what you want.

With wisdom, you drop negative thoughts, not only because you want to feel good, but because you realize that, just as good feelings are a success force, negativity is a failure force.

To be successful, identify with your forward-moving self—your friendly Dr. Jekyll, which likes the world and helps you progress—and detach from your reversed self—your unfriendly Mr. Hyde, which hinders your progress.

BECOMING REVERSED

Realize that when you're reversed your Mr. Hyde appears and turns everything upside down. When you're horrid, you're really bad. You throw the baby out with the bathwater; you're the one bad apple spoiling the whole barrel.

Psychological reversal, a primitive mode for responding to frustration and constraints, was necessary for human evolution. It was also necessary for your own development—without it you could never have separated from your parents. However, as an everyday coping strategy, psychological reversal creates more problems than it solves. Just as you are biologically wired to learn language, you have a tendency to become negative or psychologically reversed. When you become reversed, you're transformed into a maverick animal that refuses to be broken or trained.

EVEN-MINDED

Freedom from reversal comes from being nonreactive to your first-force cravings and your second-force reactions. Start to treat the first and second forces, in yourself and in others, with matter-of-fact equanimity. If someone is being overly negative with you, acknowledge to yourself, "He's full of second force, and it's not my job to fix him." When you find yourself being negative, tell yourself, "Second force happens, and it's nothing personal."

Become dispassionate toward your occasional reversals and avoid getting reversed over your reversal. You are here today because your ancestors used reversal to survive; when they encountered obstacles, they automatically fought their enemies or shut down and conserved their energy until the situation improved.

REVERSAL STAGES

At different stages in your life, you're prone to reversal. As a baby, when someone tried to restrict you, you became unhappy, inhibited, and self-punitive. Between the ages of two and a half and three and a half, you learned the power of saying no. This was the birth of your ego—your self-esteem mechanism. You felt you had a sacred duty to resist your suppressors.

When you're reversed today, you still act like a two-year-old. Your reversal gives you an opportunity to see your primitive ego in action. You may choose public places to make your stand. In grocery stores and shopping malls you become a "terrible two" and act out your reversal. You come close to throwing your food in restaurants, or kicking someone at family gatherings.

You entered a major reversal stage as an adolescent. You refined your ego or self-image through blind conformity and blind rebellion. You may have defined who you are by being the opposite of your brother or sister, or the opposite of what others expected of you.

Today you may get reversed on being single and want to get married; you may get reversed on being married and want to be single; or you may be reversed on everything and not want to be single or married.

Reversal can lead to sudden life-style changes. If you're an

125

overachiever, in your later years you may get reversed and want to become a beach bum; if you're passive, you may rebel and want to assert yourself.

REVERSAL'S ROLE IN SOCIETY

Too much uniformity brings about stagnation; to evolve and remain strong, society needs rebels, deviants, and troublemakers. You may think you're rebelling against a group when you're actually conforming to the group's more subtle demands. Similarly, your family and your employer need a few reversed "volunteers" to fight the norm and unite the group.

Do you stand up and challenge the leader of every group you attend? See that, when you're reversed and have fantasies of being a freedom fighter, all you are really doing is being a pawn of outside social forces.

At your family gatherings, you may find you are "it." You become "it" when you're in a bad mood or are going through a bad patch. Your reversed attitude and behavior help your family develop an in-group feeling and make them thankful they are not you. Refuse to be a sacrificial lamb simply so your co-workers have someone to feel superior to or your family has a black sheep to feel united against.

Although you face social, biological, developmental, and situational pressures, *you have a right not to get reversed.* Realize at a deep level that you have the right not to be negative and you'll find better ways to be independent, and to get what you want.

TRUE INDEPENDENCE

Reversal is an attempt to regain or maintain a *pseudo-independence* to boost your self-esteem. You may get reversed when someone tells you how you should wear your hair or raise your children. To give yourself a false sense of freedom, you refuse to go along with others; or, if you do go along, you engage in malicious compliance and make others sorry they asked.

To gain the illusion of freedom, you may become an outright rebel, a troublemaker, and a provocateur. When asked to sit down, you stand up. You may become a ringleader and spend your time planning office coups and feeding the fires of dissension. On the other hand, if you fear confrontation you may become a bad sport—to gain negative liberation, you rebel in subtle, passive ways.

The Africans say, "Follow the customs or flee the country." With wisdom and maturity, you develop awareness that you live in an inner and an outer world. You outwardly follow the norms of the groups you choose to belong to—you follow the dress code and play the required role. In a high state of mind, you consciously choose to play the role, all the time remembering you're playing a role.

You outwardly conform, but in your inner world, you're completely free to think as you choose. Inside, you're totally yourself. You may inwardly think, "My boss is a fool," but outwardly you treat your boss with respect. Without understanding the two worlds, you're limited to two options: you can rebel against your boss (covertly or overtly) and create problems for yourself and others, or you can suppress your true opinion of your boss in order to win approval.

With insight, you'll see that saying no to life, like blind conformity, only gives you the illusion of freedom. To become truly free, you have to move beyond reversal and see that the third-force option is the ability to say yes and no to any situation.

Your reversal comes from a sense of powerlessness; your attempt to regain control by getting reversed actually makes you feel more powerless. Recognize that feeling positive is where your strength and power (ability to get desired results) lie. Once you see that you have internal freedom, you have no need to bombard yourself with negativity to fight for your rights.

AWARENESS OF REVERSAL

Keep in mind that you're innocent—you become Mr. Hyde automatically and involuntarily. A biological switch is thrown and your whole system is turned upside down—you bring the negative to the foreground as the positive fades into the background.

Once you're aware that you're reversed, you're halfway out of it. Become objective about your subjective state of reversal. Once you can clearly see that your worst side has come forward, you stop feeding it: *you make the negative passive and the positive active.* You start to detach inwardly from your reversal.

You seldom get reversed over major problems. You typically get reversed over insignificant events, or when others act in mechanical, predictable ways. The person may be totally illogical and yet closed off to any new thinking and absolutely convinced there is only one right way. You can't win. At the moment, remember your reversal is just as predictable and just as mechanical.

Use your negative feelings—your uncomfortable physical sensations—as a sign that you're reversed, not as a sign to attack others. Err on the side of admitting you're reversed. Whenever someone accuses you of being reversed or in a bad mood, accept the possibility that, even if you *think* you're not, probably you are.

MEETING OBSTACLES

Reversal comes from running into barricades on the way to your destination and thinking, "I have either to quit or to fight." If you think you're not good enough, you give up and turn around. If you think it's unfair, you fight to the death.

Realize that when you're reversed you can only count to two—your way or no way. From a place of wisdom, you no longer see the world in black or white terms ("If I can't have this person, I can never find anyone for me"); instead, you see many ways around the obstacle, and you know that no one obstacle means you can never have what you really want.

Move to the higher third-force perspective and you become more flexible; you say yes when it's to your advantage and no when it's not to your advantage.

You have no need to quit or use negative motivation to fight obstacles. Rather than give up and turn around or bang yourself against the barricade in an effort to move it out of the way half an inch at a time, look for a third option—find a good feeling toward what you want and you'll see how you can use the good feelings as a bridge to get beyond obstacles.

When you feel yourself becoming reversed, feel the negative feeling through and then look for a higher vantage point, from which you can see over or around the barricades. Once you've located this higher point of view, you'll remember your destination.

You'll usually see that what you thought was a barricade is a tumbleweed you can easily knock out of the way.

Even if it *is* a real barricade, from your higher outlook you see ways to get over or around it—you don't see yourself as blocked. You see setbacks as temporary detours rather than as dead ends.

Good feelings move you to a third-force balance in which you exercise discretion. If you are first-force dominant, you need to be more passive toward the obstacle. Instead of fighting your foes nose to nose (and in the process cutting off your own nose), let go and relax until you can get a higher perspective. Instead of going off on a tangent, remember your original aim. If you're second-force dominant, you need to get your second wind and be more active.

RECOGNIZING REVERSAL

You are reversed when you feel irritable and out of sorts. You're cross—everything seems to annoy you. In mild forms, once you recognize and admit you're reversed, your reversal disappears. In more extreme forms, Mr. Hyde takes the wheel, and you're in for a bumpy ride.

You become reversed when faced with anything that blocks your ego's desire to have its way. You dig in and refuse to go along with the program. You want to do the opposite of what's required— *even if the requirement comes from you.* To gain the illusion of control, you rebel against all appearances of being told what you can or can't do. You refuse to clean your house, stay on a diet, or be nice to your family. You may even make up your mind to talk a potential customer out of a sale or purposely throw a tennis game. You don't know why you are being so stupid. You don't *want* to complain, take the path of darkness, and be mean to those you love; but you do it anyway.

In this alternative state of consciousness you become topsy-turvy. You lie to yourself, and you lie to others. You know it's a game, but you do it anyway. You make what is real unreal and what is unreal real. Good is bad, bad is good. You see kindness as weakness and cruelty as strength. You act worse when encouraged and better when treated badly. You get pleasure from the negative. You feel like murdering your children, kicking old ladies, and going off your diet.

Physical and mental health requires you to be congruent with your real preferences and your real values. Boris Pasternak wrote, "Your health is bound to be affected if day after day you say the opposite of what you feel, if you grovel before what you dislike and rejoice at what brings you nothing but misfortune."

MASTERY OF YOUR BODY

When you're truly free, you master your own body as well as your emotions and intellect. Observe how your body tenses up when you get reversed. You don't *want* to give in to your urge to have a drink or take a nap instead of doing your work, but your body seems to have a will of its own.

You can actually *feel* this inner struggle between what your head thinks and what your body wants to do. You may be unaware of the exact nature of the conflict, but your body feels the same way it does when you're arguing with someone.

TENSION SEEKS RESOLUTION

Psychological reversal puts you in a state of physical tension. You want to behave badly because you find pleasure and relief in reducing the physical tension. Even though you're going against your best interest, you like being bad and you enjoy breaking the rules.

Reversal puts you in a state of mind that poet Robert Bly calls "abstraction, hatred and narcissism." You react to an abstraction about reality, instead of dealing directly with reality. To get unreversed, move up to one of the higher states of mind, which Bly calls "relating," "merging," and "creating." You need to drop your abstract thoughts, your negativity, and your self-absorption and relate directly to others and the world so you can bring about what you truly want.

Your negative pleasure-seeking comes from a need to release tension. When your body becomes tense, use this as a sign to feel through your pleasure-seeking sensations, which are narcissistic and self-centered, and replace them with happiness, which comes from a mutual interaction with the world around you.

Reversal comes from reacting to your physical sensations. With insight, you realize you're not your body. Your body is an instrument, a vehicle; you're under no mandate to jump up and do whatever your body sensations demand at the moment.

The most powerful dynamic that exists is *"Tension seeks resolution."* When you're unable to catch your negative thoughts and you become reversed, negativity gains a stronghold in your body and creates physical tension. When you're unaware of your bodily sensations, they drive you to resolve the tension by seeking pleasure, which takes you away from your purpose.

HEALTHY RESOLUTION

Through practice, you can reduce the tension simply by observing with awareness and acceptance the physical sensations in your body. Experiment and you'll discover that what you observe decreases. Watch with specificity and equanimity the painful knots in your body and you'll find your awareness breaks up the knots.

By scanning your body and directly experiencing precise physical sensations (a tightness in your back or a burning feeling in your stomach), you move your awareness into the present moment; you're able to relate directly to your body and see, impartially, how sensations actually change, moment by moment.

You may know intellectually that your urge for negative pleasure-seeking will pass. However, by objectively and dispassionately observing your body's drivenness, you can know for sure that they are changing and passing away right now.

SPECIFIC REVERSAL

With third-force wisdom, you realize that you can move into "abstractions, hatred and narcissism" with anything—mathematics, a restaurant, your mother-in-law. The reasons for and history behind your reversal are complicated. The solution is simple: through direct observation, you can dissolve the uncomfortable feelings in your body, and then find a good feeling toward what you're reversed on, and you'll no longer checkmate yourself.

Keep in mind that reversal manifests itself in your body. To get unreversed concerning a specific place, person, or activity, you have to retrain your body to enjoy what is now aversive. Remember that you can create new, positive associations toward anything. If you're reversed on doing exercise, find a good feeling toward exercise. Start small. If a bad feeling comes over you, feel it through or leave until you can find a good feeling in your body toward the activity.

Aim to establish a collaborative relationship with what you're reversed on. If you're stuck on money, aim for a friendly, matter-of-fact relationship with money. Once you have better feelings toward money, you'll start to attract it instead of repelling it.

REVERSE THE PAST

If you come to a hospital with a bullet wound, the surgeon doesn't care who shot you. In any case, even though your reversal may have come from your past, there's no need to sift through your past for the answer. You carry the living past with you via your thoughts. Once you start going forward, your past memories will change. You'll no longer be able to relate to the past in the same way. You'll find that your future, as well as your past, will be different.

Because of the thought "I can't get what I want" (based on the many times you haven't), you are most vulnerable to reversal the closer you get to a goal.

When winning is almost in your grasp, drop your reversed thoughts, feel through your uncomfortable feelings, and refocus on your original aim. Remember that in a misguided attempt to protect your self-esteem, your ego tries to divert you from being successful. Once you drop your self-limiting party line, you can go beyond what you previously believed was possible.

WORK IN HARMONY

With insight, you refuse to let your body become your master. You know that, when your body wants to rebel against your true aims, you can override it by finding a neutralizing third-force good feeling in the moment. When you want to give up smoking or lose weight, let the thoughts that lead to physical cravings for cigarettes or food ("I always smoke a cigarette with my first cup of coffee"; "Why go to a movie if I can't have buttered popcorn?") pass without acting on them.

When you're reversed, you need to decide to be authentic. Get your body, mind, and heart to go in the same direction. If you say you want a job, go out on interviews. To get moving, say what you mean and mean what you say. You'll find that congruency between your thoughts, feelings, and action leads to forward movement.

DETACH FROM YOUR REVERSAL

Learn to distrust immediately your reversed thoughts and feelings. When you're reversed, you're completely wrong, but you try to convince yourself, through self-dialogue, that you're right. You try to convince yourself that ten people off the street would all agree that you're right and others are wrong.

When you're reversed, refuse to make major decisions until you feel better. If you have to do something, do the opposite of your first inclination. When you want to attack someone, sacrifice your desire to outwardly express your righteous anger and instead let the anger internally express itself through your body. Let the feeling be in your body before you give in to your urge to let off steam. After you have fully digested it, you can decide what you want to say.

REFOCUS

When you're boiling inside, stop shoveling in coal to keep the fire going. Acknowledge your anger and feel it fully and with precision and equanimity. Though operating from reversal can be temporarily effective, realize that real effectiveness comes when you operate from inspiration, not negation.

Go against your inclination to obsess on small negative details. Once you take your focus off the details, you'll see the big picture. The world will look increasingly bright as you turn your eyes toward what you want. Shift your focus from closed doors and blocked paths, and new possibilities will start to appear. What seems impossible when you're reversed seems inevitable once you're unreversed.

STOP BUILDING CASES

When you're reversed, you become like an employer who keeps a book on employees' mistakes to justify replacing them. You tell only one side of the story; you slant the facts to make yourself or others look bad. Watch yourself and you'll find that, if you're unable to express your frustration at your boss, you start building a case against the city you live in or against the people you live with. If this fails, you build a case against yourself.

Refuse to create a self-fulfilling prophecy. To move forward, stop building a case. Reversal has no life of its own, drop your litany of complaints, and you'll find that your reversal disappears.

Refuse to blame yourself for being the obstacle that stops you from getting what you want. This may be true up until now, but when you focus on a flaw—in yourself or others—the flaw continues. Decide to become more fair with yourself.

With a little common sense, you no longer indulge in the pleasure of being down on others or in the pleasure of being down on yourself; you refuse to keep a book on anyone or to give in to the pleasure of feeling superior to yourself or to others.

MOTIVATION

From a third-force perspective, you come to see that your motivation matches the direction of your thinking. With a little wisdom, you stop building a case for why you can never have what you really want. You realize that this is shooting yourself in the foot to avoid going into combat. You no longer handicap yourself and use this as an excuse for failure.

When you're reversed, you're like a tennis player who's losing. Your automatic thought is "I can't win this game," and you picture yourself losing. You then double-fault and miss easy shots. You may argue, "But I *want* to win"; yet, because you think you will lose, on a physical or motivational level you *want* to lose.

At any point, you can shift the game's momentum in your favor. Find a relaxed good feeling in your body and decide to score one point. Keep in mind that, if you score a point, you'll start to think, "I can win," and you'll picture winning. Your body's motivation will then become to play as well as it can.

When you're reversed, no matter how wildly you drive in reverse gear, you'll eventually crash and the momentum will shift. Your reversal will disappear. However, once you learn to master reversal, you will no longer back yourself into corners repeatedly—you'll deal with obstacles effectively, with the least amount of effort and the maximum amount of joy.

11

MOVEMENT

Being happy is a moving experience. The more you move in your thinking, feeling, and acting, the more you learn how the world works, how people act, and how to reach your destination. Movement in every aspect of your life enhances good feelings, and your good feelings enhance movement.

To take in reality fully, you need balanced movement in your three centers—physical, intellectual, and feeling. When you're reversed, your view of reality is biased, because your centers are unbalanced: you're overthinking and underacting and underfeeling. You need to shift your focus and activate your underused acting and feeling centers.

ACTIVE RESIGNATION

Four or five times a day, desire meets resistance and conflicts ensue. You want to jump in the pool (first force), but the water seems too cold (second force), so you freeze on the edge of the pool. The cold water may be a call you must make, reading you want to get to, or a meeting to sit through.

Remember, everything you create comes by way of the three forces. Ancient sages described this as the Tao, or way of nature. Over two thousand years ago, Lao-tzu wrote:

The Way gives birth to the One.
The One gives birth to Two.
Two gives birth to Three.
And Three gives birth to the ten thousand things.

When you fight second-force reality (your thoughts about the cold water), you get reversed and bogged down. To free yourself and find a completing third force, make peace with what you're fighting. Drop your resisting thoughts and you'll see reality more clearly. Do you have a flat tire? Quickly resign yourself to it and you'll release third-force energy that allows you to fix the tire and get on the road again.

When you're reversed, you're stuck because you buy into the illusion of permanency. Your thinking freezes the obstacle ("It's always going to be like this"). Because you see the second force as solid and immovable, what you want seems impossible. Once you find a good feeling, you unfreeze the obstacle, start to move, and reconnect with the impermanency of all nature.

Good feelings bring awareness of internal and external movement. Movement in your feeling center raises your state of mind, shifts your focus off your thinking, and puts you in touch with a direct feeling for all of life. Once your feeling center is open, you'll experience the world in a fresh way, and new opportunities will open up.

Realize that, once you have found a good feeling, jumped in the water, and started moving around, you'll warm up. The secret is to accept completely and be matter-of-fact about cold water. Get in accord with cold water, rather than fight it.

TENSION SEEKS RESOLUTION

Lao-tzu said, "Softness triumphs over hardness, feebleness over strength. What is more malleable is always superior over that which is immovable. This is the principle of controlling things by going along with them, of mastery through adoption."

The more you try to make reality bend to your will, the more tension you produce. Eventually you become exhausted and reduce the tension either by quitting or by jumping into the pool and surrendering to the cold water.

Instead of waiting until you're unable to tolerate the discomfort, surrender immediately to what is and you release your third-force energy. When you resign yourself to what is, you release tension and, like a wound-up coil, spring above the conflict. To your surprise, you become in harmony with what you've been fighting. When you resign yourself to what you've been fighting, you reconcile the subject/object dualism and merge with the moment. As you remove resistance, the pure energy flows like unimpeded electricity through you.

Just as you will always have a first force, you will always have a second force. With wisdom, you note the uncomfortable bodily sensations ("Ah, here they are"), accept them, and move on. Be happy when you encounter resistance. Realize that the third force is not far behind.

If you're been fighting your studies because you know you must pass a test, resign yourself to whatever happens on the test. Once you learn for the sake of learning, you'll find that the material begins to make sense to you. See that trying to change others is hopeless and resign yourself to how your husband or wife is acting, and a feeling of love and reconciliation will sweep over you and lift you above your differences with him or her.

Rather than battle reality to exhaustion, quickly surrender to what is. Refuse to go over the negative details; refuse to protest, silently or vocally, against the way life is at the moment. When you drop your unrealistic expectations and are able to face second-force reality directly, you're able to see clearly what is really going on.

Active resignation means you drop the thought that reality must be different. With active resignation, you know that you *could* do more (internally and externally) but for the moment you choose not to do anything and let life be the way it is. Once you relax your thoughts and become impartial to the conflict between your desires and the resistance, a third-force good feeling naturally appears and brings movement on all levels.

Disregard thoughts such as "I must change this," and look for the center of gravity within yourself. You become powerful once you acknowledge you're powerless to turn back the clock or to move time forward. Keep in mind always that power comes from your willingness to further clarify reality in the present, to tell the truth, and to align yourself with the facts.

The quicker you're able to resign yourself to the reality of the present moment, the greater your awareness and the greater your ability to see the next opportunity—which often appears immediately after a setback.

ENERGY CONSERVATION

With every setback comes a gain, but you have to be on a high level to see and appreciate this. When the moon is dark, you're able to see the stars. Accept reality quickly (stop talking to yourself about your problem) and you free yourself to see the good that hides behind the bad.

Reversal comes from letting an event or a person capture your focus of attention. You become constricted and narrow-minded. With wisdom, you refuse to let outside circumstances drain your energy and put you under house arrest. When your attention is stuck on a person or an event, actively choose to resign yourself. Detach from your resisting self-talk and free yourself from self-arrest.

Everything is temporary—impermanency is the only permanency. Accept this change and your energy and sense of self expand. Each day you have countless opportunities to resign yourself to change and create new energy. You can practice on anything—a broken fingernail, an inconsiderate clerk, or a bad cold.

Make your need for reality to be different passive and your desire to feel good in the moment active. What you always resign yourself to is *your own thinking* (what the Buddhists call "moha" or ignorance)—the illusion that life should go your way simply because you think it should.

DECISIONS

To move on a stuck decision, find a good feeling and actively resign yourself to the lost side of the equation. Let go of the thought "I must have it all." See that with every decision you have a gain and a loss. The third force is to choose what you truly want. When you have chosen what you really want, you'll gladly make the necessary sacrifices.

With wisdom, you resign yourself to the uncertainty of any outcome. Every decision is a gamble, and over the long run, what you lose on the apples you'll make up on the pears.

Find a good feeling in the present and resign yourself both to the past (which you're unable to change) and to the future (which you're unable to control). Remind yourself, "I may miss an occasional opportunity, but the energy, peace of mind, and opportunities I gain by resigning myself more than make up for it."

MASTER THE CYCLES

Robert Pirsig, in *Zen and the Art of Motorcycle Maintenance*, wrote, "You climb the mountain in an equilibrium between restlessness and exhaustion." To resign quickly, remember that everything from the stock market to your biorhythms works in an active/passive cycle. When your active energy is ascending, your passive energy is descending. To stay moving, learn to ride the crest by going with your shifting energies. By shifting your awareness to the energy in play at the moment, you can stay on top of the wave.

Initially, you may be eager to work on straightening out your closets. After a while, your energy wanes and you feel like getting back to the novel you were reading. If your energy for cleaning the closet is descending, rather than push yourself, take a break, go for a walk, or read for ten or fifteen minutes. Then, when your active energy returns, go back to cleaning the closet.

If you're really too tired to go back to the closet, go to bed, and work on the closet in the morning, when you have more energy. You might get more done today by pushing yourself, but tomorrow you will have a huge second force and find it difficult to get back to the closet project.

If you're first-force dominant, you become more efficient once you honor your passive side. Take time off during the day, go on frequent vacations, and be lazy. If you are second-force dominant, you create more energy once you focus on your active side, choose to do a little more, and go the extra inch.

PHYSICAL MOVEMENT

To rise above the second force, you often need internal and external movement. Accept reality, find a good feeling toward the finished result, and then physically move. Do what you don't want to do (exercise) in place of what you want to do (stay in a warm bed).

With just the hint of a good feeling or common sense, you'll realize you can always move physically. When you move physically, you raise your understanding and shake yourself loose from stuck thoughts.

Move your body and show yourself, "I can feel good and bring about what I want." Almost any physical movement lifts your spirits. As you move, your attention turns outward and your optimism returns.

To get unreversed, you need to move more and think less. If you are sitting in a chair, make yourself stand up and walk around the room. If you are lying down, swing your legs over the side of the bed and sit up.

OUTER FOCUS

To keep your moving center alive and vibrant, design physical movement into your life. Put away your television's remote control and get up to change channels. Park your car several blocks away from your destination and walk. Take the stairs instead of the elevator.

Physical movement takes your focus away from your thoughts and allows you to experience reality directly. Once you focus away from the thoughts about yourself, you naturally feel better. Physical movement reconnects to your larger sense of self, and as you rediscover you're part of a larger reality, your sense of well-being expands.

If you're stuck on an unknown, find a good feeling toward the newness of the situation. Look with fresh eyes. *With the right feeling and the right state of mind, everything becomes easy.* Remember, you like to travel and visit new places because of their novelty. In the same way, become like a child who is full of energy and enthusiasm because everything is new.

THE STEP IS THE VICTORY

To keep moving, focus on the steps, not on the outcome, which is outside of your control. Be willing to take the step without any guarantees. Have the courage to step into emptiness. When asked what he thought of his new baby, John-John, John Kennedy said, "We'll know more later." Tell yourself, "As I move forward, I'll know more, and once I know more, I can adjust my course accordingly."

To start moving, aim for small victories. Keep it simple: rather than think about what you should do, ignore your thoughts and do it. Your thoughts are not incoming artillery from the enemy line; they are just noise. Keep in mind that, no matter what your thoughts are, you can still move forward.

When method actor Dustin Hoffman was making the movie *Marathon Man* with Laurence Olivier, he stayed up two days and nights preparing to look tired for a scene. When he showed up for the scene, Olivier said, "You should learn to act, dear boy. Then you wouldn't have to put yourself through this sort of thing." You don't need to go through a lot of preparation to get started; you just need to start.

Remember, *the step is the victory*. Once you see you can accomplish a small step, you imagine doing even more, and you do more. With small successes, your momentum builds and your pace quickens.

NO STEP TOO SMALL

Find even a taste of a good feeling toward what you want and you'll be able to take the first step. What you want to accomplish may seem like crossing Death Valley, but once you begin to move, you'll realize it is just across the room.

Any step will work to get you unreversed. All you have to do is make a small friendly act toward what you've been resisting. Keep in mind that any small symbolic gesture will open up your constricted sense of self and get you moving.

When you're psychologically stuck, an inch of tread gets you moving. Start with a neutral gesture. Make the person with whom you're angry a cup of tea, or sharpen your pencils for the project you've been resisting. Make a sign of goodwill to yourself and others—a sign that you are not powerless. Any gesture can turn the tide, and once you move, you see that you *do* have power.

Be willing to lose face in an exchange for being true to what you really want. Remind yourself, "I need to drop my thoughts of needing to be right before I can move to a higher level of functioning." Apologize to the person you treated badly, even though it hurts; be considerate of someone you took advantage of; admit you're wrong, even though you want to keep the illusion of being the misunderstood genius.

DO A LITTLE

Use a little first force to transcend a big second-force resistance. Act against your reversal thoughts ("I don't feel like it now—I'll do it after I read the paper") by taking a tiny step ("I'll write the first sentence of the letter"). Do what you're avoiding, at least for a minute or two. After you take the step, give yourself permission to quit if you want. Then, after a period of second-force passivity, come back and take another small step.

Once you get started, you nearly always feel better and want to do more; however, keep your agreement with yourself. If you want to quit, quit for ten or fifteen minutes; then repeat the do-a-little-bit-first strategy. The combination of being active and having permission to be passive puts you back in rhythm with what you want to accomplish.

At times you may be reversed because you're too restless. Force yourself to sit absolutely still for ten minutes and feel through the restless feelings in your body. To stay in harmony, balance first-force action with second-force passivity. Realize that each invigorates the other. Rest makes your movement energetic and focused, and movement makes your rest healthy and satisfying.

BEYOND PROBLEM-SOLVING

Seeing life from a problem-solving perspective (defining the problem and testing out different solutions) ultimately puts you in a reversed state of mind. Realize that when everything becomes a problem you must solve, you eventually don't want to do anything.

You start to identify yourself as the problem that needs to be solved. This sets up an oscillation between the first and second forces. You manipulate yourself into action ("I have to solve my problems"), then inhibit your movement ("I can't do anything until I solve my problems"), and finally justify your failure ("I couldn't do anything because of my unsolved problems").

Problem-solving comes out of the assumption "If I work hard enough, I can be problem free, and thus happy." Because it gives you momentary solace and hope, attacking your problems can be addictive. Anything that reduces anxiety tends to be repeated.

Despite repeated disappointments, you probably believe that after you solve the current problem, you'll have it made. Look closely and you'll discover the first noble truth: *life is problems.* Problems are built into the very fabric of life.

PROBLEM CREATING

"Problems"—unexpected and unwanted reality—is another name for second force. See how problem-solving (the removal of something negative) is an attempt to escape from reality. Structurally it never works: first-force attempts to eliminate problems create more second-force problems.

Problem-solving will never take you to where you want to go—the best you can do is break even. Instead of peace of mind and clear sailing, problem-solving, in fact, creates a new generation of problems. How to stay on your diet (which was the solution to your weight problem) becomes a new problem. How to get off anti-anxiety medication replaces the old problem of how to get rid of your fears.

To transcend this trap, you have to see your problems as your best friend. You need to love them to death, rather than solve them away. With insight you see how problems reveal with great specificity the exact reality you need to look at and accept. Who but a best friend would do this for you?

CLARITY IS POWER

Because problems uncover your ignorance, embrace them and see with heightened awareness what they are telling you. When overeating becomes a problem, directly see what thoughts and feelings are driving your behavior and what are the immediate body consequences of overeating.

If you have anxiety, aim to know as much as you can about the mind/body building blocks that construct your anxiety. Instead of trying to escape from the anxiety that has been pushing you around, jump into your fear and discover firsthand what it's all about.

Your understanding of the second force makes it transparent. Remember that once you can see through it to your ultimate aims, you transcend it.

WHAT'S NOT THERE

Self-mastery, like all forms of mastery, comes from seeing the importance of space as well as content. By looking closely at the two doors of perception, the door of thought and the door of feeling, you discover emptiness is more significant than substance. Lao-tzu wrote:

Doors and windows are cut for a room
And yet it is the space where there is nothing
*   that makes it useful.*
Therefore, though advantage comes from what is,
Real usefulness comes from what is not.

If being tired is the current problem, or second force, sit down and look at the process in detail. Rather than identify with the obstacle ("I'm tired"), become like a scientist and investigate what is going on. You'll find the tiredness is located in a few specific areas of the body ("I have uncomfortable sensations in my forehead, left eye and right shoulder") and the rest of the body is empty of fatigue.

Next, increase your resolution power by looking at the precise body sensations. Disregard what energizes your fatigue—the thoughts that either buy into or resist the unpleasant feelings. Pour on awareness and acceptance until the sensations become transparent. Realize that by making finer discrimination between space and substance, your tiredness naturally dissolves into the pure energy of good feeling.

Discover for yourself that when you clarify your problems they solve themselves: they either dissolve into thin air or they simply become facts of life that no longer are in your way.

Van Gogh said that art is detail. As you become more skillful at the art of living (being happy) and the art of life (being successful), you have more real problems and less problem-solving problems. Each problem becomes a new opportunity to clarify current reality and a new chance to refocus on what you most want to see happen.

MOVEMENT

Clarifying reality—taking in a richer flow of information—raises your level of awareness and leads to vertical learning. Just as closing off stimuli allows you to go to sleep, bringing in more internal and external input wakes you up. Keep in mind a part of you always wants to stay asleep and hates to be awakened.

Any movement increases your input and raises your state of awareness and can get you unreversed. You don't need great durability, big injections of willpower, or extraordinary efforts to move. Simply find a feeling that allows you to understand, "I have a free mind," and use it to choose to move. No need to climb mountains or challenge oceans in a one-person sailboat; you can move without leaving your room. As long as you vary your focus, you're moving.

To feel and move more, vary your normal routine. Switch your daily habits and you'll see reality fresh again. By doing novel activities, you clarify reality and free your focus from your self-absorption. If you always get up on the right side of the bed, get up on the left side. If you always have eggs for breakfast, have cereal or a bowl of soup. Watch a different television program or read a different newspaper. Anything that shifts your focus off of what you're stuck on helps you move again.

BEARINGS

Life is like walking across hot coals: keep moving and you'll avoid getting burned. Feeling courage and keeping your sights on your destination allows you to keep your balance and move forward in the present.

Einstein said, "People love chopping wood. In this activity one immediately sees results." To move, you need an end point. Having a destination helps you keep your balance and gives you a sense of direction, and a good feeling when you reflect on it. Once you know where you're going, it's easy to keep moving.

Once you clearly know where you want to go, you're already moving. Have a destination and you rarely have to push yourself—you can graze your way home.

If you're unsure of what you want, aim for three ideals: *someone or something to love, something to do, and something to look forward to.* If you're completely unsure about what you want, turn around what you don't want ("I don't want to be bored and isolated") and make *that* your aim ("I'm going to be more interested and connected").

When you want anything, the second force or resistance is inevitable; you'll always have to make adjustments to reach any destination. Be philosophical. So what if you need to go the long way around? Keep moving and you'll eventually reach your destination.

The path will always be full of first-force distractions and second-force detours. You may end up in the slowest line or bring home the wrong size. Find a good feeling toward the result and see that detours and distractions point out the easiest and shortest way. Your destination may be farther away in mileage, but the trip is shorter and smoother when you respect and heed the signs.

REACHABLE DESTINATION

You are biologically programmed to overestimate the power of your first-force fantasies and downplay second-force reality. At the start of a project, you're like a young man marching off to war— you think, "This is going to be a picnic."

To avoid getting reversed along the way, reduce your excessive first force and aim for an accurate picture of the second force you're likely to encounter. If you take a forty-kilometer walk and think it's going to be ten kilometers, you're going to have a tough time making the last thirty kilometers. On the other hand, if you think the forty-kilometer walk is going to be a hundred kilometers, you may never get started.

Temper your enthusiasm and accurately estimate the resistance you'll encounter and you'll be less likely to get discouraged and quit halfway through. As a general rule, the second force is twice what you think it will be in your first-force state of mind. You can use the building contractors' rule of $(N \times 2 + 1)$ to estimate the second force. If you think you can finish a job in 6 months, it will be more likely to take 13 $(6 \times 2 + 1)$ months.

INTERNAL STATE

In short, you have to aim before you shoot the arrow. Although having a target is important, your state of mind is much more important. *The archer is more important than the target.* If you pay full attention to being in the moment as you aim and release, your arrow will naturally hit the mark.

To help yourself stay in the moment, break up the trip. The Indians who led the Spaniards to Mexico City never got tired, even though *they* were carrying all of the supplies. The Spaniards, on the other hand, were carrying only their swords yet were soon exhausted.

What was the difference? The Indians would throw a stone as far as they could in the distance. That stone became their destination; they could be optimistic, because their destination was always in sight. When they reached the stone, they would throw another one and have a *new* destination. Treat the second force in the same way—break it up into manageable points. Give yourself easily reachable destinations and you'll avoid getting tired or discouraged.

Break up your projects into segments and see each as your next destination, which is just a stone's throw away. At the same time, keep Mexico City in your mind. In this way, you toss the stone over and over and eventually reach your destination.

Durability is essential and keeps you moving through first- and second-force conflicts. Patience is the key to all success. Look over your life and you'll find you are successful where you persevere. If you're a successful salesperson, it's because, day in and day out, you make a set number of calls and visits. If you're a successful parent, it's because you persevered and endured the tribulations and hassles of parenting.

TRUST

To persevere, find a feeling of trust that you can reach your destination. Trust allows you to see that you can take care of yourself and get what you want, no matter what happens.

Because of trust, the world works. How do you get trust? Trust, like all forms of mental health, is the absence of thought. Reassuring yourself leads to more insecurity. Trust is nothingness. Trust comes naturally when you drop your doubts and concerns. In high states of mind, you can see how trust is built into every aspect and every object of reality. You trust there will be printing on the next page of this book. You trust that, when you flip the light switch, the light will come on.

The feeling of trust leads to the willingness to accept and embrace a future without guarantees. When you don't have a clue as to what's going to happen next, find a feeling of trust and go forward anyway. Aim to understand the wisdom and security of nothingness. Trust allows you to walk into nothingness, and once you start to live in nothingness, without the protection of thought, you'll start to understand that, when it comes to mental health, nothing is better than something.

GROWTH FORCE

Use being reversed and stuck as an incentive to move on and extend yourself. Keep in mind that you evolve only by going a little beyond your present level of ability. Through challenges, you expand your range of awareness and increase your self-mastery.

Be true to what you would love to see happen and you'll be willing to move beyond impasses. Love second-force resistance as much as first-force desire. Just because you break a nail doesn't mean you stop building the house. Realize that getting stuck is part of life and is a sign that you're alive, not a sign that you're a failure.

12

MASTER YOUR RHYTHM

Self-mastery is learning to see your psychological system as a musical instrument. Everything has its own rhythm and, with understanding, you make a melody out of any experience. You fall in tune with whatever you're doing. You stay in rhythm and in harmony and reach the high notes as well as the low.

When you get reversed, you lose your natural rhythm. You lock your keys in the car and spill hot coffee on yourself. As if you were looking down a bottomless well, your head spins and you lose your natural balance and sense of order.

When babies get cranky and colicky, their mothers rock them or sing to them to comfort them and put them back in rhythm. When you feel reversed or off balance, aim to reset your internal gyroscope quickly and regain your rhythm.

If A is the wrong note, singing it louder won't help. To get unreversed, find the right note inside you and get in rhythm with whatever you're doing. If you're in your car, get into the rhythm of driving; if you're with your children, establish a harmonious rapport with them.

When you're reversed, realize that you're looking at your current situation in a slanted and unfair way. You systematically distort reality in a negative direction. Instead of seeing the person, all you see is his or her faults. To get back in rhythm, open up your point of view and be fair with the facts.

BREATHING

Thoughts about yourself tighten you up and throw you out of rhythm. To get back in rhythm, talk to a sympathetic person, listen to music, go for a brisk walk, get back into your normal work routine. If you feel bored with the routine, embrace the monotony.

A surefire way to get back into rhythm is to focus on your body sensations. By focusing on your sensations, you get back in tune with your natural rhythms.

You get back in rhythm simply by watching your breathing. Breathe slowly and deliberately with heightened awareness. Hypnosis, biofeedback, meditation, physical exercise, and relaxation training can all get you back in rhythm, because they lead to deep and rhythmic breathing.

SELF-MASTERY

You are usually thrown out of rhythm when others are reversed and out of tune. You can use a specific place or person that chronically causes you to lose your rhythm as an opportunity to gain mastery over your own mind/body processes.

The secret is to keep *yourself* in rhythm rather than try to get *others* in rhythm. Stay impartial to others' music, focus on your own song, and you'll keep your rhythm, even when everyone around you is out of sync.

The best way for you to keep others in rhythm is to get into the rhythm of the moment yourself. Move into the present and refuse to get caught up in a battle of the bands. Stay away from struggles over who is the smartest or who knows best.

Rise above ego battles and you'll find that the good feeling that naturally comes from rising above your ignorance puts you back in rhythm. Let the other person be right, and keep your good feeling. Be willing to lose the battle for the sake of winning your own sanity and peace of mind.

SYMPATHY

How you see the other person reflects your inner state. See people in warm, caring ways and you'll move into a state of harmony. Good feelings are contagious. See others in a friendly, kind way and they'll feel friendly and kind toward you.

Sincere listening, the connecting third force, will always put you back in rhythm. Real listening forms a bond between you and others. Decide to see, hear, and understand the other person. Just as a cylinder has to be empty to become a bell, to resonate with others you must empty your mind. Keep focusing your attention back to being with the other person in the moment.

To get unreversed, aim for positive rapport. Put yourself in others' shoes. Be willing to help others get what they want, and be willing to make their journeys easier. Decide to connect with others as human beings and harmonious feelings will rise from within you.

If you feel yourself getting upset and losing your harmony, feel through your uncomfortable feelings and look for good feelings of rapport. By re-establishing positive rapport and harmony with a person (or an activity) you unlock your reversed self and move forward.

RHYTHM AND RELATIONSHIPS

Once you have learned to be in rhythm when you're alone, you need to learn how to make music with others. Just because you've changed partners doesn't mean you've learned to dance. To master the rhythm of a relationship, you need to learn the art of even-mindedness or equanimity.

If you are lucky, the people in your life will accept your occasional two left feet; if you are even luckier, you will accept their awkward moves. Good marriages, lasting friendships, and sustained partnerships consist of learning to have sympathetic joy for others' good qualities and sympathetic acceptance of their shortcomings.

To keep the good feeling in a relationship going, take the other person's reversal in stride. When a person in your life becomes negative, refuse to take it seriously. Everyone regularly goes in and out of reversal. Have compassion and equanimity and see the other person's reversal as a temporary setback.

Reversal is a human frailty. Everyone is innocent. No one consciously chooses to get reversed. Like getting a cold or a headache, everyone gets reversed now and then.

NO LONGER HOSTAGE

With understanding, you refuse to be held hostage by others' reversals. Time is always on your side. Once people become saturated with enough negativity, they automatically revert to being positive. People eventually get bored with being reversed and come around.

At times people's negativity can be subtle and subversive. The more quickly you spot their reversal, the less likely you are to be taken hostage by their states of mind.

You can always trust your feelings as a guide. Recognize that someone is reversed if everything, from his or her body movements to tone of voice, gives you the willies. You may not be able to spot it, but you can always *feel* reversal when you're around it.

Catch on when others are reversed and you stay in a high state of mind no matter what they do. The secret is to remain objective and actively resigned to their reversal.

PERVERTED PLEASURE

Remember, when others are reversed, at that moment they *want* to be negative. Many people gain pleasure from being miserable and making others miserable. The drama, stimulation, and familiarity of feeling bad keeps their reversal alive.

Misery loves company. Other people's reversed behavior is designed to get you reversed and out of rhythm. They want you to go counterclockwise. When others clam up, slam around, or pick on you, refuse to make them feel better by feeling worse.

Just as you would refuse to give heroin to an addict, refuse to react to others' negativity. Be nonreactive to their complaints and provocative behavior. Remain calm and as unaffected as possible until they lose their negative zeal. Then forget about it and never bring it up again. Pointing out to others their flaws only intensifies them. Focus instead of how you can become less reversed yourself in the future.

HANDS-OFF POLICY

Others' reversal comes from their egos (their need to be separate and special); keep your ego (your need to change others) out of the picture. An African proverb says, "Advise and counsel him; if he does not listen, let adversity teach him." Don't try to get reversed people to do something they don't want to do, even if it is for their own good. *They are reversed because they're feeling insecure and need to be in control and separate.* Your desire to change them feeds their insecurities and makes them more resolved in their negativity.

Adopt a policy of enlightened equanimity. By being nonreactive, you give others room to maneuver, room to turn around on their own.

When you are around a reversed person, always look for a good feeling in the moment. From the higher, impartial ground of good feelings, you're free from the influence of their negativity. Start to see that when people are reversed, what they really want is love, acceptance, and understanding; but because they believe they are unable to get it or unworthy of having it, they seek out the opposite. Love and gentle acceptance can help others regain their rhythm and harmony. Ideally, if you can love others unconditionally—that is, if you don't *need* them to snap out of their reversal—they often do.

WALK AWAY

Once you remember that all people live in their own separate realities, you have nothing to lose. People play at their own table with their own money. Whether they win, lose, or draw has nothing to do with you.

When people are reversed, their motivation is backward; your attempts to help are likely to get them more reversed. On a surface level, they *want* you to reject them. If you're unable to rise above their tactics and you find yourself getting reversed, walk away until you're better able to deal with them.

Mental health starts at home. If you're unable to find a good feeling, walk away. Refuse to stay out of a sense of duty. You're only good to yourself or others when you have inner rhythm and harmony.

If you're continually getting reversed around someone, stay away. Often it's better to ask a person to leave a job or a group than to let everyone sink. Just as one person can be a positive catalyst, one person can reverse a whole group or undermine a total project.

BALANCING ACT

The ancient Greeks summarized the third force in their two famous maxims "Know yourself" and "Nothing in excess." Know yourself and you'll know others. With third-force understanding, you'll naturally avoid the excesses of first-force greed and second-force aversion.

Just as machines break down, plans go awry. Remember that you and others fail to come through at times. Instead of glorifying or despising the desires or resistance you encounter, accept and align yourself with all the forces in play. To unite with reality and avoid getting reversed, you have to be in harmony with the forces in play.

Aim for balance, the middle way, in all you do; recognize that, when you're in an active first-force rhythm, your focus is all on doing, on taking control, and on being responsible. Like a sprinter before a race, your mind is all on winning. Your muscles are tense, your adrenaline is pumping, you feel compelled to move. As you leave the others in your wake, you're puzzled over why they are so passive.

In a passive, second-force rhythm, you have an "It will get

done somehow" attitude. You're unable to understand why others work so hard.

With third-force wisdom, you realize that to be in harmony with reality you need to be both active and passive, because *reality is both active and passive.* Nature is always constricting and expanding, ascending and descending. The tide comes in, the tide goes out; the sun rises, the sun sets; the seasons come and the seasons go.

To keep your balance in life and avoid getting reversed, drop your thoughts and move into the present moment and you'll shift back and forth from an active to a passive reality. If your natural inclination is to go forward at full throttle, like a runaway train, move into the present moment and you naturally start to take the opposite tack. Rather than worry about when you'll get into Grand Central Station, you'll naturally slow down and enjoy the trip.

Reconcile your desire to win at all costs with your impulse to give up when you are frustrated. Being in the moment wakes you up. If you're too excited and pushy, you'll gently calm yourself down; if you're too apathetic, you'll take a small step to make the situation a little better.

At times you have to make adjustments consciously. If you're in the passive mode and inclined to slow to a halt, do the opposite: take stock of where you are and where you are going. Focus more on getting to Grand Central Station and less on the rail crossings and overpasses.

Finding a third-force good feeling in the present moment allows you to respond wisely and effectively. You are effective with the least amount of effort. Because you're neither a Doubting Thomas nor a zealot, you avoid anarchy and tyranny.

COORDINATION

From the higher, third-force perspective, you balance your active side with your passive side. You realize there is "a time to keep and a time to cast away. . . ." When you have a good feeling, you naturally know when to step back and accept the situation and when to push forward and confront the issues.

Like a good basketball player, learn to dribble with either

hand. Rather than try to eliminate your active or passive side, develop the ability to use either hand as you move toward the basket. Don't pit your initiative against your inhibitions ("I'd better be assertive or I'll end up a wimp"); instead, let the two forces complement each other. From a higher perspective, you accept and are comfortable with all aspects of yourself. You let both the active "go-getter" self and the passive *"mañana"* self serve you.

FOCUS ON THE WHOLE

A symphony is made up of a combination of many musical parts, most of which would be meaningless alone. Yet, when you put the whole sweep together, the result is beautiful music.

You may be impatient with the first-force step you're on or dislike the second-force beat you're on, but see each as part of the whole sweep. Maybe it seems as though nothing is happening. See this point as a necessary part of the whole movement, and move on.

Accept and even enjoy every beat of the song, and every so often glance to the end of the piece. Glancing forward keeps you moving beyond the present beat and on to the next.

NEED FOR BALANCE

Nature depends on balance. The galaxy would collapse into a huge black hole if the spin of its stars failed to counterbalance the pull of gravity. With wisdom, you consciously counteract your intellect's pull toward negativity and complexity with your mind's desire for fun and simplicity.

Psychological health comes from a harmonious inner life. You need variety and balance to feel good and stay in rhythm. If you eat only one food or do only one task, you'll soon get tired of it. Too much of anything becomes aversive and leads to reversal. To stay in rhythm, balance work and play, solitude and sociability, comfort and discomfort, giving and receiving.

When you're physically losing your rhythm, go for a walk, lie down, take a hot shower, or get something to eat. Rest when you're tired and eat when you're hungry. Make an adjustment and regain your inner physical rhythm.

Refuse to let disharmony in the physical world—clutter, loose ends, inconveniences—throw you off rhythm. Rather than become Captain Chaos or obsessive/compulsive, go for the middle way. The happiest homes are the ones that have a balance between order and disorder. When you have too much clutter, or when objects seem to yell out like a roomful of children, "Take care of me; put me away," see that you first need to bring about a feeling of internal harmony and then see what needs to be put in order externally.

THE BALANCING PRINCIPLE

You have a deep desire for symmetry, balance, harmony, and beauty in your life. When you're reversed, you mistakenly think the way to bring harmony about is to change circumstances (the person you're married to, your inconsiderate friends, your unreasonable boss). You need first to go the other way and find a feeling of harmony within yourself.

From a higher perspective, you see that life constantly swings one way, then the other. Everyone calls, then suddenly no one calls; you're at the peak of health one day, the next day you're under the weather; you're in a good mood, and then, without notice, you're in a low mood.

Reality consists of a multitude of different rhythms that vibrate at different frequencies. You can be in harmony with any rhythm. To stay in rhythm, note the swing but refuse to identify with either side. Just as the days of the week follow one another, the momentum will soon shift. No matter how long the night, the day is sure to come. Become more detached and objective; before you know it, the pendulum will swing the other way.

With wisdom, you realize that reality is always in the process of change. When you're going through a bad patch, remind yourself, "The tide is turning right now, and I'll soon be in a good patch." Change is the chief feature of all of nature. Because you know that every force in nature is always being replaced with its opposite, you can roll with the punches.

NEUTRALIZING PRINCIPLE

To stay in rhythm, become impartial to both success and failure—take each more lightly and less personally. In higher states of mind, you experience a calm equanimity, no matter what happens. Because reality is neutral (only your thinking makes it otherwise), the more you directly experience reality through feelings, the more you feel the neutral, matter-of-fact nature of all life.

Use a one-two punch. Care about what you want; don't care if you don't get it. Balance attachment with detachment. Win or lose, be even-minded and go on as before. Refuse to give too much importance to the positive or the negative and you'll stay in rhythm.

You need all three forces to keep your balance. You need two wings, the active first force and the passive second force, and the connecting third force. You need to *hold on to* your vision and at the same time *let go of* the resistance you encounter.

As you ascend to a higher state, you see you must balance your first-force vision with second-force reality—the green light of desire needs to be checked by the red light of reality. Tap into your common sense and you won't get a ticket for going too fast or for going too slow. With third-force understanding, rather than try to eliminate your desire or your resistance, you use both to your advantage.

DRIVER'S TRAINING

Because you're unable to get yourself going or because you stall before you cross the line, you may think, "I need a major psychological overhaul." Nothing is innately wrong with you—you simply need greater insight or understanding of how you function.

You may be using too much first force ("I want it so bad I can taste it"). Refuse to be a frenzied driver in the fast lane, who punches the gas pedal to the floor. When you push too hard in life you either spin out of control and crash into the center divider or run out of gas and stall on the side of the road.

With too much second force, you have too many inhibitions,

too many checks on your creativity; you have trouble making it up the little hills; even on a speedway, you have trouble going over twenty-five miles an hour. To stay in harmony, refuse to ride the brake and suppress your desires for what you really want ("I don't deserve it"; "It's too hard").

PERSPECTIVE

Rather than make your desires the be-all and end-all, put them in perspective. Realize that, even if you fail to get what you want, your life will go on. Take a stand for what you want, but be non-reactive to whether you get it, and be nonreactive to the inevitable resistance you meet along the way.

Disregard your excess first-force thoughts about what you think you need. Illusionary needs are open-ended—you never get enough. If you think you need money, you'll always be out of sync with money. No matter how much money you make, how healthy you become, how many guarantees you have, how much love and adulation you get, you'll always think you need more.

Keep your real wants but drop your needs. Need (which comes from powerlessness) and want (which comes from power) are inversely related. When you need something too much, you no longer want it. A part of you refuses to be controlled. If you think you need to be nice to your rich uncle, you won't want to be. If you think you must perform sexually, your body will rebel and won't want to perform at all.

Your intellect, like everyone else's, wants to be asked, not told, what to do. Disregard "I need this," which comes from pow-erlessness, and focus on "I want this," which comes from a position of power.

To get back in rhythm, stay away from exaggerations and half-truths. Stop pretending that what you want is a need ("I must have it"), and stop pretending you don't want what you do want ("Who needs it?"). Balance your "I have to have it" and your "Whatever" attitude with the truth—"This is what I want."

Find a good feeling toward what you want and rise above your needs, musts, and have-to's. Need comes from thinking you're in the hole or deprived in some way. Believing you're lacking or deprived puts you further in the hole. If you think you have enough money, you won't feel a need to spend money. If you feel comfortable with yourself, you won't need others to reassure you.

TURNING REVERSAL AROUND

Use your negative feelings as an alarm to wake you from your negative trance, and then do the opposite of your inclination. When you're self-absorbed and negative, consider someone else's feelings. Smile, turn the other cheek, and start a normal conversation.

If you're usually broke, start a savings account. Your intellect will then assume you *want* to have money ("Who but someone who wants to have money would be this responsible with money?").

If you're a miser and insecure around money, loosen up; become more generous. Your intellect will start to assume you have enough money ("Who but someone with plenty of money would be this generous and free with money?").

THIRD-FORCE WISDOM

From a higher perspective, you realize equanimity, or radical permission for reality to be the way it is at the moment, is the proper response to the changing tides of life. You reconcile yourself to the passive and active sides of life. You discover that all of life is made up of growth and decay, advances and declines, construction and destruction.

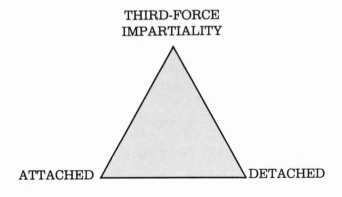

THIRD-FORCE
IMPARTIALITY

ATTACHED   DETACHED

MASTERY

To master anything, from riding a bike to doing brain surgery, you need to learn the rhythm. To master the rhythm of your own life, you have to be willing to be both active and passive.

Balance care about those you love with impartiality about how they choose to lead their lives. Balance optimism in the present with equanimity toward the past and the future. Be impartial to what you can do for people and to what you are unable to do for them.

The first and last requirement is to have an impartial awareness of both your desires and your resistance. If you can impartially observe your desires, they stay in check; if you impartially observe your resistance, it weakens and fades away.

Whether in tennis or in life, as soon as you think about winning or losing, you lose your rhythm. Serve the job in front of you, but be impartial to the fruits of your labor. Give a good talk, but be impartial to your reviews. Be patient, but be impartial to what you're waiting for. Be a good parent, but be impartial to how your children turn out.

To stay in rhythm, become as impartial as Queen Elizabeth the First, who reconciled religious strife by carrying a Protestant Bible to Catholic Mass and a Catholic missal to Protestant services. Become like successful artists who care deeply about their art but learn to become impartial to what others think about their work.

OBSERVING VERSUS FOCUSING

To stay in balance, *passively observe* what you want to decrease, and *actively focus* on what you want to increase. You weaken and decrease what you observe, and strengthen and increase what you focus on.

Observe the thoughts and actions you want to decrease, and actively focus on the good feelings you want to increase. To keep a natural, lyrical tone and rhythm, objectively observe when your voice has a sharp or flat tone to it, and actively focus on having a lighter, livelier feeling.

Psychological and physical rhythm comes from a balance of the active and passive forces. When you're restless and feel beside yourself, you're stuck between the active and passive modes. To get back in rhythm, do something clearly active (clean out a closet) or something clearly passive (take a nap).

SONG OF LIFE

By deciding to pursue truth, love, and beauty in every moment you can move in harmony with higher levels of reality. You can get back in rhythm and regain your song by focusing on the truth, love, or beauty you find around you at any moment.

To regain your rhythm, simply tell the truth. Aim to clarify reality further for yourself. Describe the facts to yourself ("Here and now I dislike what is happening, but this is what is going on"). When you're honest, you immediately feel more secure ("Who but someone who is secure would be willing to tell the truth?").

Thinking leads to ignorance. Good feelings in the moment always lead you to further clarification of the truth. Feelings are more honest than thought in that you have a wider, fairer outlook. By dismissing your thoughts, which at best are half-truths, you move into a state of greater truth.

Take a walk or a drive and look at the beauty around you and you'll be back in harmony with the beautiful feeling within you.

Look for a feeling of love in whatever you're doing. Love is the path to higher levels of reality and to higher levels of being in the world. Cultivate feelings of love toward people or activities. Love has natural harmony and forward movement to it. It's nearly impossible to hold a baby and stay reversed. Remember how it feels to drop coins in Santa's pot at Christmastime; how it feels to feed bread to the ducks; how a first kiss feels.

Truth, love, and beauty feel the same because they are the same—when you have one, you have the other two. To get back in harmony, tune in to beautiful feelings of truth and love. Once you have inner harmony, you have everything.

13

WILLINGNESS

When you're frustrated, you don't have to get reversed and go out on strike. Rather than quit working, you can drop your list of grievances and focus on what you need to be done in the moment to get what you want.

When you feel reversal coming on, use it as a chance to redirect: pause for a moment, ground yourself in your bodily sensations, and tell yourself the truth about what you really want. Replace self-talk about what you *don't* want with a clear picture of what you *do* want.

If you want to throw rocks at mangement, count to ten and look for a calm feeling. If you feel like a passive sitdown or slowdown, get active and involved in the job in front of you. Forget small procedural points—make what you want your chief concern.

Your first inclination may be to go on strike as a way to prevent something or someone from ultimately defeating you ("I'm not going camping with a bunch of people I hardly know"). Take a risk. Err on the side of getting involved, even if you think you're going to be frustrated or criticized for how you do it.

165

Though your strikes may have paid off in the past (your parents caved in when you had temper tantrums), psychological strikes become increasingly ineffective: people start to write you off and refuse to work with you on a continuing basis.

The less you demand that the world submit to your desires, the less often you will go out on strike. Learn to negotiate with reality and you'll have a steady income of successes and good feelings.

WILLINGNESS: THE THIRD FORCE

To complete anything, you need a third force. A feeling of willingness is the third force that arbitrates the conflict between your demands and reality. The feeling of willingness reconciles willfulness (the demand that you must have your way) and lack of will (your urge to give up and cave in to reality).

Move to willingness and your true self moves center stage. You rise above the willful desire to react against circumstances and the will-lacking desire to give up.

Goethe said, "If you don't feel it, you'll never get it." To transform the concept of willingness into a helpful insight, you have to experience the feeling of willingness in your body.

PARADOXES

Because the feeling of willingness is a third-force reconciliation of opposites, you can understand the feeling of willingness in paradoxical terms only. For example, when you're willing to participate

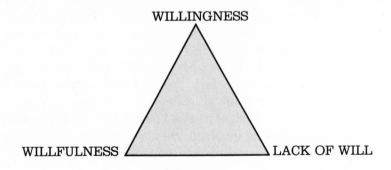

WILLINGNESS

WILLFULNESS

LACK OF WILL

in something, you feel empty and full at the same time. You are empty of your ego, your sense of separateness, and full of your true self, your connection to the world.

The feeling of willingness integrates the active and passive forces. You actively choose what you want, and you passively hand yourself over to it. If you take a job, you become a willing worker. If you go to school, you're a willing student. If you attend a meeting, you're a willing participant.

The feeling of willingness reconciles giving and taking. You fully give of yourself and you fully take from the experience. You're in a state of being and not being: you forget your false self and remember your true self. When you're a willing guest or a willing host, you lose your thoughts of yourself and gain a true feeling of self, a feeling of belonging and acceptance.

When you have feelings of willingness, the results are important and at the same time unimportant. Because you're relatively impartial toward the outcome, you have no need to work for results. You're free to participate fully and enjoy the activity for its own sake. You have no way to know if you'll be successful, but you assume you will—this leads to patience, the greatest of all virtues.

Willingness is being efficient in an easygoing way. You enjoy what you're doing and gladly give the time the task requires.

You enjoy the feeling of willingness because you are reconciling work and play. You do the job with a leisurely, playful attitude. You have no resistance to a job you *want* to do.

FROM YOUR HEART

Willingness comes from your heart. When you "put your heart" into what you are doing, your thoughts, feelings, and actions work in harmony. You move into the heart of whatever you're doing. You are wholly yourself. You are willing to do what is necessary, because you love what you are doing. You feel grateful for the opportunity to participate. What you're doing has personal meaning to you, because you feel you're becoming something greater than you were.

You expand yourself by finding a feeling of willingness. Your willingness reconciles "I" with "thou." Like a willing parent, you do whatever is necessary for the child's good. You gain by giving yourself over. Willingness is an opportunity to serve something outside of yourself and to enjoy what you do at the same time.

SUCCESS AND WILLINGNESS

Be willing to do whatever is necessary and you'll bring about nearly everything you want. The feeling of willingness is the secret to success. You don't have to *do* everything that is necessary, you just have to *be willing to do everything*.

The world responds to your willingness. Commit yourself and reality moves too. Helpful coincidences start to happen.

Look at your past; you'll see that your willingness to do what was called for was a third force that led to your successes. Your successful friendships required your willingness to keep the friendships going; successful vacations came from doing what was required from you; successful work experiences evolved from your willingness to learn and to contribute.

Third-force willingness includes doing what you don't want to do. You're willing to give up comfort and endure discomfort, and to give in and not have your way. You're willing to give up your suffering, and you're willing to be happy and successful.

BE WILLING TO LOSE

You have to make a sacrifice before you can gain. Like nature, you have to balance a gain with a loss. Both willfulness ("I have to have my way") and lack of will ("I'm afraid to have my way") come from refusing to accept loss. To gain, be willing to lose. Your strongest position—whether you are buying a car or entering into a relationship—is the freedom to walk away.

Reality is a patient teacher. If you fail to understand a lesson, reality will always give it to you again. When you're willful, you refuse to see the lesson even after it's pushed in your face; if you lack will, you avoid the lesson by avoiding the classroom.

Until you're willing to lose yourself, you'll never find yourself. Be willing to embrace the lesson that you can't have a gain without a loss. Once you understand this at a deep level, you'll no longer be thrown into reverse by the inevitable losses in life. You will not always lose, but always be willing to lose. To get to your destination, be willing to get lost along the way. Be willing to hear bad news; be willing to make a mistake and look bad. The choice to go for what you want is powerful, but the willingness to lose along the way is even more powerful.

The easiest way to find a feeling of willingness is to admit you've lost it. When you're reversed, realize that you can shadow-box with your dark side indefinitely or you can surrender and admit you've lost your willingness. Your willingness will return once you see you're only fighting yourself.

LET GO OF CONTROL

Life's lesson is simple arithmetic. Your life adds up once you learn the lessons. Just as you learn $2 + 2 = 4$, you need to learn that you're unable to control life. Once your really understand this, you're willing to face the unknown instead of trying to control it. Rather than wait until everything is known or planned out in detail, you're willing to go forward toward what you want.

When you go on a job interview, don't rehearse and try to control it; picture how you want the interview to turn out, and let the nature of the interview develop naturally. With a feeling of willingness, you can spin 360 degrees in any direction and shift the momentum to your advantage at a moment's notice.

You gain power (the ability to get what you want) by giving up control—by giving in, you get what you want. When a friend wants to control where you eat or what time you meet, look for a feeling of willingness. If the specific restaurant or time is irrelevant, keep the power by delegating the choices to your friend. If you truly care about the restaurant or the time, take a stand for what you want and be willing to surrender your need to control your friend's reactions.

FEELING OF WILLINGNESS

If you're feeling rebellious, accept the feeling in your body and then look for the feeling of willingness. Look for a feeling of rightness and authenticity. Be open and attuned to what is going on—willingness is a mutual interaction betweeen you and what you are doing at the moment.

By developing sensitivity to a feeling of willingness, you can consistently bring it into play. Willingness is being aware in an easygoing way. Whether you are on your job or on vacation, hand yourself over to a feeling of willing acceptance. Permit yourself to feel integrated and in rapport with what you are doing.

Join in the spirit of what you want to accomplish. Let the activity strike a deep chord within you. Instead of *enduring* your way through a family gathering, a meeting, or a dinner party, be willing to *participate* your way through. Be willing to make the party or meeting a little better; act friendly and extend yourself in some way.

WILLINGNESS AND FRIENDLINESS

At the heart of willingness is the feeling of friendliness. Aim to feel friendly toward whatever you're doing. If you're with people, feel friendly toward them. If you're working on your house, feel friendly toward your house.

Friendliness is an inclusive feeling that allows you to unite with something outside of yourself. Treat your body in a more friendly way instead of pushing it relentlessly. Treat the part of you that wants to have fun and enjoy life in a more considerate and friendly way.

GOODWILL

Replace your reversed ill will with goodwill. Drop the silent as well as the vocal ill will against others and the world. You are at your best when you have goodwill. What you send out is what comes back. The more goodwill you have, the better your life works.

Cultivate goodwill toward everyone you meet. When others tell you about what they want or about their difficulties, picture in your mind the situation working out for them.

When you're reversed on others, ask yourself, "How can I earn their goodwill?" If you're reversed on someone at work, ask yourself, "How can I go out of my way to earn this person's goodwill?" If you're stuck on finishing a project, ask yourself, "What can I do to earn the goodwill of the project?" You'll find that even inanimate objects appear to get on your side (the mountain becomes easier to climb), when you have a friendly attitude toward them.

WILLFULNESS

You need the feeling of willingness to deal effectively with the runaway excitement of the first force and the denying power of the second force. Where there's a real will, there's always a way. But you need true will. Your lack of will increases the second force by avoiding it, and your willfulness increases the second force by fighting it. The feeling of willingness, which is a psychological summit, allows you to rise above the lower forces.

When you're reversed and willful, drop the demand that you must have your way. Instead of going into a second adolescence and becoming rigid when you encounter resistance, be willing to bend and become more mature as well as more flexible.

Occasionally your survival switch gets stuck and your dislike of what you *don't* want propels you forward ("Remember the Alamo," "I'll show them"). This is like wildly driving to your goal in reverse—you may get there, but you'll have many accidents along the way. At these times, calm down and remember what you really want. See that, whereas negative strength can help you win in the short run, positive strength makes you the winner in the long run.

POSITIVE STRENGTH

If you're unusually willful, realize that you can excel even when the crowds and umpires are *not* against you. Don't confuse control over others and the physical world with mastery over yourself. Drop your normal reversed strategy. Don't pick fights to make yourself feel stronger. Don't get angry to justify your actions.

Learn to replace negative strength with positive strength. Rather than react, play a creative game with life. Discover that you can be happy and energetic, *even when life is going well*: you can spring to life without crises.

From a willingness perspective, you do the opposite of what you do from your reversed perspective. You are able to look equally and fairly at what is right as well as at what is wrong.

With understanding, you give up your negative stance, which comes from insecurity. You see there is no need to be constantly vigilant or to fear falling asleep on guard duty. Start to see that you don't have to be aggressive—life is not a battle.

Operate from the positive strength of good feelings, and re-place control, the illusion of power, with real power. *Be willing to make peace with your enemies.* For example, rather than fight the clock, see, "Time is on my side—if I'm willing to be on time's side." Instead of fighting the traffic, slow down and enjoy the trip. Rather than fight with your children, enjoy them.

WIN BY LOSING

Develop an awareness and a distaste for your own willfulness. Getting reversed is a throwback to an atavistic, primitive way of responding to the world. See that from a higher state of mind you can relate to the world in more enlightened, gentle, and effective ways.

A feeling of willingness allows you to drop your need to win on every point. You find you can relax and still win the game. Experiment and prove to yourself that you can give in a little and not become a doormat. You are better at giving once you discover you have an infinite source from which to give.

You can be right or successful. To be successful, be willing to lose face. Plant the seeds of success by your willingness to be vulnerable. If you want others' respect, be willing to lose their respect and tell the truth.

KNOW YOUR PURPOSE

Replace willfulness with willingness and you'll no longer say, "My only regret is, I did it my way." When you refuse to play by the rules of the game ("My way or no way"), you lose.

When you're willful, you forget your original aim and you become like Richard Nixon, who defeated himself when he said, "I don't care what happens. . . . Stonewall, cover up, or anything else if it'll save the plan." Instead, always go back to your original aim.

Care more about power than about being in control. If you are trying to get in shape, focus on the result (being in shape) instead of how to stay in control. With willingness, you transcend your willful all-or-nothing thinking ("I'm in control or out of control"). Stay result-oriented, and if you miss a day or two, you'll be willing to get back on your program.

SELF-TALK

To move into willingness, catch and drop your willful self-talk. Refuse to make a federal case out of your grievances and complaints. See that, when you're trying to make yourself right, you're wrong. Refuse to have interior monologues with your boss, your client, or yourself—refuse to self-justify and self-condemn.

When you're reversed and in a room with another reversed person, there are four of you in the room—your two exterior selves and your two inner self-talkers. You can be outwardly cordial even though the feeling is not quite right between you. The two inner self-talkers have their own separate, unspoken, and unpleasant conversation, and this conversation has much more to do with what's going on in the room than your two exterior selves.

Self-talk is a negative, one-sided argument against someone who has failed to appreciate you adequately. You may even be debating with someone you last saw twenty years ago. Self-talk is innately unfair, because others have no chance to defend themselves.

Self-talk drains your energy and keeps you reversed. Refuse to line up your arguments, your defenses, and your witnesses so that you can build a case for your position. Instead of brilliantly dismissing any indication that you could be wrong, drop the whole matter.

Self-talk against yourself is equally one-sided. Your ego has the upper hand. Self-talk is a no-win game. Your ego demands that you get up and do some housework, yet you ignore the demands and refuse to budge. The harsher and stronger the self-talk, the more you rebel against yourself.

All of your self-talk is counterproductive ("Who but someone in the wrong would need to talk so much about being right?"). To regain your willingness, disregard your self-talk, focus on the feelings you're having in the moment, and regain the natural interaction between yourself and the world.

OBJECTING AND WILLFULNESS

To find a feeling of willingness, refuse to object to what is required of you. You can dislike what is required, yet agree to it. You can dislike paperwork or cold calling, yet refuse to object internally to doing them. Drop your objections and you'll move out of willfulness and into willingness.

Try to ignore or battle the second force and you increase it, but will the resistance to be there and you decrease it. Choose to have your resistance ("If this is what I have to deal with, fine. . . . I let it be this way") and align yourself with reality and you become more powerful.

Use your free will to focus away from your objecting self-talk and toward willing reality to be the way it is at the moment. Your free will—*your ability to direct your focus of attention*—is always accessible. At any moment, simply by choosing to, you can end your self-talk. Stop focusing on it and it falls away. Just as you can walk away from an unpleasant conversation about religion or politics, you can always walk away from your self-conversation.

LACK OF WILL

The other side of willfulness is passive second-force lack of will. When you lack will, you lack backbone. You become passive and obedient, like a well-trained dog.

To move to willingness, refuse to let circumstances run your life. First feel through your bodily sensations of insecurity, and then look for a good feeling of courage. Take a stand for what you care about, and be willing to accept the consequences. Drop your fantasy of being taken care of by authority figures. Be willing to develop your own inner authority and be responsible for your own life.

The willful attitude is "To hell with the consequences." A will-lacking attitude is "I'm afraid of the consequences." When your will is gone, your life is run by fear of punishment and hope for outside help. To move to the reconciling state of willingness, refuse to identify with the outcome. Know what you want, but be wise enough not to let the fear or hope of consequences rule your life.

PLAY BY THE RULES

When you're willful, you refuse to play by the rules. You stick your tongue out at others and do what you like. When you lack will, you play strictly by the rules of the game others assign you. You are resentful that those who play loose with the rules often surpass you.

With a feeling of willingness, you choose the games you want to play and you play by the rules. If you choose to play basketball, you don't tackle the other players when you start to lose.

When you're willing, you stay within the rules of the game but invent new ways of playing. You point your whole self toward your next move. You want to win, but you also want to enjoy the game.

Instead of oscillating from willfulness to lack of will, look for willingness. All weekend, instead of talking about work ("The boss can't push *me* around"), enjoy your time off. Then, on Monday morning, instead of meekly doing whatever you're told to do, talk to your boss about what's troubling you.

To move to willingness, drop your expectations that you must always have your way, and drop your expectations that you can never have your way. To be successful, keep your expectations low and your willingness to do what is necessary high.

14

BEYOND SELF-ESTEEM

As a child, you had the motto "I say it's spinach, and I say to hell with it." You were naturally in tune with your true self—you knew what you liked and what you disliked. You were in touch with your real values and your real preferences.

As you grew up, you covered over your true self. To help you fit in, others expected and even demanded that you ignore your true impulses. You willingly went along and concluded, "My true feelings must be unacceptable."

While you were going about the business of growing up and fitting in, your true self, or essence, was being covered over by your ego or self-images. Over time you came to think of your ego voice as "the real me."

176

FRIENDS LIKE THIS

You were born with a true self and the programming to develop an ego. Your ego, which is part of your intellect, is set up to protect your self-esteem and help you survive in the world. Your ego's job is to protect the fixed ideas and pictures you have of yourself. Your ego fears that, if you fail to live up to your self-images ("I'm a good daughter," "I have a weight problem," "I'm good with money"), you won't survive. Your ego is like an overprotective friend that relegates you to a dependent role and keeps you addicted to your self-images.

Your ego lacks basic trust in your ability to deal effectively with reality. To protect you from pain and disappointment, your ego may go on the offensive ("You can't fire me—I quit") or on the defensive ("I won't quit—you have to fire me"). Your ego is a defense system designed to protect you, but in the process it stops you from finding your true nature and purpose.

TRUE POTENTIAL

Your potential for self-perfection is an unlimited wellspring to draw from; however, your ego believes your potential is finite and your vulnerability is infinite. To protect your potential, your ego holds you back from fully committing to what you truly want ("What if I try and fail—then what?"). Fearful of losing your self-importance if you drop your self-images, your ego maintains the illusion that you're separate and distinct from the rest of the world.

The greater the perceived threat to your self-esteem (pictures of your ideal self), the stronger your defense system. Your true self appears when you feel good in the moment and forget all about yourself. Fearful of losing its job, your ego distracts you with thoughts ("What if . . .") to take you away from your good feelings—your real self.

SELF-IMAGE

The liberating insight is to realize that the self-images you live and die by are an illusion. They are just thoughts, and all thoughts are distortions. Your self-images consist entirely of concepts you arbitrarily adopted as the real you. Alan Watts wrote, "Trying to define yourself is like trying to bite your own teeth."

Your self-images or adaptive selves are simply mental constructs, a collage of assorted thoughts and images you developed to help you survive in your family and in society.

Your self-images are illusions to be dispelled, not deities to be worshipped. Free yourself from your limiting concepts about yourself. Become an atheist toward your self-images: see they're merely myths that exist inside your head. Because the images you're trying to prove are at best half truths, all your striving for self-worth and self-esteem is in vain.

Your ego is like a public-relations person for a fraudulent corporation. In the face of embarrassing disclosures, your ego has to work harder and harder to protect the company's image.

Your ego constantly scans for threats to your self-esteem, ever-terrified you'll be exposed as an impostor; your ego hands out alternately self-congratulatory and self-condemning press releases. However, you can never feel secure when you try to defend and prove something you know in your heart is untrue. In your heart of hearts you know you're neither as bad nor as good as you are trying to make yourself out to be.

You can only feel secure when you're real. Trust that, once you're willing to give up your striving to prove and protect your self-images, you'll find your real self.

SOURCE OF CONFLICTS

Your ego, whose twenty-four-hour job is to protect your self-esteem, operates on the assumption that the world revolves around you. This assumption once served a vital purpose. To survive the long process of growing up, you needed to think you were the center of the universe. Now you need to realize you're just one five-billionth of the world's population. When you become an adult, your greatest childhood asset—your ego—becomes your greatest liability.

The trouble is that your ego can be a true believer and fanatic about protecting your self-images. Your ego can even convince you to kill yourself to protect your self-esteem.

All of your conflicts are between your true self and your false images of who you think you must be. Your ego will readily sacrifice your true desires to protect your self-esteem. Your true desire may be to give yourself over to a relationship, but your ego's insecurity causes you to hold back and sabotage the relationship. Your true desire may be to be an artist, but you suppress the desire and choose a more conventional career.

SELF-SABOTAGE

To protect your self-esteem, your ego sabotages you in countless ways. Your real desire may be to get to know your date honestly, but to protect your self-image you spend the whole evening trying to impress the other person. You may want to be successful in your career, but to protect your self-esteem you hold back and give yourself an excuse ("I didn't get the promotion because I didn't try").

Start to see the different ways you handicap yourself to protect your self-images ("I could have made a good speech, but I was too anxious"; "I could have gotten the job, but I was hung over"; "I could have written a good paper, but I waited until the last minute and didn't have time").

PSYCHOLOGICAL REVERSAL

When you're reversed, you're held hostage by your ego and move directly away from what you really want. Your ego (the you of little faith) believes you're powerless to get what you really want; so, to protect your self-images, you stop wanting it. To get unreversed, surrender thoughts of who you think you should be. Go for what you truly want and give up your need to be right and save face.

Remember, when you're reversed, your motivation is the polar opposite of what you really want. When you ditch your need to protect your self-esteem, you move out of your failure pattern and out of the blame system ("I'm to blame for others' problems and they are to blame for mine").

To move into your success pattern, do the opposite of your

inclinations. Be willing to sacrifice short-term self-esteem in favor of long-term gains. If you want to be loved, go against your ego's impulse ("You're unlovable, so act unlovable"). If you want to be successful in your career, give up your ego's desire to protect your image ("I'm always right").

PUSH, PULL

Look at the subtext of your ego in action and you'll discover why your ego is inherently self-defeating. Your ego gets most of its information about your self-images directly from you. Your ego says "yes" to whatever you tell it. If you tell yourself, "I'm not good enough," your ego says, "Yes, you're not good enough and I'll help you prove it."

As a backup system, your ego makes inferences about what you tell it. If you try too hard to belong, your ego reasons, "Who but someone that doesn't belong would try so hard to belong?" If you become dependent on self-affirmations ("I'm worthy . . . I'm worthy"), your ego reasons, "Who but someone who's unworthy would have to keep affirming 'I'm worthy'?"

When the first force is active, your ego pushes you forward to prove that you're great. While you're trying to prove yourself, you're strengthening your ego's conviction that you're inadequate ("Who but someone who's inadequate would need to prove himself or herself?").

Your ego hates the unknown, because of the possible threat to your self-image. When you move into the unknown and are close to reaching your goal, you switch into the second force. Your ego, more convinced than ever that you're too inadequate to be successful, attempts to sabotage your goal in some way. By doing this, your ego maintains the image "You're inadequate." Your ego is fearful that if you were adequate you couldn't survive.

THIRD FORCE

The reconciling third force is to see how you use your ego to protect your self-images. See how you try to prove and defend your illusionary self-importance by alternately pushing yourself forward and holding yourself back. Because your ego operates from faulty assumptions ("I alone am special"), you can never feel secure when you're ego-driven. Only the full truth will make you feel secure ("In the big picture, I am as ordinary and as special as everyone else").

SELF-ADDICTION

Your ego has no sense of reality (it even believes it's real). Your ego, which manifests itself through self-talk, is real only because you *think* it is real. The truth of who you really are can be found only in a quiet, serene state of mind—a state of mind free from self-talk. First, see that your ego is an addiction to a thinking process dedicated to boosting your self-esteem; second, see that you have the freedom to disregard any thought, and break the habit.

No need to hit bottom and see your impression in the mud before you give up this addiction. Your real self is more subtle and immensely bigger than your ego. Your true self includes your individuality and your connection to all of existence. Simply realize that you are larger and greater than your ego. Just as schoolchildren are part of their classes, their schools, their school districts, and the whole world's educational system, you are part of a much grander scheme than your ego, in its blind devotion, believes.

To reduce the ego's role in your life, see your ego as an overzealous guardian angel. Watch and disregard the insecure thoughts ("I'm in trouble") that bring the ego to your rescue. The more insecure you make yourself, the more your ego comes to your rescue. If you're totally insecure, your ego gets grandiose: you start to believe you're Jesus Christ or Napoleon.

Use insight to actively reduce your ego's sphere of influence. When others criticize you, have the presence of mind to see, "I'm sure I have room for improvement." Go against your ego's automatic reaction to defend yourself. A fault confessed is half redressed. Let the bright light of day shine on your errors.

Catch your need to impress others, and then let go of it. Rather

181

than give in to the urge to show how smart you are, tell about a time you tried to be too smart. When someone is rude, remember how often you're rude in the same way.

After an ego binge, you nearly always feel awful ("Why did I have to brag and make a fool of myself?"). Use your second-force hangover to nonverbally decondition your ego's hold over you.

Suffer effectively: fully surrender to the physical pain you experience from being untrue to your real self. Drop your self-condemnation and self-justification and feel through, with precision and equanimity, your body's pain. Let your awareness teach your deep mind the folly of an ego-driven life.

GIVE IN TO WHAT IS

Success in any endeavor comes from giving up the struggle to prove you're successful. Success, by definition, is lack of struggle. The struggle is always between the fiction of your ego and the fact of reality. Give up your need to prove and cover your false self, and your real self appears. Your ego desire to prove your importance is like an organic illness; you never know when the symptoms will appear. The cure is to give up the struggle (even though your ego believes, "If I give up the struggle, I will perish") and disregard your thoughts of needing to prove and defend your self-image.

The easy way to resolve the conflict between your true self and your ego is to shift your focus of attention onto what you really want. If you have trouble with co-workers, be truthful about what you want ("I want to look forward to work each day and enjoy my job"). Once you know what you want, you can rise above the conflict and move toward it ("I'll forget about having to look good to others and bring a good feeling toward work").

FEELING OF PRESENCE

When you're caught in a conflict between your true self and your ego, to see where reality lies, look for a feeling of truth. A feeling of presence, or truth, is the third force, which reconciles your true desires with your ego's misguided attempt to protect your self-image. If you have any internal conflict ("I want it but I don't want it"), look for a feeling of presence and you'll be able to reconcile the conflict in favor of what you really want.

To neutralize your ego's dominance, pull back from your self-image identifications ("my house; my job; my children; my husband; my wife") and move into the moment. Live in the present tense and you'll see who you really are and what you really want.

FEAR OF THE PRESENT

Your ego evaporates as soon as you move into the present. Because your ego believes you'll die without its help, your ego's first priority is to stay in business. Your ego avoids bankruptcy by distracting you from the present with countless thoughts about the past and future.

Although well intended, your ego's fear of the present is unfounded. The greater your sense of presence, the greater your ability to deal with reality. A crisis, such as a fire, brings you into the immediate moment. Your real self springs forward when you need to be at your best—and your real self comes from being totally in the moment.

When you're in the here-and-now, you have a sense of ease and a feeling of being in command. You are congruent with yourself and with where you are at the moment. You are right there and completely real—you are simultaneously tuned in to the details and to the larger picture of reality.

FORMLESS SELF

Unlike your static, illusionary self-image, your real self is formless and dynamic. *Your real self is found in a feeling of presence.* You are your real self when you are mentally, emotionally, and physically right in the moment. Feelings of being in the moment are a sign that you're operating from your true self. No longer distracted by self-esteem thoughts, you're awake and fully conscious.

Presence is a gift you were born with. To reconnect with this feeling of pure aliveness, simply drop your distracting thoughts. Listen fully to the other person. Do one task at a time with full attention to the job at hand. *Being present means remembering what you're doing.* At any moment, once you remove the diluting thoughts, you are left with pure presence.

MOMENT OF TRUTH

Relax and be open to the moment and reality becomes more real, more colorful, and infinitely more interesting. When you no longer let your thoughts filter out reality, and instead shift your attention to the moment, the moment enlarges and becomes real.

Your best performances come from your sense of presence and truth. A feeling of presence is contagious. If you write a letter or cook a meal in a state of presence, when others read the letter or eat the meal, they will likely be drawn into a state of presence.

To find your real self, drop your self-involved small talk and embrace reality. Just as light causes shadows to disappear, a feeling of presence causes your ego's cravings and aversions to disappear and frees you to come home to yourself.

RETURN TO PARADISE

You were in touch with your real self, your sense of presence, when, as a child, you lay on the grass and watched the world go by. Everything from seeing a bee on a flower to examining the cracks in the sidewalk was fascinating.

When you're in the present, you experience reality in a qualitatively different way. You have a primordial feeling of joy and completeness. Because you are reconnecting with your childhood essence, you can experience the sweetness and innocence of the moment.

To find your real self, look for what lightens and lifts your spirits in the moment. Let the feelings of presence pull you into the future and lead you to your true purpose. A feeling of being in the moment leads to a direct communication from what is genuine within you—the feeling opens the way to your true mission in life and allows you to live under the law of destiny—you're led intuitively to what you should be doing with your life, and the steps you need to take next to fulfill your destiny appear naturally.

Writer Ernest Becker said, "If I were to write a manual on seduction for young men, the first and foremost precept would be: Keep your mouth shut." The first and foremost precept for capturing a feeling of presence is inner silence.

Thoughts that distract you from the moment are your only downfall. You can learn to do anything if you can stay in the moment. Teachers have found that any person can learn to draw if he turns the object or picture to be drawn upside down. Once you are no longer thinking about what you must draw, you are forced to see what is there, and this enables you to draw it.

FLOW OF THE MOMENT

Follow the ancient and enduring wisdom "Be present at every breath and don't let your mind wander." Live each second as if it's your last. The wisdom of a life-style based on being fully in the moment swept Asia twenty-five hundred years ago and became the basis for many of the Eastern philosophies. The rallying call became: "Look to this Day! For it is Life, the very Life of Life." With insight, you emulate the early discoverers of presence and live more of your life in a state of pure wonder and joy.

A feeling of presence snaps you out of your amnesia and leads you to see who you really are and what you really want to do with your life. With wisdom, you let what you think, feel, and do originate from this authentic feeling, rather than from external circumstances.

LARGER SELF

Presence is a feeling that moves you into a reality that is both larger and grander than your small concerns. You feel powerful because you're connected to a higher order of reality. When you're no longer caught up in your small thoughts and petty concerns, you become like a soaring eagle; you can see where you came from, where you are, and where you're going—the past, present, and future merge into one.

Subtle, unifying feelings of being fully in the moment give you the real picture of who you are. When you're in the eternal moment, you see that your true self is bigger than your self-image and striving for self-esteem. Your true individuality comes from expanding the present moment to a point where you know you're part of a larger order of reality. Once you realize you're part of everything, you rise above your self-limitations and your self-imposed rules on how you must think, act, and be in the world.

15

BE TRUE
TO YOURSELF

Your true self is a feeling of truth you have in the moment. "Self" is another word for "experience." When you are true to yourself, you have an intrinsic experience of rightness. You always carry the potential for your true self with you. You don't have to hire private detectives or conduct a nationwide search. Find a feeling of truth and you discover your true self has been with you all along.

Like a soap-opera character, you have been suffering from selective amnesia. With understanding, you can reconnect with what is authentic within you and use this as a third force to guide you in life.

Your feelings are a built-in truth detector. (Keep in mind that wisdom is the *pursuit* of truth; you can never get to the bottom of it all—truth is infinite.) You feel what is true both inside and outside you. When you see a movie, read a novel, listen to a speech, you can feel when it's truthful and you can feel when it's false. The more you practice feeling and saying what is true, the more sensitive you become to truth.

BE REAL

Your emotions (excitement, anger, anxiety, depression) come from your ego's reaction to circumstances. Your ego's automatic attempts to protect your self-images create your reactive emotions.

To be true to yourself, move into the moment and let your true feelings guide you. Your feelings, in contrast to your emotions, come from within you—they come from being in communion with your real self. When you transcend your reactive self and find a feeling or flavor of truth, you're no longer a machine: you have command over your own life; events no longer determine what you think, feel, and do. Instead, your true feelings allow you to create the events in your life.

TRUTH AND GOOD FEELINGS

Good feelings are a sign that you're in touch with your true self. To ensure that you're true to yourself, refuse to do anything until you have a good feeling toward it. If you want to stay in truth, refuse to get out of bed until you have a good feeling toward the day. If you're unable to get a good feeling about going to work, stay home. If you truly want to go to work, even if you're afraid of going, a good feeling will well up in you, and you'll move into the moment and go.

If you're unable to get a good feeling, you're better off staying home than going out with a bad attitude. If you're unable to trust your own true feelings, what can you trust?

Keep a good feeling and a sense of truth and you'll finish what you start and gladly receive and enjoy your successes. When you're able to stay true to yourself, you enjoy the process as well as results. You'll feel a deep fulfillment and deep satisfaction with your accomplishments.

TELL THE TRUTH

Bring a feeling of truth to whatever you do and truth will come to you. Telling the truth sets up a magnetic field and pulls the truth to you. When you're truthful with others, they become truthful with you.

Your thoughts and labels cover up the real. Move to the side of further clarifying reality by discarding fixed thoughts and beliefs. You become real by dropping yesterday's thoughts and seeing what is happening right now.

Become like a true scientist and let greater clarification of reality surpass your outdated models of reality. Once you develop a taste for it, you'll be encouraged to be more real with yourself and others.

UNDERSTANDING

You don't get wisdom overnight; ultimately, however, only wisdom allows you to move to higher levels of living in the world. Your level of psychological functioning depends entirely on your level of understanding. Understanding who you are and how you function is the yeast that allows you to rise above your current state.

You gain understanding piece by piece. Playwright Samuel Beckett could have had the acquiring of wisdom in mind when he wrote, "Grain upon grain, one by one, and then one day suddenly there is an heap, a little heap, an impossible heap."

To reach wisdom, you go through three levels of self-understanding. In the first level, the principle or facts of how you function make sense to you—you know the truth on an intellectual level. In the second level, you remember the principles in everyday life and are able to use and explain them to others. In the deepest level of understanding, you know yourself and how you function on a nonverbal level.

Use your feelings as a guide to how much understanding you're gaining. Look for *insight happiness*. Just as recognition of confusion or ignorance leads to a bad feeling, the further clarification of reality leads to a good feeling. The better you're feeling, the more you know you're internally verifying and appreciating the truth of who you are and how you're functioning.

The deepest level of understanding takes a lifetime of work and practice. Just as you can have no tenure, no permanent promotion to happiness, your level of understanding fluctuates. However, have patience: over time, your base level of understanding will gradually increase. Each time you go down, you'll come back up with a little more understanding.

GAINING UNDERSTANDING

Seeing is different from being told. Understanding is knowing something is true from your experiences. Understanding *comes from direct experiences filtered through truth*. Real experience plus a feeling of the truth is the best teacher. You need both life experiences and a higher perspective on reality to grow in understanding.

Understanding is the reconciliation of your daily experiences with seeing directly into reality. All real understanding comes through truthful observation of your thoughts, feelings, and actions. When you catch yourself hiding from the truth of an experience, ask yourself, "What is really going on? How can I further clarify reality? What principle of functioning am I now operating from?"

The more you understand yourself, the more powerful you become. When you know yourself and how you function, you're also able to know others and how they function. You're able to draw on internal and external resources to bring about the life you want.

THE BEST POLICY

You gain the greatest understanding by bringing truth to unwanted and unpleasant experiences. Be willing to face reality and do the unpleasant jobs (return merchandise, make difficult requests) and investigate the uncomfortable bodily sensations. Vigorously go after the relevant internal and external facts. Look under the bed even if you are frightened. Open your mail, go to the doctor, return the phone call, look at your tax records.

Make it easier for others to tell you the truth. Encourage others to tell you what is really going on even though on one level you don't want to hear it. If others tell you, "You are off course," listen.

Care enough about others to connect with their real selves. Have the courage and faith to let other people know what is going on with you. Say how you think and feel, even though your self-image may suffer in the process.

TRUE VALUES

To bring truth to your experiences, look for discrepancies between what you say and what you do. Discriminate between what comes from your ego and what comes from your true self. Your self-image may be that of a loyal marriage partner, but your current situation may be that you're having an affair. Be honest with yourself about what you're doing and you can raise your level of understanding a notch.

If you have any internal conflict ("I want it but I don't want it"), look for a feeling of truth to clarify the experience; once you're clear about what you're doing, you'll naturally be able to be more honest. The truth is that you always want one thing more than another.

Remember that you need truth to reconcile any conflict between your real desires and your ego's agenda. If you tell your family, "This is a democracy," and then veto whatever displeases you, bring truth to the experience and separate your true feelings from your ego's need to safeguard your self-esteem.

The reality of any contradiction is that you have two choices: a true choice, and a choice designed to protect your self-esteem. Keep in mind that your ego, as well as being a well-meaning idiot, can be a pathological liar. Find a feeling of truth within yourself and tell yourself the truth about what you really want ("I want a clear conscience more than I want to be right").

At times, to clarify reality further, you have to force yourself to make a choice. Which do you value more—your children's independence or getting your way? With greater self-understanding comes self-accountability: you refuse to let yourself off the hook and force yourself to tell the truth about what you really value.

TRUE CHARACTER

When you need to be true to yourself, refuse to give yourself the benefit of the doubt. Force yourself to look inside and see what is true. You need moral courage, which is rarer than physical courage, to be true to yourself.

Each time you refuse to compromise yourself (which expresses itself in a queasy, uncomfortable feeling), you gain a little more understanding and a little more inner strength.

You always know when you are true to yourself and when you're not. Just as you are smart enough not to jump off tall buildings, be smart enough to be honest with yourself and others. Find the moral courage to keep your word and to force yourself to follow through on your aims. Keep in mind that the action may be small but the benefit will be huge.

Make being true to yourself your touchstone, the center you always return to. You'll find that, just as compromising wears you out, being true to yourself rejuvenates and reenergizes you.

LET THE CHIPS FALL

To find what is real with you, chip away at all that is false. Catch yourself telling others what you think they want to hear, instead of what you really feel. Endure the discomfort and be honest about what you like and what you dislike. Let the chips fall where they may. Forget about what others think and tell the truth.

Pay attention to what is real for you. When you catch yourself being swept away by what you think others want to hear, find a feeling of truth and force yourself to say and do what is congruent with your true values and true feelings.

Any movement toward the truth liberates you from the tyranny of your false self. To become more real, be honest in small ways (order what you want at a restaurant) and big ways (leave a job that operates against your values). Do more of what you really want to do. Go to the party because you *want* to, not because you think you have to. Walk away from a loss, even though you'll lose face. Refuse to let your ego run the show. Quickly admit your mistakes and tell the unfaltering truth about yourself.

MAKING A DONKEY OUT OF YOURSELF

To clarify reality, strive to be honest with yourself and with the relevant facts. Stay away from your ego's theories and rationalizations. If people dislike you, no amount of analyzing your childhood will make them like you. If many people reject you because you're unfriendly, what you can do to become more friendly is important, but how you got to be unfriendly is unimportant.

Trying to figure out what a problem means is like trying to pin the tail on the donkey. Keep in mind that your ego is an idiot— well meaning, but an idiot. The essence of any situation is simple; your ego tries to fog reality by making everything complicated. See that your speculations take you out of the moment. To stay in the truth, refuse to try blindly to fix a meaning on a situation.

Once you stop trying to figure out what your experiences mean, you can move toward clarification of what is really going on. Move into the moment—look, listen, and feel what's going on inside and outside, and cast aside your analyzing and pet theories.

STRIPPING AWAY

The path to inner freedom is found through being honest with yourself. To make room for being yourself, catch your false self in action and drop your vanity and pretensions; be real with strangers as well as with your family, co-workers, and friends.

Just as you have to remove coats of paint to get to the true grain, to reunite with your true self you have to strip away all that is false. In the process, you'll find unsightly flaws and scratches that you've tried to cover over in the past. Keep in mind that you purify your awareness and raise your state of mind by feeling through and letting go of whatever negative thoughts and feelings arise.

You have to dismantle your self-image to discover who you really are. Be thankful for all the flaws you've unearthed and processed through—you're making progress. Each time you strip away a coat of self-illusion, you're closer to your real self. Remember, your true self is formless and expansive; the images you try to paint of yourself are always too rigid and too limiting.

With wisdom, you'll feel good each time you find out you're much worse or much better than the self-image you painted for yourself. The ability to clarify the reality of who you are is your greatest resource. In the long run, you always feel better and act better when you admit and accept the full, unvarnished truth about yourself.

TELL THE TRUTH

Only when people are honest does trust flower. You trust those who consistently tell you the truth. To trust yourself, you need to tell yourself and others the truth consistently.

An African proverb says, "All of the truth is good, but it's not always good to tell the truth." Refuse to use truth as a weapon. You're at your best when the truth comes from a feeling of authenticity and at your worst when the truth comes from your need to prove and defend your self-esteem.

When your ego is the governing force, you use the truth to hurt and tear down others. Your pleasure, however, is short-lived. The glee you feel soon turns to a guilty conscience. Putting others down to build up your self-esteem leaves a bad taste in your brain. When you feel an ego impulse to tell the truth, bite your tongue. See that through the eye of the ego you tell only part of the truth: you're never emotionally honest.

Honesty from your true self is a comfortable and natural relationship with the facts. You tell what is helpful and what needs to be told. From a feeling of truth, you're impartial: you honestly and simply report the news.

TOLERATE THE TRUTH

When you feel inclined to shade the truth, do the opposite— force yourself to shift your attention to the complete picture and tell the whole truth. T. S. Eliot wrote, "Humankind cannot bear very much reality." Just as you can increase your capacity to feel good, with practice you can increase your capacity to *bear the truth*. As you begin to live in an atmosphere of truth, you want to breathe more of it.

To avoid being cast down and thrown about by life, you need inner strength. Inner strength comes, first, from being a fair witness of your total self and, second, from being able to tolerate what you see. All of your major mistakes and flaws come from your need to protect and defend your self-esteem. To rectify your mistakes rather than deny them, find a feeling of truth and admit your errors—at least to yourself. If you objectively and impartially see your shortcomings, nature will naturally correct them for you.

With practice, you become more adept at being true to yourself. You'll find this means being ethical—you naturally make decisions based on your true values. When you have to face yourself, you discover that personal integrity is your only real asset.

TRUTH AND SUCCESS

Be honest about your true values and have the courage to act on them and the rest of your life will fall into place. Act from your true feelings and you serve the job in front of you instead of your ego. From the higher vantage point of serving the truth, you confront the issues, write the letter, and ask for what you want, regardless of how your image could suffer. You make the phone call to find out where others stand; you tell others where you stand; you see your shortcomings so you can do something about them; and you see what you really care about and so are able to bring this about.

REAL IMPORTANCE

When you lessen the hold of your illusionary self-esteem, your real importance comes forward. Let go of how you look, how much money you have, how much you're admired, and your true importance becomes readily apparent.

This is not false humility. In a higher state of presence, you come to appreciate all of the people and events you have positively influenced over the course of your life. You see the importance of smiling at your neighbor; you see the importance of doing a good job at work; you discover the real importance of raising your children and helping your parents; you see the importance of listening to a friend and participating in activities and causes you truly care about.

FEEL THE TRUTH

Life is structured to be a shattering experience. On one side, to protect your self-esteem, you're programmed to think, "Everything revolves around me"; on the other side, you soon discover you're a drop in the universe. With understanding, you no longer try to hold off the structural conflict between your ego and reality; instead, you welcome it. You know that the loss of ego heralds the rebirth of your true self.

Actively go after the conflict between truth and reality rather than wait for it to hit you in the face. Realize that eventually the facts will come out. At some point, the contradiction between your ego and reality becomes too extreme to ignore.

The beauty and power of being true to yourself lie in its simplicity—you need only to acknowledge and accept what is going on and you become real and powerful in the moment.

16

WILLING TO BE ORDINARY

To find your true spirit, use the realization that you're ordinary as a third force to rise above your first-force need to be important and your second-force need to protect your image.

Catch on to your ego's two opposing modes. Your ego's first force developed when you were a baby. You needed to cry out when you were hungry and cold. You needed to make your needs the most important issue on the table. Still today, your ego tells you that you're number one in the universe and you need to assert your importance.

Your ego's second force developed between the age of two and three. You started to cover your eyes to avoid others' gazes and wanted to hide behind your mother's skirt. Still today, your ego knows that those who stand out are likely to be shot down.

TWO MODES

Your ego, in its misguided attempt to help, gets you coming
and going; your ego pushes you to argue with others and then
criticizes you for talking too much. Your ego wants you to be better
than others, but it also wants you to be anonymous and fade into
the background.

The two modes (to stand out and to hide), like the sympathic
and parasympathetic nervous systems, balance each other out.
When one becomes too extreme, it is balanced by its opposite.

Like other mind/body processes, such as anger and anxiety
(when you get too angry, you get anxious; and when you get too
anxious, you get angry), the two modes help the species but inhibit
you as an individual.

THIRD FORCE

The willingness to be ordinary is the third force, which allows
you to transcend the two primitive modes. Along with giving up
your first-force need to be self-important, you give up your second-
force desire to protect your image.

A feeling of being ordinary sets you free. Give up your desire
to prove the lie of your self-importance and be honest about being
ordinary and you'll feel comfortable anywhere; you'll feel secure
because you've eliminated the gap between fact and fantasy.

NO WIN GAME

Your ego throws out sticks for you to chase. The thought "If
I can find and bring home the right stick I'll have it made" is an
illusion. When it comes to proving yourself, you'll discover this is
an endless and thankless task. Your ego's attitude will always be
"What have you done for me lately?"

Refuse to play the game. Refuse to be an obedient dog who
chases after whatever stick your ego says you need. Why spend
your entire life chasing after more money, approval, and love than

you need? Once you no longer need anything to prove your importance, you'll see you have everything you need.

Rise above your need to prove yourself and you'll look back at your life and think, "What was I doing? Was I crazy?" At the time of your death, you'll see that the ego dream was the ego treadmill: there was nothing there. You can transcend the boundaries of time and get that insight right now. Your true priorities radically shift once you see the illusion and futility of trying to prove your importance.

LOOKING BIG

Your ego's need to prove your importance shows itself whether you brag or berate yourself. You act big because you feel small on the inside, or you act small on the outside to feel big on the inside.

To discover your real self, become comfortable with all sides of yourself. Realize that once the truth that you're ordinary is out in the open, you have nothing to hide. Your tendency to be touchy or defensive naturally disappears once you admit you are an ordinary human being.

Your self-talk ("What will people think?"; "This is going great!") is your ego in action. To connect with your real self, turn off the self-talk radio as soon as it appears. Disregard your pursuit of self-importance and see what is highest in you—who you truly are and what you truly want.

FIRST-FORCE EGO

To reduce your ego's excess first force, put yourself on an equal footing with others. See yourself as another player on the field. Keep your need to be important out of the picture and you can enjoy the game as well as score a goal.

Have the insight that you're ordinary and you no longer see the world and other people as mere backdrops: you include more in your world view. With insight, you discover, "I may shine in some areas, but overall I'm another human being."

199

SECOND-FORCE EGO

To weaken your ego's desire to be anonymous, refuse to put yourself in a blender and be homogenized. Speak up at meetings. Tell the truth, even if it's unpopular. Drop the thought "I shouldn't talk too much," and go against your impulse to give in to the forces of uniformity and conformity.

Life has infinite variety. No need to try to fit in—you already *are* in. Accepting that you're ordinary allows you to follow your own lights and to forget about trying to impress others—with insight, you know it's nearly impossible anyway.

Trying to prove you're special so you'll be approved of and accepted leads to blind conformity. Let go of the need to be special and allow your real self to emerge. Own up to the fact that you're an eccentric and live in your own reality; your whole experience of reality is quirky. Rather than hide your eccentricities, relax and enjoy them.

Appreciate your exclusive view of reality. No one like you has ever been here before or will ever be here again; if you fail to acknowlege and act on what is truest in you, it will be lost forever.

Stop trying to prove you are unique and you discover you already are. You have nothing to prove; you merely need the wisdom and courage to be your eccentric self.

RELAX INTO THE TRUTH

The ability to relax allows you to be your real self. Relaxation comes from your willingness to be ordinary. When you're relaxed, you glide across the finish line. You're active when you're passive and passive when you're active.

If you're relaxed and in the moment while you watch a movie or listen to music, you actively focus on what you watch or listen to. If you're relaxed while you play tennis, you can be active and passive at the same time; you can let go of the need to control the outcome of the game.

Drop your need to prove and defend your importance and you'll relax into any task. The more relaxed you are, the better you perform and the more open you are to learning. You're receptive and able to assimilate the new input. You excel at your job and in your personal life. Be willing to be ordinary and give yourself the message "Who but someone who is going to be successful could be this relaxed?"

Relax your concerns and your intellect assumes you're safe and sends you feelings of well-being. Once you find a feeling of relaxation, you are a success. Take the pressure off ("I'll do the best I can") and get out of your own way. Let go of the thought "I must prove myself" and your natural abilities come out and lead you forward. Nothing succeeds like success. Because you're already a success, what you bring about is a bonus, not something you need before you can be happy.

EGO CREATES INSECURITY

Your ego comes from insecurity and leads to more insecurity. Your ego's desire to prove you're extraordinary is a compensation for feeling insecure. As a child, you had real reasons for feeling small and powerless. With wisdom, you discover that trying to prove you're extraordinary only brings about extraordinary insecurity ("Who but insecure people need to prove themselves?").

Ultimately the process is self-correcting. Your need to prove your importance carries the seeds of its own destruction. You bring about the opposite of what you want. Rather than wait for your ego to self-destruct, be willing to be ordinary and take your chances along with everyone else. Drop the thought "I must never get sick" and you'll stay away from extreme diets and exercise programs that undermine your health. Drop the thought "I must be rich" and you'll stay away from fraudulent get-rich-quick schemes. Once you accept that you're ordinary, you bring a balanced, common-sense approach to what you want.

BE CONSIDERATE

Gradually free yourself of your compulsive need to prove your importance. Learn to recognize and drop the urge to prove yourself, and learn to be alert to what you can do for others.

As you grow older, you naturally see you're more ordinary than you once thought. You can escalate this liberating process and connect with your real essence by being more considerate of others. Once you take others' feelings and thoughts into consideration, you automatically shift your focus off your self-importance.

To lessen your ego's hold, drop tasks at will. Get up and serve coffee rather than expect someone to serve you. Be on time rather than make others wait for you. Call when you're going to be late even though it's inconvenient. Take a moment to write a note to a friend. Immediately lay the newspaper down and do what others ask of you. Hold your tongue rather than complain and lower others' feelings.

Don't expect others to be objects to make you look good; allow them to be who they are. Accept your children, friends, and relatives unconditionally. Refuse to tie your self-importance to others in your life. See them as separate individuals instead of means to boost your self-esteem.

RESULTS = VISION MINUS EGO

If your ego is 90 percent out of the picture, you're assured a 90-percent chance of getting what you want. The less you try to prove your importance, the more energy and awareness you bring to your aims in life.

Find a feeling of being ordinary and you'll be able to effortlessly bring about results. Relax your overpush and give yourself breathing room. Get your ego out of the way and you'll learn and assimilate what you need to know to be successful. Once you no longer expect life to cater to you, living becomes easy.

Stop thinking, "I should automatically know everything," and be willing to take the steps to learn the drills and take in the necessary information. You'll read the directions on the box and look at the fine print on the contract.

FEEL FREE

Your ego's focus is on how to find techniques and formulas to prove and maintain its importance. The drive to be important keeps you insecure and defenseless. Once you have nothing to defend and nothing to prove, you feel secure.

Grasp the insight that you're ordinary and you see that everyone else is too. You stop calculating your every move to protect your image. You no longer put others above you or below you—even if they have special traits or accomplishments.

Be willing to accept that you're ordinary and you can disregard the false front. You drop your social mask and allow yourself to connect with others: Eliminate self-absorption and make room in your heart for others. Overlook slights and listen to others, even if what they have to say is unflattering.

You have the same hangups and shortcomings as each of your neighbors. See, first, that all your flaws come from your ego and, second, that you weaken your ego through awareness. All you have to do is watch your ego in action, and nature will do the rest. Begin to look for your ego. Rather than criticize others or complain about them, ask yourself, "How do I act in the same ways myself?"

ROLE OF EGO

Getting beyond your ego's fixations is necessary to evolve into your true self. Your ego is an elaborate system of beliefs and reactions designed to protect and maintain your constructed personality. To become a functioning adult, you need a stable identity. Developmentally, you need to be somebody before you can become nobody.

After you construct a working personality, you have to start to dismantle it to evolve further. If you become too attached to your personality, you'll fail to advance to higher order functioning.

CHIEF FEATURE

As a young child, you were completely open to the world and fully expected to have a friendly merging with all nature. Then the second force suddenly appeared: you discovered the world could be unfriendly, frustrating, and frightening. In response, you became reactive and defensive.

Through trial and error, you developed one predominant coping strategy for dealing with life's second force. Your behavior was repeatedly reinforced, either positively ("Hey, Mom, look at me") or negatively ("What's wrong with you?"). The strategy reduced your anxiety and brought you pleasure and attention. Over time, this became a conditioned way of dealing with the world.

Your heuristic coping mechanism became the chief feature of your personality, or ego identity. You began to think that this strategy, which was used to habitually prove and protect your self-esteem, was the real you.

Your chief feature has become such an all-encompassing part of your makeup that you're largely unaware of its existence. It is woven into the fabric of how you see reality; it's your last thought at night and your first thought in the morning. You take for granted that everyone sees the world as you do.

NINE PERSONALITY TYPES

Your chief feature becomes the axis for your personality type. Because there are a limted number of effective coping strategies, only a limited number of personality variations exist.

You gain freedom and power by clarifying the nature of your personality type. Your type develops out of what you are good at. Your gift, however, is ultimately what does you in. Your virtue becomes your vice. Start to see how your personality type consists of ways you use your intrinsic talent to compulsively avoid your worst fears.

Your ego type, according to the enneagram (an ancient system which developed out of painstaking observation), is one of nine variations. While you have elements of each, one will be predom-inant. You get to know your type through careful self-watching: look at your internal motivation, not at your behavior.

Just because you get all A's doesn't mean you're a perfectionist. You may need to get A's for one of nine reasons: to get others' approval; to show you're a winner; to suffer; to prove how smart you are; to avoid fear; to avoid the bad feelings; to be in control; or to avoid conflict.

Type One: The Perfectionist
If you're a perfectionist, you want all A's because it's the right thing. Your chief feature is to reform yourself and the world. Realize the drive for perfection is your biggest imperfection. Your anger,

criticism, and pickiness make it hard for others (and yourself) to be around you.

Your need to be above criticism leads paradoxically to your failures. Like a hawk, you're constantly looking for a flaw to attack. This destroys your relationship with yourself and with others.

To find balance, no matter what your personality type, force yourself to go against your natural inclination—do what you don't want to do and don't do what you want to do. If you're a perfectionist, you need to become lighter and more flexible. Be patient and give yourself and others room to grow and develop.

Realize that when you gain wisdom and move to higher states of functioning, you don't lose your natural gifts; rather, you are able to use them to the fullest. As a perfectionist, your genius is in seeing what you need to do to become a better person and make a better world. As you gain insight, you're able to put this talent to full use.

Type Two: The Helper

Each type has a core belief or assumption that drives the behavior. The helper believes, "I can get others to love me by serving them." Giving becomes a compulsion that hurts you and others. In the process of trying to help, you cripple those who become too dependent on you, and flatter yourself into thinking you do it all for the sake of love.

Your personality type is often the opposite of what you think it is. Do you think you're too generous? Who but selfish people think they do too much for others. You gain power by clarifying the nature of your personality type.

Structurally, each type brings about the opposite of what is hoped for. Compulsive giving reinforces the giver's fear (the helper's chief feature) that at heart they are unlovable: who but someone that is unlovable would work this hard to be loved?

The behavior of each type also brings about the opposite reaction from others than is hoped for. Helpers, or love birds, instead of being cherished, end up being taken for granted or resented. Gurdjieff said, "The first time you help people, they want to kiss your hand, but by the ninth time, they want to sue you."

If you're a helper, your gift is the ability to deeply love. However, you need to develop yourself first. Realize you need wisdom before you can have true compassion. Clarity before charity. By working on developing yourself and nurturing your creative side, you can transcend your false flattery and compulsive need to be loved.

Type Three: The Performer

The ego is motivated by deep and powerful fears that are often only felt subliminally. The behavior of each type momentarily reduces the anxiety; however, under the surface, the insecurity is being reinforced and kept alive.

As a performer, the driving force behind your need to win is not the satisfaction of success but the fear of failure. Realize that by acting as if losing is the worst thing in the world, you increase your fear of being a loser.

Your chief feature, deceit, is designed to make you look special and important. You may lie and avoid getting too close for fear of having the illusion of being a winner exposed.

The characteristics of one's personality type generalize and color every aspect of life. As a performer, you work excessively to appear successful. You are intolerant of others' inefficiency in helping you look good—you overlook that you get all of the upside. Being a performer, your talent is talent. You are gifted at knowing what others want to see and hear. However, being a peacock and needing to show off sabotages your real desire to be authentically loved for who you are.

To protect what is most important to you, your ego checks your true desires. The chief feature of your type (whatever it is) protects your self-esteem by having you not go directly for what you want. This reaction safeguards your potential ("Someday I'll get what I want") and is a way to reduce a perceived major threat to your self-image—the biggest blow to your self-image would be to lose the potential or dream of what you most want.

As a status seeker, your chief feature (deceit) stops you from being loved for who you really are. You need to go the other way: risk rejection and work toward establishing authentic relationships with others.

Type Four: The Artist

In your ego's relentless desire to be special, your identity can become attached to anything. As an artist or tragic romantic, you become self-identified with suffering. Feelings of longing, melancholy, and unfulfillment become addictive. Your chief feature is suffering and like the "Raven," you feel close to the dark forces.

The true quest for everyone is to get in touch with the real self. Without insight, your chief feature appears to be leading you to your essence. Actually, your compulsive striving gets in the way of discovering who you really are. Your personality type causes you to look in all of the wrong places.

Just as performers look to their achievements to define them, if you have the Raven personality, you look into the black hole of self-absorption to find yourself.

In every case, the personality type's solution to the problem of being human is the problem. If you are the artist type, start to realize that more process journals and more soul searching only cause you to be less in touch with your real self. See how you try to fill your inner void with beauty and associating yourself with the best instead of actually taking constructive action.

When you know your personality type, you know the direction you need to take to evolve. With wisdom you use recognition of the emergence of your personality's characteristics as a signal to look for a way to enhance its opposite—the true qualities you really want.

If you have the artist's personality, you need to see your salvation is through hard work. Focus on creating something positive in the external world and your internal sense of self will naturally and organically develop on its own. Your talent and extraordinary sensitivity can then be used to create something real and beautiful.

Type Five: The Thinker

Each type needs to learn how to accept and process the unpleasant feelings that have been systematically avoided. If you're a thinker, you need to learn how to stay with the uncomfortable feelings of not knowing. Aim to learn the wisdom of not having all of the answers. Instead of holding back and watching like an owl, decide to participate without first having to know everything there is to know.

Realize your personality type is the trigger for what causes you to get reversed. This is why two people of the same personality type usually cross each other up. If your driving force is success, for example, you are likely to get reversed when others are more successful than you.

Because thinkers are identified with their ideas, they get reversed when their thoughts are attacked. This is one of the reasons their chief feature is withholding—of themselves, their knowledge, and their time and energy.

Each personality type's strategy works paradoxically. You get less of what you want and more of what you don't want. To evolve you need to go against your ego's agenda and actively deflate your need to prove yourself in some way. Realize that your ego is the container and the characteristic of your type is the contents. You need to empty the container rather than fill it up with more of the same.

If you're a thinker, see how the more you try to fill up the void with facts and knowledge, the more insecure you feel. The more you try to know, the less you know. If you are a thinker, you need to stop protecting your ideas (which you have become morbidly attached to) and allow your ideas to be used and abused: only by entering the real world can you allow your talent for wisdom to flourish.

Type Six: The Doubter

Your personality type is driven by a specific dread and by a specific compulsion. The different personality types have been called idiots and for good reason. Your compulsion brings about the very fear you're trying to avoid, which in turn creates more compulsion.

If you're a doubter, or chicken, your fear is fear. Your compulsive demand for certainty causes you to be hyper-vigilant for any deviation from the expected. Because acute awareness of deviation is the very mechanism of fear, you are always afraid. Your anxiety leads to chronic ambivalence and a host of other problems.

The bad news about any personality type is that you are stuck with it. The good news is that you can forget about trying to change your personality. You can go for psychoanalysis for fifty years and you will never change your personality type. However, by accepting who you are, you can learn to skillfully work within its parameters. In one sense, this makes the job easier. You don't have to tackle every psychological problem that ever existed.

At any one moment, the manifestation of your personality type will range from the healthy to the unhealthy, depending on your state of mental health (how much awareness you have of your mind/body process). Simply by acknowledging and accepting your personality characteristics, you increase your self-tolerance and raise your level of awareness.

As a fear type, you need to see and accept that you are addicted to fear. Realize that this is no more than a bad habit that you can gradually let go of. Worry and dread have no magical qualities. You can lead your life quite well without it. As with all addictions, allow yourself to completely feel in your body the unpleasant sensations of fear and you will start to naturally surrender it.

Transcend your fear of fear and you can fully develop your talent for close, interdependent relationships. Discover that it's okay to be scared and take action anyway. You'll learn real security comes from accepting your insecurity.

Type Seven: The Pleasure Seeker

The chief feature of every chief feature is excess. Your predominant way of responding and reacting to the world becomes way overdone. Too much of even a good thing becomes a bad thing. Wisdom and real success are always found in the middle.

If you're a pleasure seeker, your excess is excess. Your chief feature is always wanting more. Like a hummingbird, you are driven to be constantly moving. You are known for worrying and hurrying. You probably have had many interesting experiences in your life, but unfortunately you weren't there to experience them—you were too busy planning the next event.

While every type wants to avoid some discomfort, as a pleasure seeker you want to avoid all unpleasant sensations (pain, boredom, confusion). The inability to tolerate bad feelings in yourself or others sets you up to be easily manipulated.

Because your overriding concern is to have fun, people generally like you. However, if you'll look closely, you'll see that you rarely relate to anything or anyone in depth. This is the clue to what you need to do. See that you have to fully experience your experience. Realize that your constant pleasure-seeking is a way to run from your anxiety. Be willing to slow down and accept whatever uncomfortable feelings arise: you'll discover that they pass away on their own and you've been running for nothing.

You can bring your talent for enjoyment to full bloom by aiming for quality rather than quantity. With insight, you can get more of the joy of life you want with less effort.

Type Eight: The Boss

What keeps you locked into your compulsive personality traits is believing your chief flaw is your chief virtue. You have it upside down. More of the same will not solve your difficulties—it is the source of your troubles.

If you're a boss, or leader type, your chief feature is needing to dominate the situation. Your chief fear is appearing weak and being taken advantage of by others. The troubles in your relationships will not be solved by more controlling of others. Realize that trying to protect yourself and those you care about is how you defeat yourself.

Your failure pattern, no matter what your type, comes from identifying with your ego or personality type. If you're the boss type, you're like a rooster: you're more interested in ruling the roost than getting what you want. In your failure pattern, you spend all of your time and energy trying to be in control and, in the process, lose sight of what you really want.

Rather than constantly trying to be the boss and have your way, allow yourself to become more vulnerable. Get in touch with your innocence, that part of yourself that you cover over out of fear. See that while you can dominate the physical world, the same strategy destroys relationships.

Your talent is for making things happen. By gaining insight into how you and others work in the psychological world, you can become an effective champion for justice and, in the process, earn the love and respect that you really want.

Type Nine: The Peacemaker

Your adult ego, or personality type, largely develops on its own, but will only take you so far in the evolutionary process. If you want to go further and complete yourself, you need to create a working super-adult. It's a do-it-yourself project. Your super-adult is to your adult as an adult is to a child. As a super-adult, you learn to lovingly guide yourself to higher levels of maturity.

If you are a peace lover, your chief feature is to go to sleep or tune out to avoid conflict. Like the condor, you endlessly circle around what you want, trying to make up your mind where to land. In the process you're likely to get shot down and become extinct. A nice person, you're more than willing to take a backseat role. Unfortunately, you tend to go to sleep while you are in the backseat and miss life in the process. Your easy-going strategy, which covers up an underlying cynicism about doing anything, prevents you from fully developing yourself.

As with all of the types, you need a super-adult to oversee your adult personality. Aim to create an unbiased witness that is willing to tell the truth and point you in the right direction. Your super-adult will show you how to use your talent for equanimity to take a stand for what you really care about.

DREAMLIKE STATE

Although you may believe that circumstances betray you, only *you*, via your ego and thoughts, can betray yourself. Your ego becomes insecure when you feel good and follow your true purpose. When you're off work and free from external demands and have the chance to feel real and be yourself, your ego starts to make up negative scenarios to distract you.

See how thoughts of needing to prove or defend yourself put you into a dreamlike state, a state of temporary insanity. Your vanity moves you out of here-and-now reality. You're unaware that you're asleep and daydreaming—you think your thoughts are reality. In your daydream, everything has great impact on your self-image. Whether you daydream about being adored or ridiculed, you're the center of attention.

As in night dreams, you weave some facts into the scenario. Refuse to take a small fact (someone criticized you) as proof that the daydream ("Everyone hates me") is real, and refuse to give in to the urge to keep up the daydream by analyzing it. Understand, "I'll never know what a daydream means until I'm psychologically awake. The quicker I wake up, the quicker I'll learn the lesson."

BEYOND NARCISSISM

Poet Antonio Machado said, "Narcissism is an ancient fault and has become a boring fault." Catch the times when you focus all on yourself and make a caricature out of who you really are. Once you're willing to be ordinary, you allow your interesting and subtle nuances to come to the foreground. Rather than focus on a small slice of your overall life, remind yourself, "I'm more than what I'm good at, and I'm more than what I wish I were good at."

With wisdom, you start to separate from your ego and follow your true path. Pay attention and you'll find reality always tells you, "It's time to get real." Find a good feeling and take off your ego's eye mask and earplugs; you'll move into the present moment. Let good feelings wake you up from your ego daydreams and put you on the right path. Gently wake yourself up and come back to here-and-now reality.

DRAMAS

Your success pattern comes from being true to yourself and from forgetting about proving yourself. Whenever you catch yourself acting out your dream of self-importance, find a feeling of presence and walk off the stage. Drama situations (where you get caught up in the details of a crisis) always revolve around your self-importance ("If I don't help my friend, there will be no hope for him").

Drama is your ego's attempt to avoid the reality of being ordinary. The drama could be in your mind—small and quiet—or it could be a full-blown Hollywood production for all the world to see. No matter what part you play in the drama, your importance is always center stage.

See your self-dramatizations as a reaction to the reality of your being ordinary. Reality is knocking at your door, trying to arouse you from your sleep with the facts. Acknowledge that you're ordinary. If you try to avoid answering the door, reality will come though the window; board up the windows and it'll come down the chimney.

Use reality as a wake-up call: "I'm ordinary." You make mistakes, you get rejected, you're like everyone else—you're unable to control all of life. From a higher vantage point, you forget about your small self. Once you see you're ordinary and no one special, you become part of everything.

THOUGHTS AND THINKING

Your ego projects its insecurity onto the outside world. The more insecure you are, the louder the voice of external circumstances becomes. When you walk into a room, you can hear everyone thinking about you. If you are in a higher state of mind, the voice of circumstances is silent and your real voice is clear and strong.

In high states of presence, you care about what you truly value and you treat external circumstances and yourself in an even, matter-of-fact way. You are in alignment with reality, which is completely neutral; you are as neutral toward yourself as you are toward others.

Thinking that you must prove your importance is an automatic, involuntary, and harmless process. The difficulty comes when you become stuck on a thought (the product of your automatic thinking). When you hang on to a self-important thought ("I have to look good"), the thought stays in your system and colors all of your perceptions.

To become attached to any thought of self-importance is to invite pain into your life. Refuse to fixate on or give credence to any thoughts of self-importance ("No one has suffered as I have"). Your idea that you're great or terrible is just an idea. *Realize that your need to prove yourself is nothing more than a thought* that rises up and passes away. Refuse to tie your self-esteem to thoughts of your successes, the ways you have been mistreated, or what you have endured.

TRUE PURPOSE

Your true self has its own essential feature, which is your true purpose. Following your true purpose is a third force that allows you to bring about what you most want in life. You don't have to invent or create your true purpose—you already have it within you. You simply need to recognize and live it.

Your true purpose is like an old friend; it's the part of you that you love best, and it's what matters most to you. Others are attracted to this quality in you. When you operate from your true purpose, you enrich the lives of those you touch.

The essence of your true self might be to lead, teach, love, create, know, nurture, initiate, build, complete, master, serve, connect, express, search, enliven, facilitate, encourage, bring together. A balance always exists in nature. People unable to care for themselves have a life's purpose to be helped; they provide the means for others to help and serve.

DISCOVER PURPOSE

Your true purpose is a common thread that runs through your entire life. When others think of your most positive trait, this is what comes to their minds.

Your feelings of presence give you the strongest clue to your deepest desire. You feel the most alive when you're engaged in the real purpose of your life. You feel real, powerful, and inspired— you're in your element.

Your true purpose is what you most value and what you're the best at. You become a genius when you operate from this essence quality. Your true purpose comes from a feeling within you, but is expressed outward, toward reality and others.

The more you focus on your true purpose, the more authentic you become. Rather than ask yourself, "What *should* I do?" ask, "What do I *really* want to do?"

Develop a life-style that supports your true purpose. If your true purpose is to appreciate nature, design a life-style that maximizes your ability to be close to nature. Whatever your true purpose, use your life to express it. Rather than selectively and sporadically follow your true calling, make it central in your life.

PAY THE PRICE

Be willing to pay the price to be true to yourself. The price of being true is giving up your ego, your false self-image: be willing to look foolish and ordinary; be willing to have others think poorly of you. You'll always pay a higher price by being untrue to yourself. Realize that paying the price to be true to yourself is ultimately a bargain.

When you're true to yourself, you feel as though you've been released from solitary confinement. After years of worry about what you're allowed to do, you'll find that a tremendous weight is lifted; you'll realize that you have choices, that you can do what you want to do in life.

DON'T WAIT

When you have true self-esteem, you accept being ordinary and forget about proving anything. You find that, the less you *think* about your importance, the more you *become* yourself and the higher your real self-esteem rises. True self-esteem comes from having all-encompassing good feelings, not from feeling good about being special or from feeling good about what you do or have.

Inevitably you'll have the liberating insight that you're ordinary. You may have this insight next week, or twenty-five years from now ("My lifelong need to prove myself was a case of chasing my own tail. . . . I never got anywhere, and I wore myself out in the process").

Why wait until it's too late? Right now you can eliminate time from the equation and see the connection between having a good life and accepting that you're ordinary. Realize now, or later you'll know what is important: love and appreciation for the everyday experiences in life.

With wisdom, you refuse to squander your precious time trying to prove you're special ("What is important is that I'm alive and can enjoy life; what is unimportant is my need to prove my importance").

Clear your mind of self-importance and you'll develop room for wisdom, intuition, and compassion. Turn a deaf ear when your ego tries to convince you that you are the favorite child, the chosen one, the lord of lords. Drop your self-importance and separateness. You are part of the vastness and power of the universe.

The benefit of disempowering your ego is immediate and far-reaching. Instead of looking for your reflection from others, see yourself and others in a more direct and honest way. You'll find you can lead a special life once you're willing not to be special.

17

WILLING
TO BE
HUMAN

Every time you have a
first-force desire, you're going to run into second-force resistance.
Look closely and you'll see that your mind is constantly shifting
from cravings to aversions. One moment, eating is heaven, but
soon another bite will be hell and going for a walk becomes the
new heaven—which will shortly become the next hell.

The body's metabolic system keeps a delicate third-force balance between the growth-producing anabolic process and the destroying and eliminating catabolic process. The expanding first
force and constricting second force are built into the structure of
all life and have nothing to do with you as a person. Without this
understanding, you're likely to take personally the second-force
humiliation of falling on your face. Your humiliation then becomes
a reason to quit or to detour away from what you really want.

Humiliation *skillfully* handled is the best way to dissolve the
power of your ego; conversely, if unskillfully handled, humiliation
solidifies your ego's hold over you.

With third-force understanding, you see that humiliation is an exercise in humility—a way to become free from your false pride. Acceptance is the alchemy that changes a perceived loss of face into a gain of true self. Humility, the means to freedom, nearly always comes via humiliation.

When humiliating feelings (which can range from slight embarrassment to utter mortification) arise within you, be as open as possible to them. Don't try to think them out or act them out; instead, feel them through.

Be as relatively accepting and nonreactive with your bodily sensations as possible. Allow the feelings room to move. Painful self-conscious feelings, when fully processed, turn into charisma, or richness of personality. Many performers are charismatic on stage and awkwardly self-conscious offstage. The difference is that when they are on, they fully accept their self-consciousness, and when they are off, they resist the same feelings.

Humiliation can become a psychologically and emotionally uplifting third-force experience of humility if you allow it to destroy your false image and reveal your real self. With wisdom, you use humiliation as a friendly reminder that you are human, rather than as a sign that you're a failure.

False pride and self-idolization ("I am distinct from all other life") set you up for a fall. The bigger your ego, the harder the fall. Second-force reality breaks through your defense system and shows you that your first-force pride is a sham, a self-imposed hoax.

THIRD FORCE

Allowing yourself to be human is the third force, which frees you to reconcile yourself to the big issues in life. No matter what your current concern (your job, your relationships, your health, your appearance), you transcend it by acknowledging, "I'm human."

See how humility frees you from the thrall of your ego and you'll no longer sacrifice your true desires to avoid feelings of humiliation. Accept that you're human and freely welcome your painful self-consciousness and you will suffer much less humiliation in the future. Accepted and processed humiliation teaches you that you're human. When you learn the lesson, the humiliation disappears and true humility takes its place.

Let go of the idea that you're special and you'll create meaning and order out of your life. Reconcile your real power with your powerlessness. Understand that you are alone and at the same time connected to the world. Discover that you're human and you no longer fear the prospect of death, the ultimate second force. You see that being mortal is part of being human.

Once you let go of the belief "I'm the jewel of the universe," you give yourself the gift of freedom. You discover that, because everyone is special, no one is special.

WINNING THROUGH LOSING

Accept your own humanity and learn to be comfortable in your own skin. No matter what your situation, once you let go of your image of self-importance, living becomes a joyful experience. The more human you're willing to be, the more freedom and latitude you have to bring about the life you want.

Dag Hammarskjöld wrote, "To reach perfection we must all pass, one by one, through the death of self-effacement." You win by being willing to lose face. Accept that you're human. Be willing to go down and you'll move up in the psychological world. Rather than egotistically insist, "I'm always on top," be willing to be wherever you are. You come in first in the art of living once you're willing to be last in the art of life.

Your ego is a primitive mechanism that tries to help you sur-

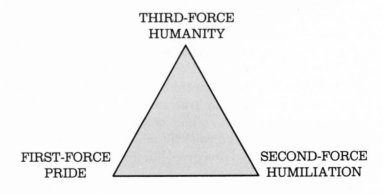

THIRD-FORCE
HUMANITY

FIRST-FORCE
PRIDE

SECOND-FORCE
HUMILIATION

vive by proving and protecting your identity. To stay motivated, your ego has pegged you as the most important person that ever lived. To protect your identity, the ego will even sacrifice your life. You are the most important person to yourself, but your ego thinks you are the most important person in the world, period.

Try to prove your illusionary importance and you'll live in insecurity; disregard your ego and you'll start to feel secure. Reduce the downward pull of your ego's mission and ascend to higher states of being. You move up once you drop the burden of trying to protect your self-image.

A man found such long lines at the main gate to heaven that he was unable to get in. Around to the side he found a gate with no one in line. The sign over the gate said "Humiliation." By going through the gate of humiliation (what the Sufis call *malamat*), he was able to walk right in. Though humiliation may be the last door you want to walk through, you'll find that *malamat*, skillfully experienced, is the best way to liberate yourself from the prison of your own self-importance.

HEALING

Humiliation is a naturally occurring catabolic antidote to egotism: it slows down the anabolic growth of your self-importance, and leads to third-force humility. If your system is riddled with self-image toxins, you will inevitably live a life of humiliation. Shame and humiliation work on your self-images the way chemotherapy works on cancer—the stronger the dose you can tolerate, the better.

Humiliation is like a near-death experience. The pain you feel is your illusionary self-images being eradicated. While this is not recommended, you do have the potential to get the most out of humiliating experiences that take you to near–psychological death.

Unwelcomed humiliation can be a terrible shock to your system, but if you use it therapeutically, you'll emerge healthier and happier. Humility cures the malignancy of arrogance and strengthens your psychological immune system.

With understanding, you realize that small daily doses of humiliation are blessings in disguise. Destroying your illusionary self-image allows you to be your real self. Once you have accepted that you're human, you have accepted the worst. You have nothing left to hide. There's no need to care or worry about what others think—it's all out in the open and out of your hands.

LEVELS

The deeper you're willing to let an ego-shattering experience penetrate your being, the freer you'll become.

First, you need to accept your inability to prevent feelings of shame and embarrassment. Like everyone else, you will have automatic and uncontrollable feelings of shame every day.

Second, let the feeling from public humiliation rise up and pass away. Fully experience with awareness and acceptance the sensations in your body. Accept yourself and your feelings when you look foolish in others' eyes. Embrace the times when your image slips in public. Learn to love the fact that you've made a fool of yourself, instead of trying to reject it and push it away. You become free by learning not to care any longer what others think of you.

Third, let humility come in and penetrate to the marrow. On the deepest level, you're shattered because your ego's fantasy is destroyed. Once you drop what's most important to your idealized self and accept that you're human, you can make fundamental shifts in your whole life orientation.

FANTASIES

Humiliation destroys fantasies, and only by giving up your fantasies can you ever be happy. As long as you fantasize about the perfect relationship or being idolized by your peers, you can never be happy today. Your idealized future makes you disdain what you now have—it's never good enough.

The healthy get healthier. The happier you are, the less you fantasize; the less you fantasize, the happier you become.

Your fantasies are illusions because they have no second force, no reality to them. Your fantasies are picture-perfect productions. Your intellect tries to compensate for the illusionary nature of your fantasies through your night dreams. Pay attention to your dreams and you'll find they bring in a second force to counterbalance your positive daydreams, and a first force to counterbalance negative daydreams.

Your troubles really begin when you try to bring your fantasies into reality: your daydreams turn into nightmares. The affair you fantasized about ruins your marriage. The business empire you pictured in your mind becomes your jailer.

Take heart. Reality is always in the wings to destroy your fantasies. Welcome the destruction of fantasies with open arms. Once you're rid of your fantasies, you free your imagination to create visions of what you truly want.

If you lose money because of a poor business decision or get fired from a high-powered job, you'll have automatic feelings of shame and embarrassment. Experience the feelings through, and appreciate that you're human and how others are able to see your humanity. The greatest gains come from the loss of your fantasies. This loss frees you to bring about what you truly desire—what is highest in you.

LOVE AND HUMILITY

Shattering experiences shock you into asking, "What do I *really* want?" Your answer may show you that you're feeling bad about something that you've outgrown ("I was fired from a job that I'd lost interest in years ago"). Use the shock as an opportunity to stop and see where you are and where you want to go.

Let the experience snap you out of your trance of self-absorption. Having someone leave you can shock you into seeing how you took the person for granted. Use the rude awakening to reevaluate what you're doing with your life.

Your response to humiliation should always be "Thanks, I needed that." Use the near-death experience of a shattered relationship to learn to love. After being humiliated by seeing the truth of your life, you become like Scrooge—you're free to connect with humanity through love.

True love is possible once your need to be special is out of the way. With true love, you care more about the other person than yourself. Your ego's self-love inhibits real love. Let the fire of humility burn out the impurities in your heart and you'll be able to truly love.

Like Mary Magdalene, after experiencing humiliation, you have the possibility to be redeemed by love. Love, like freedom, is another name for nothing to lose. Once you've let go of your ego's agenda, you're free to surrender yourself. Sacrifice your self-love and you're free to open your heart to others.

HIGHER PERSPECTIVE

To create order out of your personal chaos, you need initially to raise your perspective. You can use understanding as a beanstalk to rise to higher levels—but first you must defeat your giant ego.

To digest your humiliating feelings and complete the experience, you need to *focus* on the uncomfortable bodily sensations, and at the same time mindfully *observe* them. When you focus on the sensations, initially the pain will increase; however, by simultaneously observing them with acceptance and heightened observation, you'll discover they start to metabolize and fade away.

Focus with precision and specificity on your bodily sensations. Your focus holds the sensation in place and your mindfulness, like a laser beam, melts away the uncomfortable sensations.

Your instinct will be to tighten up and close yourself off from your painful feelings. Go the opposite way. Have the courage and clarity to open yourself to your pain and to feel it through. The quickest way to have your painful feelings leave is to not want them to leave. Nature will work out the pain as quickly as it can. Your job is simply to stay with the bodily sensations, to observe them with specificity and equanimity, and to stay out of the way of the purification process.

Your ego will try to interfere with your feeling the sensations through. Your ego will try to distract you from your feelings by getting you to think about the humiliating incident or by trying not to think about it.

Your ego wants to protect you from experiencing the raw feelings, but, even more important, your ego wants to protect the self-image that is under attack.

When your ego's self-talk starts up, note to yourself, "Thinking," and return to feeling through the sensations. By continuing to feel the sensations, you'll eventually reach a critical mass of understanding. At that point, you'll have a sudden wordless insight: you'll realize the self-image you're trying so hard to protect is just a thought and not reality. This insight will free you from the prison of your self-concepts and self-images. A burst of good feelings will signal your insight into the truth.

Rather than try to figure out what happened, rise above the debris. Obsessively going over the humiliating experience, looking for a lesson, reduces your awareness of the truth of the current moment. You mentally grind any learning into dust.

You reduce your awareness by replaying the experience over and over like an instant replay of a football fumble. Instead, look for a way to process your feelings and raise your state of mind. Once you accept and complete the experience, you can let go of it. Refuse to grind away on your humiliation and the insight will be there when you need it.

WISER

You start out ignorant and become wise through your experience. Be impersonal toward your inevitable falls. Anything you inflate too much explodes. Having your image shattered is built into the human condition; it's a natural check against human pride. Humility is your greatest resource. Your only enemy is the ignorance of your errors. If you conceal your illness, you can't expect to be cured. By acknowledging with humility the existence of your flaws, you weaken their hold over you and eventually you eliminate them.

An Arabic proverb says, "One camel does not make fun of the other camel's hump." Once you are honest about your own shortcomings, you are more tolerant of others' shortcomings.

The courage to acknowlege your humanity allows you to transcend setbacks and move on. After you rise above an embarrassing incident, make a full confession to yourself ("I'm only human"), then forget about it.

HUMOR

Quickly create a sense of poise and a feeling of being in the present with your humiliating experiences; see on a deep level that destroying your self-images is your only chance to be truly free. Once you understand this, you can even turn past losses into present gains.

People in the theater say you can turn a tragedy into a comedy by having the actors sit down when they deliver their lines. Humor is a third force that allows you to reconcile your pride with your fall. Humor reconciles your illusionary self-concepts with reality. Have fun with your quest for humility. Laugh at how serious and pompous you were and join in others' laughter at your foolishness and you'll be able to integrate your real self with reality.

TRUE PRIDE

Reality destroys your ego's false pride and makes room for real pride. True pride is centered in what you've accomplished, not in yourself. With true pride you focus on the task, rather than on trying to make yourself bigger than you really are.

To gain mastery, which leads to true pride, you have to let humiliation, skillfully experienced, destroy your fantasies of having it all together. To produce anything of value, be humble to the task; be willing to serve the task instead of your self-image.

Disregard the thought "I'm above putting in extra effort." Be willing to persevere and do the job right. The less special you think you are, the more you're willing to do what is necessary.

Realize that you're human and you'll let go of losing situations. *A loser is someone who refuses to accept a loss.* Be willing to endure small losses and you avoid big losses. Quickly accept your mistake and you turn the tide in your favor; you stop throwing good money after bad. Recurring humiliation is a sign that you need to accept the truth: you're not special. Once you have the insight that you're no one special, you become free.

When you discover you're not special, you become free to do, be, or have what you really want. As soon as you disregard thoughts of needing to be special, your fear of humiliation disappears.

With insight, you know that nothing outside of you can ever

humiliate you. There are no humiliating circumstances. Only your thoughts about your self-image can humiliate you. Once you start to accept yourself as you really are, your humiliation starts to disappear and is replaced by true humility.

LOSING FACE

Your ego has you put on a series of social masks. Where you have no ego, you have no role-playing. Once you remove the mask, you can see your true face. Let your feelings of shame and embarrassment point to where you need to lose face and show your real self.

Refuse to hold back from life to avoid losing face. With wisdom, you see the futility of trying to prevent losing face—it's an inevitable part of life. Once you let go of face-saving maneuvers, you can put yourself on the line for what you really care about.

You are unable to beat reality, no matter how hard you try. Reality is relentless—just when you think you have it beaten, it blindsides you. Collaborate with all aspects of reality and avoid the false pride of thinking you won the war and the shame of losing the war. Instead of trying to make life turn out exactly as you want it, understand the forces in play and work with them to your advantage.

Humiliation shows you where you need true humility. Stop being attached to the thought "I must be the boss" and you no longer feel humiliated when you think others are directing your life. Let go of your attachment to needing to be the star and you no longer feel humiliated when others take you for granted.

Listen to humiliation the way you would listen to the wisest person you know. Just as pride is the foolish first force, humiliation is the second force that teaches you exactly what you need to know; it's the reality principle that teaches you to tune into relevant reality.

BEYOND APPEARANCES

Reality breaks through appearances and lets you know you're not special, you're human. You may think, "But I *am* special. I have accomplished more than others, I'm better-looking, I have more money, and I have a better education."

If you bake the best peach pie in the neighborhood, you are special in the peach-pie department, but it's small stuff. Your pies may win every blue ribbon at the country fair, but grasping the fact that you're an imperfect, nonspecial human being is what sets you free.

The moment you want to *be* something or someone, you are enslaved. If you're honest and look closely, you'll see that nothing you ever do remains special for long. If you get married, after a while marriage becomes ordinary; if you have children, after a while parenthood is nothing special. If you make a million dollars or win an Academy Award, you soon discover that fame and fortune don't remain wonderful for long.

FACE THE TRUTH

Who are you? Let the sunshine in and take a look. Just as a shadow falls, when hit by sunlight, your self-illusion weakens when held to the light.

You'll never have a better opportunity to free yourself from self-pride than right after you've fallen on your face. Use every mistake and failure as an opportunity to correct your errors and weaken your ego's hold over you. Use your shameful feelings as a signal to pull back the curtains and let reality's fresh air and sunlight in.

Rather than blame others, admit your mistakes. Be objective about who you really are ("I'm not special; I do the best I can"). Embrace ordeals, learn your lessons, and disregard the rest.

As you move up in states of mind, everything becomes more subtle; but because it's more subtle, it can easily trip you up, without your even realizing it. False humility leads to conceit. The worst conceit is spiritual conceit—Lucifer thought he was the best angel. Refuse to pretend to be humble and nonassertive to boost your self-importance. False humility leads to self-concepts that make you feel separate from, different from, and better than others.

MAKE PEACE WITH REALITY

Directly or indirectly, your choices and actions create your humiliating experiences. Own your role in all of your experiences. Try to escape an ordeal and you'll only make the ordeal worse. Ordeals are turned into wisdom and mastery when accepted with humility.

Repeated losses let you know exactly where you need to relax your fight with reality. Give way and realize you're human and not special. You may think, "I can control the horses, the stock market, the aging process, and my in-laws." With understanding, you collaborate with reality rather than try to keep up the fiction that you're bigger than life.

Once you realize you're not special, you can relax and transcend what you're stuck on. Your ego believes you should be able to control all of life. If you have a drinking problem and think, "I can beat the bottle," you'll be humiliated until you see the folly of this thought. With insight, you transform your humiliation into willingness to be nonspecial: you humbly admit, "This is something I am unable to control."

Reality is unforgiving. You can put your last cent into a losing business, and reality will demand more. If you refuse to see the writing on the wall, reality will advertise on billboards. Reality stops harassing you with humiliation once you cry "uncle" and admit you've run into something bigger and more powerful than your thoughts about yourself.

Be willing to be nothing special and accept that you're powerless to change the reality you're trying to control, and you become powerful. Humility allows you to take in reality's message, and lets this message lift you to a point where you can see clearly.

In the end life wins. You can wait until you hit bottom before you start to catch on, or you can gain insight right now. To win, accept your losses. You can turn your life around in an instant, once you see your pain comes from false pride ("I'm bigger than ordinary life").

Do you think, "I can eat all I want and still be thin"; "I can be arrogant and still be liked"; or "I can spend money on whatever I want and stay out of debt"? Your humiliation will always let you know the part of reality you are banging your head against.

ROAD TO SUCCESS

The road to success must be traveled with humility. To be a successful salesperson, you have to be willing to call on a customer eight or nine times before you get a sale. To be a successful author, you have to be willing to accumulate a stack of rejection slips. To be in a successful relationship, you have to be willing to expose your flaws to another person.

Learn to appreciate humility and you'll be better able to endure the ordeal and find the understanding you need. Refuse to be intimidated by feelings of humiliation. Ask for what you want and you'll take a stand for what you want—even though you may look foolish in the process.

RITES OF PASSAGE

To move to higher levels of mastery, you have to go through humbling rites of passage—doctors serve internships, lawyers must pass the bar, mechanics serve apprenticeships, college students must register for classes, kindergarten children must face the teacher on their own.

See ordeals as necessary steps and you can move forward. Be willing to go through the ordeal of having your self-image attacked. Keep in mind that you never have to experience all that you imagine—you just have to be *willing* to experience it.

Rather than spend time and money in an effort to save face, realize there is no way out. *Dropping out is just as humiliating as going forward.* If you're going to lose face anyway, why not move forward to what you want?

Be powerful. Move forward toward what you want and accept both the applause and the risk of humiliation along the way. Ask for what you want even though you risk being turned down and embarrassed. Take a stand for your position and accept that you might lose others' respect. Make commitments and risk failure. Acknowledge unpleasant facts, rather than filter them out to protect your image. Move out of your small circles of predictable outcomes ("Nothing ventured; nothing gained") and be willing to have your self-image destroyed.

TRUE WISDOM

Being human is understanding at a deep level that your real value consists simply of being alive and having experiences. Identify with your empty container—your humanity and essence— rather than with the contents—the images and concepts of who you think you are. True humility is the absence of any thoughts about yourself to be proved or ashamed of. Your ego's fixed concepts of who you are severely limit you in every area of your life. Your ego doesn't want you to be less than your image of yourself or more than your image of yourself. Katia Kaft wrote, "It's very nice to feel. You're nothing. You're just nothing when you're near a volcano." When you're happy and in the moment, you're free of any concepts about yourself. You're happy out in nature because you feel empty and invisible, as if you're nothing.

With each image-shattering experience, choose to accept fully that you're more than your fixed self-images. When someone points out your flaws to you, rather than defend yourself, see this as more proof that you're human, and when someone says you're better than you think you are, accept this too.

UNIFYING

Accept that you're not special and you'll connect with your essence, which is part of a larger reality. False pride strengthens the illusion "I'm separate from the rest of life." Living your life from false pride is like being in a big city where you're unable to see the stars. You lose sight of your connection to something bigger than your small self. Just as the lights of the city dim your view of the universe, your false pride prevents you from seeing your part in the universe.

See through the illusion "I'm distinct from and superior to life." Though you're not responsible for this thought (it appears involuntarily and automatically), you do have the capacity to disregard it when it appears.

Let your losses as well as your gains show how you're like all human beings and subject to the forces of reality. Humility realigns you with reality. Reality is completely neutral and is unconcerned about you as an individual. Remind yourself, "Like everyone else,

I have my ups and downs and go through good and bad patches."

Refuse to be blinded by your ego's artificial light; dim the lights of your false self. Be human and see the true mystery of life. Look for life's higher creative order. As you reconnect with the mystery of life, you'll feel your true humanity return; you are willing to be affected by something bigger than yourself.

Being in touch with your humanity leads to a profound sense of gratitude for being alive. Sip your cup of coffee or listen to your favorite tape on the way to work and see, "I am at the foot of the universe." At these moments, you are empty, invisible, and in touch with the mystery of life. You know that everything is a mystery. No one has a clue as to how everything came to be. Stay with your feelings of awe and mystery; you'll come to see, "I'm a part of everything; the separation I make in my mind between my self-importance and the rest of life is just artificial thought."

18

SELF-MASTERY

T he road to success is found through third-force mastery. The more skills you have, the more third force you have at your disposal. You'll find all of your difficulties come from lack of mastery and all your successes come from mastery.

What is valuable lasts, and what lasts is mastery—physical or psychological. Once you learn to ride a bike, write a brief, disregard a thought, or find a good feeling, you always have this mastery within you.

You can use the forces in play in a creative or a reactive way. You can use the first force for intoxication or for initiation. You can use the second force to build you up or tear you down. You can use your ego overpush as a third force, or you can use mastery (know-how) as a third force to rise above the resistance.

You need more skills to cook a gourmet meal than to boil water, and even more to create a new way of cooking. As you live your life, why be content to psychologically boil water? Why not develop the mastery to make your life into a feast?

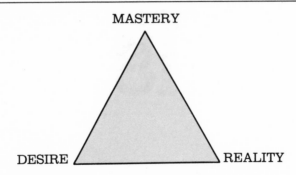

MASTERY

DESIRE

REALITY

Aim for mastery in your career, in your relationships, and in your self-development. You add to your psychological estate when you master the way to organize your house, deal with difficult people, and relax on your days off. Van Gogh wrote, "If one is master of one thing and understands one thing well, one has at the same time, insight into and understanding of many things."

Mastery is vertical, unconditional learning—you're learning the generic principles you can apply to any condition. Because all forms of mastery involve the process of learning to learn, you can use the mastery of any skill to help you master mastery. By paying close attention to the general principles of mastery, such as the need to clarify reality and the need to keep coming back when you're stuck, you can increase your overall capacity for mastery. Mastery can be cumulative. Not only do you add to your living trust fund, you earn interest. When you develop mastery over your car maintenance, you can increase your mastery in how you deal with your children and handle your boss.

PERFORMANCE VERSUS MASTERY

To master anything, focus on learning rather than on proving yourself. Disregard your ego's ultimatum "I must perform flaw-lessly," and adopt the attitude of a beginning student. Make your overriding concern to gain greater skills and greater abilities.

If you want to master public speaking, see the lesson in each of your speeches. You'll lose your terror once you see each speech as a chance to learn, instead of a mandate to prove yourself. The deck is stacked in your favor: if your speech is good, you learn from that; if your speech is bad, you learn from that.

If your goal is to impress the audience, the best you can do is walk out the same door you came in. Even if you succeed, you've failed to learn. *There is no rest for the insecure.* Aim for mastery and you'll stop thinking, "Well, I've escaped the guillotine . . . this time . . . but what about next time?" Refuse to identify with your performance and you'll be impartial to the outcome—good, bad, or indifferent.

Negative thoughts ("I'm worthless; I'm stupid") reduce your awareness and learning. You punish and decrease your awareness, not your errors. Be as objective as possible when you catch your mistakes ("I'm seeing how to improve") and you'll reinforce your learning.

OTHERS AS RESOURCES

Take the long view. Use each experience as a means to learning, rather than an end in itself. Switch your focus away from desiring applause and avoiding jeers, and instead focus on your natural ability to master the physical and psychological worlds.

When your desires encounter an unsolvable second force, use others as a third force. Follow the ancient adage "Pay a doctor; pay a teacher." Actively search out teachers and mentors. If you want to master your job, rather than see your co-workers as rivals or critics, approach them as resources.

No need to reinvent the wheel. Others are a deep source of knowledge and wisdom. Err on the side of inclusion; ask for help, even though you may be turned down. Use the accumulated insights of others. Be willing to engage others, to listen and learn from them. As a general rule, however, take with a grain of salt the advice of those who want to do what you're doing but never get around to it. Their criticism of your work, like their own self-criticism, is usually one-sided and unfair. You'll get more reasons why you can't do something than why you can.

Sincerely move toward mastery and respect others on the same path. Treat with equal respect those who know less and those who know more. If people don't know one thing, they know another. Refuse to put others' heads higher or lower than your own, and realize, "I can learn from everyone."

COMMON SENSE

When you have good feelings and a sense of presence, you increase your practical intelligence. Mastery consists almost entirely of practical or applied intelligence—the rarest and most valuable form of intelligence.

The main players in any endeavor—from Harvard Law School to an automobile assembly line—are those with common sense and practical intelligence. Street smarts means you understand how the world works. You see all of the pieces, and you know how they all fit together.

With practical intelligence, you know how to find and employ people with the creative and analytic intelligence you lack. You have something more valuable: *insight into what is going on.* You're able to grasp the whole picture. Rather than be attached to your ideas of how it is, you *see* how it is. Because you see more clearly than others, you take steps that to others seem obvious only in retrospect.

To excel in anything, you need practical intelligence. Unlike analytical and creative intelligence, you can develop unlimited practical intelligence. You gain practical intelligence by keeping your eyes open as you gain practical experiences.

MEMORY

Mastery is taking in and using reality in fresh, innovative ways. The memory that makes up mastery is a living, synthesizing, and creative phenomenon—not merely a mental recording device.

Mastery is the ability to create out of your past experiences the exact memory you need at the moment. To enhance your ability to remember, first move into the present, find a good feeling, and raise your state of mind. The relaxed, synthesizing ability of your higher states of mind creates a climate for learning. You learn the most when you're relaxed, and the least when you're uptight and trying to analyze the data or forcing yourself to remember something. The less you strain, the more you take in and the more you recall. If you are calm and tranquil, your mind, like a body of water, takes in and reflects back clear images.

Always aim to be a beginner and you create room for new

learning. The beginner's mind is empty and open to new possibilities. Disregard the myth of being a virtuoso, and be willing to be a student. To master your moods, for example, disregard your fantasy of always being happy and focus on being a little happier each day.

Mastery is active relaxation: you're effective in a relaxed, easygoing way. You learn the best when you can have fun with the material. You experience the joy and lightness that naturally come with learning once you disregard your ego's agenda ("I need to perform perfectly").

LOVE AND LEARNING

To gain mastery, make results secondary to learning; learn because you want to learn—not to enhance your superiority. Drop your desire for the fruits of learning and make the enjoyment of learning noncontingent on how well you are doing and independent of what the learning means about you.

Decide to master what you love and you'll have good feelings toward learning and be motivated to move past the second force. Practice because you enjoy it and you rise above the frustrations and setbacks you meet along the way. Good feelings toward what you want to master allow you to stay with the learning, and make it easier for you to know what you need to do next to gain mastery.

Style, a manifestation of mastery, comes from being true to what you love. As your mastery deepens, develop the flair and courage to be yourself. Give yourself the freedom to develop your own style and put your own signature on your accomplishments.

BALANCE AND FRIENDLINESS

Aim to complete and master all sides of yourself. Balance your feeling, thinking, and action centers. Seek to gain mastery where you're out of balance. If your intellectual ability is well developed, sign up for a physical-fitness program. If your sensibility to art and music is your strong suit, find an intellectual challenge (take a science class or read a difficult book). Decide to master something that's out of character but that you always wanted to do.

When you need to prove yourself, you either hold back out of fear or you give 150 percent in an effort to overpower your fear. To gain mastery, use energy, not effort. Bring in the completing third force: disregard the underpush and overpush and leisurely hand yourself over to what you're learning.

If you want to master your weight, be willing to learn from whatever happens. Have a friendly and collaborative relationship with eating and with your body. Appreciate your successes and gladly accept slips along the way.

To learn anything, from swimming to conducting international negotiations, you have to discover how to balance the active and passive forces. You need to balance the effort you put out with the resistance you meet.

HUMILITY

Mastery is knowing your limits. If you've mastered law, you know when you have a case and when you don't. If you've mastered medicine, you know when you can treat the patient and when you need to refer out. If you've mastered parenting, you know when to guide your children and when to back off.

Even if you gain a degree of mastery, you have to keep your ego from pushing past your limits. The best mountain climbers are the ones that keep their egos in check. When you get close to your goal, avoid summit fever—the urge to push past your capabilities to prove how great you are.

Before you can have mastery, you must first admit you don't know what you're doing. The truth will come out anyway. Learning to do something well naturally humbles you. You'll find that, the more humble you become, the more quickly you gain mastery and the better your work becomes.

USE LOSSES

Your loss of face guides you to what you need to learn next. If you want to learn to invest money, welcome your losses and let them teach you prudence. If you want to learn to master good relationships, appreciate your misunderstandings and let them teach you compassion and empathy.

See failure as a step in learning. Be an alchemist and turn every loss into a gain. If you want to learn to play tennis, use the times you hit the ball out of the court or over the fence as opportunities to make adjustments and improve your game.

Karlfried Durckheim wrote, "By tirelessly practicing a given skill, the student finally sheds the ego—sheds it so completely that he becomes the instrument of a deeper power, from which mastery falls instinctively." Embrace each ordeal and find the lesson that helps you move on to the next stage of mastery. Love your shortcomings and you'll weaken your self-pride and hasten your mastery.

Realize that you're a quick study in some areas and slow in others. You live in your own invisible reality. You have your own separate learning curve for each activity you undertake.

The real value of gaining mastery is that in the process you become less arrogant and a better person. Mastery over the external world leads to internal growth. Be willing to confront your lack of development. Develop your skills and discover the liberating paradox "The more I master, the more ordinary I realize I am."

COMMITMENT

To master anything, you have to be willing to commit yourself and make sacrifices. Take a stand for what you want to learn and let go of the ego's doubts ("Something better might come along").

Decide to learn even though you have no guarantees you will be able to stick it out and gain mastery. Be willing to accept the uncertainty and move forward anyway.

To gain mastery, you have to be comfortable with voids and losses. If you want to master being a friend, you have to give up your willfulness and be willing to go along with another's agenda. If you want to master law school, you have to sacrifice activities you're good at and face what you're not good at.

LOOSEN UP

Your ego wants to make the learning process rigid, formalized, and complicated. The first and last lesson is: *let go of your need to control the learning process.* Learning through a textbook will take you only so far. To gain real mastery, you have to go forward without a hint of what you are going to do next.

Let learning be simple and unfold in its own way and own time. Drop your willfulness and be willing to serve your apprenticeship. Obey what you're trying to learn, rather than make it obey you. Make reality the coach or teacher, and willingly do what it shows you. If you want to learn word processing, obey the written instructions and the menu on the screen; use mistakes as feedback—don't ignore them or try to control them.

Mastery is the opposite of control: you have to let go of trying to arrange how you're going to learn. Focus on what you can learn in the moment and not on what you want to prevent (making a mistake or a fool of yourself). Make whatever happens grist for the mill—a point from which you can evolve and grow.

Because you have to be in tune with the impermanent flow of nature, learning is the art of letting go of control. Whether you're learning to dance, swim, make love, talk to others, or do brain surgery, you have to relax into the moment and then let go.

Because you have to let go of fixed ideas, learning often feels wrong; however, instead of letting your feelings get the best of you, relax and be attuned to what you're learning—join with what you want to learn rather than try to dominate it.

MASTER THE RHYTHM

To master anything—riding horses, chairing a meeting, making glass sculpture, relating to your in-laws—you need to learn the rhythm. You need to know when to lean to the left and when to lean to the right; when to press on and when to hold back.

The great philosopher Wittgenstein said, "Don't think: look!" To find the rhythm, *think less and experience more.* In the past, as you learned to type, drive a car, or take care of your baby, you gradually talked less to yourself and found the feeling for what you were doing.

Be willing to take the next step on the road to mastery even though you're unsure how it will turn out. Be your own scout and advance into uncharted territory before you feel you're completely ready for it.

Refuse to postpone action until you have it "down pat." Learning is a process, not an event. Keep in mind that you'll learn more about the step you're on as you move forward. Walk before you know everything about crawling. Move forward before you feel completely ready and you'll master the steps you left behind.

SECOND FORCE

When you want to master anything, you'll inevitably encounter a second-force resistance. The external second force could be the person across the chessboard, the mountain you're trying to climb, or the cost of the equipment you need.

Your real opponent is your internal second force; your ego distracts you with thoughts, feelings, and actions that move you away from learning. You may think, "I'm not smart enough, strong enough, or capable enough to learn." You may feel too tired or too excited to sit down and learn.

When your first-force desire to learn meets second-force resistance, you experience tension. The temptation is to resolve the tension by quitting. Instead, let go of the resisting thoughts that created the tension, clarify the present moment, and find a good feeling. Once you move to a higher state, refocus on what you want to learn. Create a structural discrepancy between where you are and where you want to go. Continue to do this until you resolve the discrepancy in favor of gaining the mastery you want.

The more mastery you have, the less effort you put out. Mastery is learning to deal with first- and second-force conflict with minimum effort. Because the second force manifests itself on the physical level, your first thought is "I need to change something physically." Resist your urge to double your effort to fix yourself or the situation.

With insight, rather than problem-solve or fix the outer world, you need first to raise your psychological functioning (calm yourself down, find a good feeling, and move to an open and receptive state).

DETAILS

Mastery, like art, is detail. The high in any form of mastery, like the high in any form of life, comes from losing yourself in the details. With mastery, however, you have to earn the right to work with the details. You have to write the novel before you can enjoy the process of rewriting it. You get into trouble when you try to circumvent the natural process that goes from the gross to the subtle.

Love the second force; it lets you know exactly where you are in your development and what you need to learn next. Once you've calmed down and can see the whole playing field, look for what level of detail you need to master at this moment. If you're stalled in your career, see that you don't need to change yourself or the situation—*you need to become more skillful.* You may need to learn how to run a computer, deal with authority figures, or better tolerate frustration.

Once you've pinpointed what level you need to master, be willing to do whatever is necessary to master the lessons. Realize that anything you're unwilling to learn will haunt you until you are willing to master it.

VALUE THE SECOND FORCE

Once you no longer invisibly handicap yourself, you use the second force as a ladder to step over obstacles to learning. Remember that, just as a weightlifter needs the resistance of the weights to develop, only through the second force can you grow and develop.

Your second force is a psychological knot you feel in your body. The more you fight the resistance, the tighter the knot becomes and the less you learn. Take the opposite tack and make your internal reaction passive. Relax and let the knot unravel on its own. See that the time for nonaction is when you're uptight and unable to think of any constructive action.

CREATE ROOM

To make room for new learning, be willing to let go of the old. Disregard the thought "This is the way things are." Be like a child and let go of preconceptions that could smother new learning.

To create anything of value, you have to be willing to destroy the old. If you can't destroy, you can't create. Picasso, who embodied third-force mastery, said each of his paintings was "the sum of its destruction." He said, "In each destroying of a beautiful discovery, the artist does not really suppress it, but rather transforms it, condenses it, makes it more substantial."

To learn, you need to reedit and re-create on an ongoing basis. Let go of the last moment, move into the immediate second, and then let go of that. When you're present, you see more of what needs to be done next, and you gladly do it.

Children have a much easier time learning, because they have few fixed concepts of what they can or can't do. You often need to unlearn what you previously saw as the truth. Your ego is invested in the status quo: your ego wants to freeze your self-image and your knowledge. Your past thoughts about the way things are are the chief barriers to new understanding. When you're stuck, consider the possibility that reality is actually the opposite of what you think it is.

You find that, as you let go of outmoded self-concepts and unlearn old ideas, you rise above the second force to a new level of understanding.

You have many fixed thoughts that can stop you ("I'm not mechanical"; "I'm not musical"). Refuse to be entrapped by your overlearned, conditioned thinking. Remind yourself that you have the right to remain silent in the face of reactionary thinking. Rather than fight with fixed ideas about yourself, prove them wrong by learning what you previously thought you were unable to learn. Don't buy into them or fight them. Instead, simply dismiss the thoughts and focus on what you want to learn.

Realize that the ideas, expectations, and principles you've been operating under are just thoughts, and thoughts are not holy—you can dismiss any thought at will.

Choreographer Martha Graham, in talking about creativity and mastery, said, "You do not even have to believe in yourself or your work. You have to keep open and aware directly to the urges that motivate you. Keep the channel open."

PATIENCE

You may avoid learning because you think it will take too long. Mastery, no matter how long it takes, is the shortest way to get where you want to go.

You gain mastery through gradual refinement. Great inventions, from zippers to computers, evolve through a process of refinement. Your first attempts at mastery may be clunky, complicated, and ineffective. Stay with it and you'll eventually develop grace and fluidity.

To evolve, you need to develop the greatest virtue—patience. What you learn in a slow and steady way stays. Dedicate a full year to learning how to take off an extra fifteen pounds and by the end of the year you will have lost weight and gained mastery. If, on the other hand, you go on a two-week crash diet, you'll fail to learn anything and will quickly gain the weight back.

Keep the attitude of a patient beginner. Kafka said, "There is only one cardinal sin: impatience. Because of impatience we are driven out of Paradise." Mastery requires staying with it. You can learn to ride a bike in a few days, but you need fifteen years of training to become a heart surgeon. At times you'll hit plateaus: on the surface you seem to be standing still, but beneath the surface you're assimilating and processing new learning.

Because mastery is never complete, there are no final exams. Time is on your side. Because there is no end, *when* you gain mastery is irrelevant. Keep in mind you have more to learn, and you can get better.

MOVE ON

Mastery is complementary. You complement what you master, and what you master complements you. To master skiing, you have to allow yourself to get on the side of skiing; to master a relationship, you have first to let yourself belong to the relationship.

Because everything is constantly changing, you have to move

beyond your current level of mastery. Mastery is an ongoing and unlimited process. Don't let your self-image of mastery stymie you. Refuse to become too satisfied with what you've already mastered; be willing to surpass yourself and break your own records.

Once you feel you have mastered an activity, let go and move on to a new one. After you have mastered Spanish, move on to master woodworking. After you have mastered being a good son or daughter, let go and move on so you can master being a good partner to someone. After you've mastered your friendships, master your relationships with the community and with the world.

See, "What I was unable to master in the past is irrelevant." Start with where you are and aim to become more skillful at whatever job, tasks, and relationships you have in front of you.

Mastery is like magic: you continually surprise yourself with what you can do. What seems overwhelming becomes commonplace. As you gain mastery, you instinctively begin to make the right move nearly every time. You know intuitively what is the appropriate action.

Know you can do the job, but refuse to let your ego use your mastery to put your head higher than others'. When you have mastery and know you're ordinary, no one can touch you. You do what you do for its own sake and not to impress others.

19

SELF-REALIZATION

Mastering the physical world leads to mastery over your psychological world. Master the external world and you start to discover at a profound level that you're a living being, with an inner existence separate from your outer life.

As you become aware of your inner existence, you're able to observe yourself impartially in different contexts. Once you're free from thoughts about yourself, you're able to step back and see your outer as well as your inner existence for the first time.

To turn awareness of your existence into self-mastery, remember that living is the container and your life (job, family, friends) is the contents. With wisdom, you reorder your priorities: you make living bigger than life. At a deep level, understand there's more to living than life and more to dying than death.

Living is more real and more immediate than life or death: you can feel you're living at any moment. Life is always just out of reach, something off in the future; death is a vague possibility, more real for others than for yourself. Living, on the other hand, is as close and as real as your breath.

THREE FORCES

You can easily go through life unaware that you exist. In the first force, you're intoxicated with how good life will be. When you encounter the second force, you blot out the experience of living with thoughts about how bad life has become.

Find a third force to wake you to the reality that you're alive. Refuse to sleepwalk through life with only dim awareness that you exist here and now. Refuse to defeat yourself at the deepest level: balance awareness of life with awareness of living.

To transcend the trance of life, use first-force *recognition*, second-force *renunciation*, and third-force *reconciliation*—recognize you're alive, renounce overattachment to life, and reconcile living and life. At the point of self-realization, the three forces come together and become one: *you live your life*.

WITNESS PROTECTION PROGRAM

Your ego's agenda depends wholly on your being unaware that right now you're living your life. Your ego hypnotizes you into thinking, "This is all preparation, and I'll really start living once I get my life together." Your ego tries to convince you that you'll be able to do it all over again for real next time.

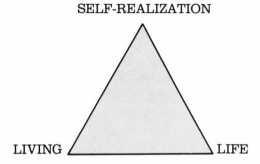

SELF-REALIZATION

LIVING   LIFE

To remember consistently that you're alive, set up a witness protection program. Protect yourself from your ego's desire to kill off any awareness that you're living each moment. Leave your old identity and psychological residence and move to a place where you can freely and nonjudgmentally see yourself in the context of your life. Separate gathering evidence about being alive from judging how you're living.

When you know you're alive, every experience is good. Objectively watch yourself as you're angry, greedy, funny, or lazy; use each state of mind as evidence that you're living. At first you'll be able to observe your aliveness only in retrospect: then, gradually, you'll be able to do it in the present. Relate what you've discovered in the present to how you've lived in the past and how you can live in the future.

Bring your existence into explicit awareness as you go through the day. Regularly remind yourself, "I'm living in this moment." Use the power of suggestion. Get interested in living through daily exposure: stop four or five times a day and feel the glow of being alive. Remind yourself, when you get up in the morning and when you go to bed at night, "I'm alive." Become so absorbed in the miracle of your existence that it becomes as familiar and real as the bed you sleep in each night.

As you step back and observe yourself, you'll find a coherence to your internal world. Under the immunity of your witness protection program, you find that your thoughts about yourself are based on fraudulent documents. You discover you're not at all the way you thought you were. Gradually you discover the central point—you realize you have a here-and-now inner existence independent of your physical existence.

Knowing at a deep level that you exist right now requires awareness, understanding, and practice. This is what separates humans from animals and the foolish from the wise. As your understanding deepens, you'll stop taking yourself for granted; you'll be aware of being alive more of the time, and you'll carry this awareness with you.

FEAR OF FEELING

Your authentic feelings are a gauge of your aliveness. The more you feel, the more meaningful and more beautiful being alive becomes. Your life becomes bigger and more real. The menu expands, and you see more possibilities and more choices.

If you think about existence, it becomes absurd. If you feel your existence, the experience becomes wonderful beyond description. Just as repressing feelings decreases your sense of being alive, feeling your feelings increases your awareness of being alive. The better you're feeling, the greater your awareness that you exist.

Good feelings help you focus in on the reality of being alive. Like adjusting a microscope, looking for a good feeling makes the reality of living come into sharp focus. Finding a good feeling honors living. The better you feel, the more you know that living is more important than life.

Good feelings come from the recognition and appreciation of all existence. You feel happy when you glance at a smiling child, see a beautiful sunset, or hear a moving piece of music. Bliss, the pinnacle experience, comes from fully realizing, "I'm living." You have total appreciation for the gift of existence. Your deep joy springs from the recognition that your living is part of all existence.

BECOMING REAL

Give living equal billing with life. Drop *thoughts* about life and make room to *feel* alive. You can affirm your existence at any moment by *feeling* it. You're unable to describe the reality of being alive adequately; you can only feel it.

You can think and hear about being alive, but it's all hearsay until you *know* you're alive by *feeling* alive. In the past, both great sorrow and great joy may have jolted you into the insight "I'm alive." You may have felt real and alive after someone close to you died or you survived a serious accident or illness. A veil was lifted, and you saw the miracle and wonder of being alive.

When you're bored, you're out of touch with living. Your awareness of being alive would fit in a teaspoon. Use a sense of deadness as a signal to feel your aliveness. Turn physical discomfort and negative feelings into reminders that you're alive.

All of your feelings, if you fully accept, feel, and complete them, will give way to higher feelings. Through a feedback mechanism, the more you become aware that you're alive, the better you feel.

When you feel a feeling, you send your intellect the message that you're alive; your brain then, out of gratitude, sends back a good feeling.

APPRECIATION

As soon as you realize you're living, your life becomes perfect as it is. Just as being in a beautiful setting is meaningless without appreciation, life is meaningless without appreciation. Fully feel you're alive and you'll know it is valuable in and of itself. No matter how you articulate being alive, the reality is always more beautiful than any description.

In high states of mind, you see everything sparkle with life. Use beauty as a barometer of living: the more beautiful life looks, the higher your state of being or aliveness. Keep looking for good feelings until life becomes more beautiful. Use the immediate surroundings as a feedback mechanism. When you find yourself surrounded by beauty, you know you're totally alive.

REVOLUTIONARY SHIFT

Find a feeling for your internal life and you discover you have a free will. You move from appreciating being alive to being an active participant in your own existence. As you find you can actively choose the thoughts you want, you are transformed from an observer to a practitioner.

This new understanding leads to a major insight. For the first time, you're able to direct your inner as well as your outer life. Rather than life being something that happens to you, you live your life. You become responsible for both your life and your relationship with your life. Free from fragmentation, grounded in the awareness of your own being, you're able to love the simple fact that you exist.

THREE LEVELS OF AWARENESS

At first you become aware of the products of your thoughts (actions and emotions); then gradually you become aware of the thoughts you've been reacting to; and, finally, you become aware you're alive.

Once you have this awareness, you no longer fall asleep at the wheel. You see that Descartes had it backward when he wrote, "I think, therefore I am." In fact, it is "I am, therefore I can think." For the first time, you see, "I can bring about the experiences I want." You dismiss your conditioned thinking and live independent of your history and biography.

With insight and practice, you can consistently remember you're alive. You move from experiencing life as a dead, artificial flower to experiencing it as real and alive. You can experience the joy, love, and beauty that naturally come with the awareness of the gift of existence.

HOTEL STAY

Your first-force desire to feel alive will inevitably encounter second-force resistance. Your biggest obstacle is your ego, which continually gets you caught up in life. In your trance logic, you believe, "If I can get my life together, I can be happy and live forever."

Life is like spending a night in a strange hotel. At times the service will be good, the bell will be answered promptly, and the beds will be comfortable; then suddenly it will all change. You'll hear the people in the next room fighting, the employees will be sullen, and mice will run across the floor.

Even though you want a positive life-style, refuse to think you can turn life into an infinite stay in a five-star hotel. You can move to a quieter room, but the plumbing may be out and you may lose your good view.

Instead of trying to control and manipulate life, collaborate with it. Drop the myth that, if you suffer enough, work hard enough, or are good enough, you can beat life.

With the right attitude, you can have a wonderful visit any-where. To enjoy your stay in life, see that your inner life is separate from your physical experiences: you can be anyplace physically and be in a deluxe hotel psychologically.

The way to be successful in life is to begin to live. The solution isn't to escape life and live in a cocoon (wherever you go, you take life with you), but to see living and life as complementary. Ground yourself in living and you'll let go of your quarrels with life.

DISTRACTORS

Refuse to confuse life intensity with living. Both positive intensity (you get high from making deals and having sexual affairs) and negative intensity (you get high from crises and self-dramatization) are counterfeit living. They are surface experiences that come from external stimuli. Real living is a deep experience that comes from being fully in the moment.

Ambivalence about any life decision ("Should I stay or go?") is a strategy to avoid living. With insight, you choose *being* over *becoming*. You decide to be in the present instead of thinking about what you could become or might become. Trying to live life to the hilt is as much an avoidance of living as is hiding in bed. Make the quality of life as important as the quantity, and time as valuable as money.

Choose to live life rather than put all of your energy into having "the good life." Through determination and effort, you can have many successes, but without living your life, you have nothing. Material wealth without happiness is poverty. Playwright Eugene O'Neill, after much acclaim, said, "Success, spiritually speaking, is just as flat as failure."

DIRECT LIVING

When you go for indirect living ("After I get it together, I'll start living"), you can get hooked on any detail of life. You may do drugs, food, ideas, work. You may use failure as a distraction and compound your nonliving with a nonlife.

Refuse to let your existence on earth flow unnoticed through your hands while you're trying to figure out what to do with your life.

Realize that you're going to be dead for a long time. Sickness, old age, and death get everybody. "Life passes quickly by, and is gone." When people die, whether a fourteen-year-old girl or a ninety-five-year-old man, they all say essentially the same thing— "It went so quickly."

As you gain a deeper knowledge of being alive, you lose both your infatuation and your fight with life; you gain an appreciation for living. In the process, life becomes meaningful, and thus valuable. You start wearing seatbelts, quit smoking, drink less, and get in better physical condition.

You no longer need a "problem of the week" to occupy your time; you become free to enjoy your own company without the need to distract yourself with food, fiction, or fantasies. Once you're in touch with the reality of your own existence, you feel complete and content: you come home to yourself.

Rather than try to outwit life, relax and enjoy it. Being alive is the original note; the life you create is the echo. If you find life flat or a pretense (acting "as if" you're living), go back to the original note. Get into the rhythm of your aliveness, and let your life flow from that note.

When you're lost in life, get grounded in the reality of living; return to your center, find a feeling within yourself, and experience the depth and breadth of being alive. Detach from the details of life and focus on living in the moment. Remind yourself, "I'm here through the grace of being alive."

FIRST THINGS FIRST

Being alive is the first cause, the first form. Your existence is the underpinnings. Your life comes as an afterthought, a shadow. You'll never get to living through life ("I'll start living after I get married"; "I'll start living when I retire"). Forget about getting your life together before you start living.

When you catch yourself waiting for your life to begin, see that you're putting the cart before the horse. Shift your priorities: let your feeling ("I'm alive") lead and your life follow.

What you're able to see and do is determined by your level of being. With wisdom, you work on being first and your life second. Through affinity (like attracts like), your being, or state of aliveness, attracts your life.

Life should follow, not lead you. Get in rhythm with living and life will follow in harmony. You'll know what is right for you because it is coming from your center—not from your reactions to life's circumstances.

FEAR OF ALIVENESS

Your second force may be fear of feeling alive. You may be afraid because it's unknown territory ("I feel out of control"), or you may be afraid because you think you'll be unable to get back to life. To transcend your fears, you need to reconcile any false dichotomy between living and life ("I only feel alive on weekends").

Find feelings of aliveness in whatever you do and you bring together living and life. Feel alive at work as well as at leisure; with friends as well as with strangers. Refuse to put your life on hold while you wait for the big "thing" to happen. See that living right now is the big thing.

You may think, "I need to earn the right to live"; or "I need to be worthy enough to live." Go back to the most profound fact that you're alive right now. Understand at a deep level, "Who but someone that exists would have the right to exist?" No need to find a reason for living; you have nothing to prove. You're alive; therefore, you're worthy of being alive.

FEAR OF LOSS

Your resistance to living may come from a fear of loss. When you feel grateful for being alive, you often experience a poignant feeling of sadness; the sadness comes from recognition of the eventual loss of what you have.

At times it can be frightening to see how wonderful being alive can be. You may fear that if you feel alive you will be punished for enjoying it. Drop the primitive fear "I'll be punished for existing in my own right." Find a good feeling. Raise your state of mind and you'll see your existence as a celebration, not a challenge to the gods.

PASSING AWAY

One way you may avoid thinking about dying is to pretend that you're not alive—that you're like an inanimate object that will be around forever. You sacrifice living to avoid facing dying. Only by coming to terms with the reality of living and dying can you ever feel secure.

To live your life fully, accept the transitory nature of your existence. Life is to be felt and transcended, not dwelled upon (if you're eternal, you can't get out of it; if you're not, you can't get into it).

Stay with good feelings and you'll rise to a point of wisdom where you'll be able to reconcile your being and nonbeing. You'll adopt a relaxed self-acceptance of your eventual nonexistence.

A Yiddish proverb says, "It's a great boon to old age to die when you're young." Let unplanned and unwelcome changes remind you of the transitory nature of all existence. Fully accept this reality and you find great solace. Whether you lose a good feeling or a good pen, let your loss show you how everything, including yourself, eventually passes out of existence.

Even change changes. Keep in mind that you're a process, not a stable event. Use both the changes you see in the mirror and the changing seasons you see out the window as reaffirmations ("I'm part of an ever-changing process").

FREEZING

Your ego, which wants to be special and permanent, fears living and clings to life, because existing is not special and not permanent. Your ego tries to make you into something that never ages, never breaks down, and never passes away.

After a period of feeling good, you no longer have to allow your ego to come in and try to freeze it ("It was too good to last"; "I know that everything will always be bad"). With understanding, when your ego tries to create permanent images of yourself or of others, you can let them go. You know images are false because reality is bigger, more real, and more dynamic than any still picture.

You no longer freeze a wonderful picture of the past or a picture of what your future life will be. You know, whether they are negative or positive, both are undesirable. You enjoy a good experience without trying to hold on to it; you let go of suffering in the same way.

Refuse to freeze your theories or ideas about how the world is. As you let go of willful and addictive thoughts, your mood rises. Rather than hang on to a good or bad experience, remind yourself, "Living goes on."

Warm and alive feelings free you from your ego's influence. See reality as a panoramic moving picture instead of a series of still photos. Everything is in constant motion. The up will soon become a down, and the down will soon become an up. When you feel good, it's okay; when you feel bad, it's okay. You live in the warm, alive feelings of the moment, instead of in frozen images of the past or fear of the future. You get in the rhythm of change.

INCREASE ALIVENESS

By being considerate of others, you're affirming their aliveness and you're affirming the reality of your own existence. Focus on the feelings and aliveness of others. Think about others' feelings when they are with you and when they are out of your presence. When you feel good about anything, you validate your own existence as well as what you feel good about.

Affirm the existence of anything and you affirm your own existence. You release internal energy by feeling and connecting with the outside presence. The inner becomes the outer, and the outer becomes the inner.

You confirm your aliveness when you refuse to focus on what you don't have or have failed to do with your life. You energize your aliveness when you focus on and are grateful for what is.

Any experience can be exquisite torture or exquisite enjoyment, depending on whether you accept or reject it. A child elaborately describing the plot of a movie can be wonderful or torturous.

Walking in the wind on a rainy day is beautiful when you love it, and painful when you feel the opposite.

Feel your aliveness and be in harmony with the world. Reconcile the dichotomy between yourself and the world and the existence of the world takes on new meaning. Your feelings, which go out into the moment, bring you into a point in the present. Because what is real is satisfying, you find satisfaction in the smallest activity.

CLOSE TO REALITY

Call off your all-out assault on life. To balance living with life, buy less, do less, talk less, and feel more. Move closer to the direct experience of reality, and be more appreciative of being alive. When you're hungry, appreciate food; when you're tired, appreciate rest. As you go through your day, appreciate your moment-by-moment aliveness.

The moments that you're aware of being alive stay with you: *they are all that count.* You may remember where you were when John Kennedy was shot or when your first child was born. When you feel life deeply, your life becomes full of daily surprises and wonderful memories. When someone asks what you've been doing and you say, "Nothing," realize that this means you need to experience living more deeply.

Your existence is a gift. Treasure being alive so that, when it's time to pass on, you won't wonder, "Where did it all go?"

Feel your aliveness and be in concert with universal existence. Lose your sense that "I'm special and separate" and become part of everything. Stay with the moment—the experience expands, and you feel the aliveness of everything as you capture a sense of eternity.

THE QUESTION

At any moment, you face the eternal question: *to be or not to be.* You can focus on beating life or on being in life. Choose being and a sense of peace and contentment will cascade over you.

Focus on being alive and the experience is deep and becomes

more real. Life is real when *you're* real. When you're real with yourself, you have nothing to hide from others; you no longer fear and dread life.

The main quest of life is to be real. Life's journey is a circle. You always come back to the beginning—back to what you most want and most avoid—the realization that you're alive and that you exist.

A complete list of books and tapes by Dr. Gary Emery is available from the Los Angeles Center for Cognitive Therapy, 630 South Wilton Place, Los Angeles, California 90005 (213-387-4737).